The Treasury of
HORSES

by Walter D. Osborne & Patricia H. Johnson

PHOTOGRAPHED BY WALTER D. OSBORNE

A Ridge Press Book / Golden Press / New York

The Treasury of Horses

by Walter D. Osborne & Patricia H. Johnson

Dust jacket and title page:
Under the watchful eye of
his mother, a Thoroughbred foal tests his speed at
Darby Dan Farm, in Lexington, Kentucky.

Editor in Chief: Jerry Mason
Editor: Adolph Suehsdorf
Art Director: Albert Squillace
Art Associate: Allan Mogel
Art Associate: David Namias
Associate Editor: Moira Duggan
Associate Editor: Frances Foley
Art Production: Doris Mullane

Prepared and
produced by
The Ridge Press, Inc.
Printed in the
United States of America
This edition prepared
for distribution by
Crown Publishers, Inc.

Published by
Golden Press
850 Third Avenue, New York 22, N.Y.
Copyright © 1966 by
Western Publishing Company, Inc. and
The Ridge Press, Inc.
Library of Congress Catalog Card
Number 66-19427

Contents

FOREWORD

Although the working association of man and horse has virtually ended in America, the traditional bond existing between them has refused to die. It may even be said that in the American world of sport and recreation the horse is flourishing to a greater degree than at any time since the invention of the automobile. And all signs point to an even brighter future for this most enduring of man's animal partners.

The demand for information and instruction posed by this equine renaissance has quite naturally prompted an outpouring of literature on the many and varied aspects of the equestrian arts. Much of this material, while excellent, is highly specialized and intended primarily for trainers, veterinarians, breeders, and others who derive their livelihood from the care and management of horses.

Another sizable segment of literature has been devoted to invaluable but extremely detailed research in the fields of archaeology, paleontology, history, and sociology. Again, this is not directed at a public interested in horses in general, but at scholars with specific academic goals.

And inevitably there are books of instruction in horsemanship aimed exclusively at students of riding.

Aside from these specialized volumes, however, the authors have long felt there was room for a concise, not overly technical discussion of our essential knowledge of horses today. While roaming freely through the vast literature of horse stories and legends, such a book would also present the latest findings of archaeologists and paleontologists in determining the origin and evolution of the horse.

The complete scope of horses and horsemanship is large and complex. While in recent years many hitherto unknown facts have been brought to light, there remains much about the horse—his background, his care and training—on which valid differences of opinion exist. It would not be possible within the covers of a volume of this size, or indeed a dozen such, to present a total picture of the horse in past and present America and, at the same time, to do full justice to the opinions and beliefs of the many dedicated horsemen and women who have brought the horse to his present pinnacle of excellence in this country. It should be possible, however, to discuss the salient facts about the various kinds of horses in America, the backgrounds of the individual breeds, and how they are used today.

In preparing *The Treasury of Horses*, photography has been widely employed to illustrate points which would otherwise require many pages of explanation in text. Moreover, the best examples of horses of any type or breed are creatures of singular grace and beauty, as well as of great ability in the various tasks for which they have been bred and trained. It has been one of the authors' aims to present them faithfully, each in the geographical setting where he has achieved renown. Quarter Horses are seen working on the cattle spreads of the West; Appaloosas in the northwest home of the Nez Perce Indians who bred them; Thoroughbreds in the traditional Kentucky Bluegrass, as well as at many of the leading racing establishments from coast to coast. Better than seventy thousand miles of travel were logged in an effort to bring together a collection of the best of each breed and type performing his assigned task. Hopefully, the result is a unique photographic record of the American horse as he is in this day and age.

Many men and women who are outstanding in their particular spheres of horsemanship have given wholehearted cooperation and assistance to the preparation of this book. The authors would like here to acknowledge their very great debt to:

Mr. E. L. Adamson, Mr. & Mrs. Irving T. Alderson, Jr., Dr. Donald J. Balch, Miss Mary Lou Bartram, Mr. Lynn Beutler, Mr. Stanley Bergstein, Mr. H. C. Biddle, Jr., Mr. James H. Blackwell, Mr. Max A. Brewer, Mr. William Bryan, Mr. William C. Buchanan, Mr. Knox Burger, Mr. William R. Burns, Mr. Lewis Burton, Mr. August A. Busch, Jr., Mr. George B. Cassidy, Mr. Marshall Cassidy, Mr. Harold Clark, Mr. Leslie Combs II, Miss Margaret Conner, Mr. J. P. Conway, Mr. Paul I. Cook, Mr. Waldo B. Craig, Mr. William Cruikshank, Mr. John I. Day, Mr. H. D. DeLashmutt, Mr. Edward T. Dickinson, Miss Lucy Drummond, Mrs. Richard C. duPont, Mr. Dale Easter.

Also, Mrs. Courtney Ellis, Mrs. Marcella Alt Falbee, Mr. J. B. Faulconer, Mr. Milton Feldman, Mr. J. Cecil Ferguson, Mr. Lewis G. Ferguson, Mr. Lawrence Fleischer, Mr. William Foster, Miss Louise P. French, Mr. Walter J. Fultz, Mr. & Mrs. John W. Galbreath, Mr. Olin Gentry, Manuel A. Gilman, D.V.M., Mrs. Leonard Goldsmith, Mr. Joseph Goldstein, Mr. Theodore F. Gussenhoven, Mr. Stewart A. Hall, Mr. George A. Hamid, Mr. A. B. Hancock, Mr. Carl Hanford, Mr. George Hanneford, Jr., Mr. George B. Hatley, J. Y. Henderson, D.V.M., Mrs. William Hewitt, Mr. Eric Holm, Mr. Seth P. Holcombe, Mr. C. Maury Jones, Mr. James M. Kahn, Mr. Samuel Kanchuger, Mr. Robert F. Kelley, Mr. John F. Kennedy, Mr. Horace L. King, Mrs. William C. Kyriakis, Mr. Hugh Lamb, Mrs. Nancy G. Lee.

Also, Mr. Emmanuel Levine, Mrs. Mae Lyons, Mrs. Elaine E. Mann, Mr.

Hugh J. McCarten, Mr. Frank McKernan, Mr. Alex Mackay-Smith, Mr. Don Merritt, Mr. Carl Miles, Mr. Czeslan Mroczkowski, Mr. William A. Murphy, Jr., Mr. Patrick W. O'Brien, Mr. Joseph O'Farrell, Mr. Ralph D. Osborne III, Mr. J. Ralph Peak, Mr. James Reed, Mr. Fred H. Ryan, Mr. Burnett Robinson, Mr. Jerry Rybolt, Mrs. Dean Sage, Miss Blanche A. Schmalzried, Mrs. Mildred Searcey, Mr. L. C. Smith, Mrs. Dick Sparrow, Mr. William C. Steinkraus, Mr. Whitney Stone, Mr. Dave Stout, Mr. Robert P. Strub, Mrs. Evelyn Stuart, Mrs. Sidney S. Swett, Mrs. Bazy Tankersley, Mr. Earl Teater.

Also, Mr. Maurice Telleen, Mr. Til Thompson, Mr. H. C. Tilford, Jr., Mr. Roy Tolbert, Mr. Robert Uihlein, Mr. & Mrs. Frederick Van Lennep, Mr. Edward Walsh, Lieut. Bryan Wasson, Mrs. Charles J. Werber, Mrs. Alfred G. Wilson, Mr. S. Bryce Wing, and Mr. Wilbur Yount.

The authors also wish to thank the editors of *Life* magazine for permission to reproduce the Osborne photographs appearing on pages 76 and 77; the Harness Racing Institute for those on pages 198-199, 201, 203, 205 (top), 207, 210, and 214; the New York Racing Association, Inc., and Mr. Pierre Bellocq for permission to publish the photograph of Mr. Bellocq's mural appearing on page 70; and to express gratitude to The Jockey Club, Inc., the American Horse Shows Association, and to the officers and personnel of the Harry M. Stevens Company for many kindnesses along the way. Nikon Inc. was generous with technical advice on photographic equipment. And a particular debt of gratitude is owed to Mrs. Amelia King Buckley, of the Keeneland Association Library, Lexington, Kentucky, for her invaluable assistance in producing the text, and to Mrs. Seville Osborne for researching the photography.

Walter D. Osborne, Patricia H. Johnson

1 THE DAWN

OF THE HORSE

However you look at it, a book about horses is also a book about people. The horse as he is today is in many ways a creation of man. From the great wild herds that foraged over a large part of the earth in prehistoric times, man has fashioned an array of handsome animals, each peculiarly adapted to perform a specific task. And whatever special qualities of beauty and performance the modern horse breeds may have were put there by man over a span of some four thousand or more years of selective breeding.

On the other hand, the story of people, and the level of civilization they currently enjoy, is also a story of horses. For however large a debt the horse may owe to man, that which man owes the horse is infinitely greater. Of all the creatures man has domesticated for his service (or dinner table), only horses have had an impact on human history so massive that, without them, it is impossible to imagine how far back civilization might now be lagging.

From the end of the "crooked-stick" era of prehistoric agriculture until the dawn of the mechanical age, it was the horse who tilled the fields. It was the horse who became man's indispensable partner in war and in the exploration of new lands. It was the horse who dragged raw materials to the manufactory and finished goods to the market place.

Today, except where he has survived as a farm animal, the horse has been superseded by the gasoline engine in the performance of these time-honored roles—although man acknowledges the old relationship by grading his machinery in terms of its horsepower.

Nonetheless, in the United States the horse is more than holding his own. In fact, he is staging a strong comeback, both as a pleasure animal and as an athlete—one of whose activities, Thoroughbred racing, is the leading spectator-sport attraction in America. Individual horses have won great fame. The modern coun-terparts of Alexander's Bucephalus and Robert E. Lee's Traveler are the Kelsos and Bret Hanovers of the flat and harness tracks, the Wing Commanders of the show ring, and the Baby Dolls of the rodeo arena. They are also the entertainment stars Silver, Trigger, Fury, and the other "wonder horses" of almost human wit and capability.

And, thank God, we still have the "just plain horse," the old dun or Paint, of free-form conformation and dubious pedigree, who stands patiently behind the farm house. He would scarcely command a horse fancier's second look, but when school is out he becomes a magical animal who can turn a youngster into a knight, a saber-swinging dragoon, or a six-shooting cowboy of the Wild West. Perhaps he is the most important horse of all.

Obviously, the horse comes in a considerable assortment of sizes and shapes. His biological species—Equus caballus—ranges from the smallest varieties of Shetland pony, which stand about 9 hands, to the herculean draft breeds, which occasionally measure as much as 20 hands.*

Two general sources supplied the strains from which all modern breeds are descended. One was the coarse, "cold-blooded" stock that once ranged wild over Northern Europe and Asia, and whose modern descendants include not only the big draft animals, but several pony breeds, among them the Shetland and the Icelandic. The other roots are those which originate with the "hot-blooded" desert horses of North Africa —the early Arabian and Barb types—which were first domesticated by the ancient peoples of Libya around 2000 B.C. Bred for innumerable generations with the utmost care, these animals in early times spread eastward into Asia Minor and westward along the southern shores of the Mediterranean. They were far more refined than the Northern type and, while most modern breeds are based on blends of both hot- and cold-blooded strains, it is the heritage of the desert horse that supplies the qualities of fineness and

* A "hand," the common unit of equine measurement, is four inches, and a horse's height is measured from the withers to the ground. One inch over 16 hands would be 16:1. Sixteen and a half hands is 16:2.

mettle in today's horse and pony breeds.

In all the clans within the equine species, a standout specimen has a distinct character—the look of a champion—that is peculiar to his breed. The best ponies have an alert, cocky bearing, snappy movement, and trim lines that immediately catch the eye of the show judges. The compact, well-muscled body and darting action of a good Quarter Horse tell the rancher or rodeo hand that here is a top cutting, roping, or dogging animal, just as the sleekly powerful look and smooth running gait of a classy Thoroughbred bespeak speed and stamina to the racing man. Even among the giants of the family, the mighty Percherons, Belgians, and Clydesdales, the best animals have a majestic bearing that recalls the Middle Ages, when these titans carried the armored chivalry of Europe into battle.

There are likewise many qualities common to all good horses, regardless of breed. Shakespeare summed up most of them in his description of the young huntsman's "lusty courser" in *Venus*

and Adonis:

"Round-hoof'd, short-jointed, fetlocks shag and long,

"Broad-breasted, full eye, small head and nostril wide,

"High crest, short ears, straight legs, and passing strong,

"Thin mane, thick tail, broad buttock, tender hide:

"Look, what a horse should have, he did not lack,

"Save a proud rider on so proud a back."

In these few lines, Shakespeare provides a concise word picture of a good-looking horse. But had the Bard intended buying Adonis' steed, instead of merely rhapsodizing over its appearance, he would have viewed it not only with an eye to its fine conformation, but with due attention to its soundness as well. Some of the best-looking creatures in the horse world, particularly among race horses, have been notorious cripples, so unsound that they were rarely, if

ever, able to reach their full potential. To the experienced eye, therefore, soundness is actually part of a horse's looks.

Evaluation of a horse, from the ground up, first requires close examination of the hoofs. In most breeds these should be dainty in proportion to the rest of the body, and nicely rounded, the rear hoofs slightly more so than those of the forelegs. The soles should be firm, but with sufficient springiness of texture to cushion the footfall from jarring contact with the ground. Overly hard soles are a common cause of lameness. The hoofs, which are composed of an insensitive material similar to human nails, should be wholly free of rings and of cracks or fissures.

A sound horse or pony will stand squarely on all four feet. His forelegs, viewed from the front, are straight and broad-kneed, and set well enough apart so that he does not have a "narrow" look. His hind legs are straight and perpendicular to the body when seen from behind, and are planted so that the hocks are well separated, but not so far that he has a spraddled appearance. His limbs are flat, rather than round-boned, and there should be no indication of puffiness—a sure sign of unsoundness—about the joints. The tendons of the foreleg, which run behind the cannon bone, are likewise of great importance. They should be straight and well set out from the bone. Those which tie in too closely at the upper end are weak and those which bend outward have been "bowed" by injury.

The quarters should be plump, well-rounded, and evenly balanced crossways, ending in a croup that slopes away gradually. The tail is fine-haired and full, set high and carried stylishly. The back is short and of a piece with the quarters, or the animal is likely to give the disjointed appearance of a two-man vaudeville "horse." The chest is full and deep, without being overly square, the shoulder sloping. The head-on view of the body should approximate the profile of an egg set on the bigger end.

The neck should be long and gracefully

Hot- and cold-blooded breeds. Top: Arabians, at Quentin, Pennsylvania, show, are source of hot-blooded strains. Tiny Shetlands (center) and giant Clydesdale (bottom) are historically related "cold" breeds.

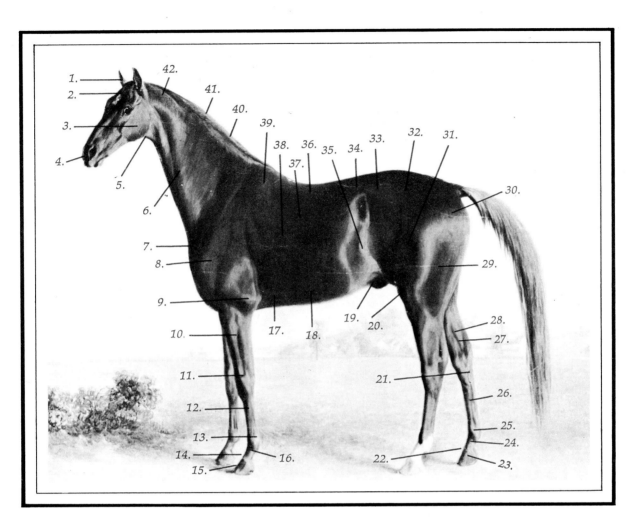

THE POINTS OF THE HORSE

1. Ears	11. Knee	22. Coronet	32. Croup
2. Brow	12. Cannon Bone	23. Hoof	33. Haunch
3. Cheek	13. Fetlock	24. Pastern	34. Loins
4. Muzzle	14. Coronet	25. Fetlock	35. Flank
5. Throat	15. Hoof	26. Cannon Bone	36. Back
6. Neck	16. Pastern	27. Hock	37. Barrel
7. Point of	17. Girth	28. Leg or Gaskin	38. Ribs
Shoulder	18. Abdomen	29. Buttock	39. Withers
8. Shoulder	19. Sheath	30. Point of	40. Mane
9. Elbow	20. Stifle	Buttock	41. Crest
10. Forearm	21. Night Eye	31. Thigh	42. Poll or Nape

*Thoroughbreds are top equine
athletes. Steeplechasers make light
of this jump, taken at full run.*

formed, arising from distinct withers and arching through a high crest ending at the poll. The mane should be thin and fine. The ears are small, the eyes large, clear, and prominent, with a bright and kind expression. The head is small, but not out of proportion to the neck. It should be lean, rather than fleshy, with visible bone structure and the surface blood vessels showing plainly. The nostrils are wide and flaring. The nose, in profile, squares away sharply and does not droop downward, like the end of a banana.

If the animal is in peak form his coat will have a natural luster that seems to emanate from within. A dull coat indicates poor condition, while one that is "washy" (sweaty) often betrays extreme nervousness.

As to the color of the coat, Izaak Walton once observed that "No good horse is of a bad color." Perhaps this is true to the extent that caution should be used in undertaking to relate a horse's quality to his color. Nevertheless, since as far back as the ancient breeders of the desert, there have been theories attempting to do just that. The Arabs believed that chestnuts were the fastest, bays the sturdiest, and light-colored horses least able to stand the heat. To this day, some ranch hands will tell you that Paints make the toughest cow ponies, while others proclaim the same virtue for duns. There is a coterie of horse-racing fans which bets on grays and another which will advise you never to wager on a horse of that color.

All pure breeds of horses are either solid-colored or hereditarily of mixed colors. That is to say, a horse of two different colors does not result from the mating of one solid color to another. Among the true breeds of solid color, white markings are quite common on the face and lower leg areas, but if they appear elsewhere on the body they are almost certain proof that the animal has a color-breed ancestor somewhere back along the line.

The solid colors of the horse are:

BAY—Ranges from a yellowish tan called light bay, through a bright reddish color known as blood bay, to a mahogany shade called dark bay. The mane and tail and, usually, the lower legs are black.

BROWN—From a lustrous, rich shade of brown to almost black.

BLACK—A true black coloration which is quite rare. Very dark bays and browns are frequently mistaken for blacks.

CHESTNUT—From a light, yellowish red to a deep, liver-colored hue with many red, gold, and coppery tints in between.

DUN—A dull yellow-brown or yellow-gray which ranges from a creamy shade, called Isabella, to a darker color called buckskin.

GRAY—Actually a mixture of white and black hairs which gives an over-all gray look. Ranges from a deep gun-metal hue to almost white. Many horses called white are, in fact, just very light gray. Dappling is common among grays.

ROAN—Like gray, roan coloration is a mixture of different-colored hairs. There are two types: strawberry roan, which is an intermingling of reddish, white, and yellow hairs, and blue roan, a similar mixture of black, white, and yellow. Like grays, roans come in a fairly wide range of shades from light to dark.

SORREL—Similar to dun with more stress on a reddish tint.

WHITE—Pure white, an extremely rare color occurring in animals with over-all pink skin. Most often found in albino horses which quite commonly have sun-sensitive eyes.

HEAD MARKINGS

STAR—Small patch of white on forehead.

BLAZE—Larger such patch. When it covers the entire face, the animal is called calf-faced or white-faced.

STRIP—A patch starting between the eyes and running part way down the face.

STRIPE—A thin white line running down the face to the bridge of the nose or lower.

SNIP—A small white or flesh-colored marking on the lip or nose.

LEG MARKINGS

STOCKING—White almost reaching the knee of the foreleg and hock of the hind leg.

HALF-STOCKING—A stocking which only reaches halfway or so to the above joints.

SOCK—A white anklet which reaches about to the fetlock.

The above are the only markings permissible on any purebred horse of the solid-color families. Except in the cases of rare congenital freaks—the Thoroughbred race horse Candy Spots being one—white or colored markings on any parts of the body except the head and legs are an indication of breeding irregularity. This, of course, does not hold true in cases where an old injury may become overgrown with white hair. The markings of Appaloosa horses, Paints, and Palominos are discussed in Chapter Five.

The solid-color breeds trace back to the earliest written history of the desert peoples. (Indeed,

"Action" can
differ dramatically
among horse breeds.
Top: Low, long-striding
running gait of
Thoroughbred racer.
Below: Extremely
elevated action
of fine-harness horse
(left) at Devon,
Pennsylvania, show,
and swift
but mannered gait
of a top pacer.

their carefully preserved breeding records are among the first documents of any kind.) But there is plenty of evidence that painted and spotted breeds go back as far and even farther, since horses with such markings appear in the primitive cave paintings of Spain and southern France. What color, or pattern of colors, distinguished the horse's early ancestors is not certain. Some paleontologists believe these prehistoric prototypes may well have been striped. Striping persists to this day along the spine and on the legs of some dun-colored horses.

So much for similarities. Perhaps even more important are the minor structural differences which distinguish each breed, for what is highly desirable in one breed may be quite unwelcome in another. As noted earlier, each of the various horse families was developed through selective breeding to perform a specific job. The Thoroughbred was created to race, the Standardbred both to race and to provide fast harness transportation at a time when there were no automobiles. The durable Tennessee Walking Horse, with his unique, gliding gait, was developed for the express purpose of carrying plantation owners and overseers of the Old South over the vast reaches of their estates, and the versatile and tough little Morgan was made to satisfy the multiplicity of uses demanded by the New England farm folk.

A number of the coaching and saddle horses, among them the English Hackney horse and the three- and five-gaited American Saddle Horses were developed to meet the requirements not only of stout service, but of high fashion.

Gaits can be characterized generally in terms of action: the "low" action of the long-striding Thoroughbred race horse and the unusually "high" action of the gaited show horses and ponies.

The Thoroughbred is a beautiful animal, but primarily designed for speed. His good looks are the by-product of extreme functionalism. He is characterized by a sloping rump and long legs. There is great length in the measurement from point of hip to the hock—that portion of his anatomy sometimes described as his "drive shaft." Like any well-built athlete, his muscling is long and flat. Though tall—he occasionally reaches 17 hands—he is lean, weighing less than many horses of smaller stature. His great, pendular stride, which can cover upwards of twenty-four feet in one sequence, is loose and flexible, and the best of his breed will go "low as a Southern houn' dawg" in chewing up yardage on the track.

At the opposite extreme there is the very high action of the American Saddle Horse, who was created with style in mind. He is typified by a slender, arched neck, short back, and well-rounded barrel. His comparatively slighter hindquarters terminate in a long, nearly level croup. His pasterns—the short links between his hoofs and fetlock joints—are elongated to a degree that would be undesirable in most breeds, but which, in his case, enhances the "elevation" of his showy gaits. Of a top Saddler it is said that he "can canter all day in the shade of an apple tree."

All horses must be trained to perfect their natural gaits—the walk, the trot, and the gallop—and sometimes to modify them to movements that do not come naturally. One example of such a gait would be the pace, a highly mannered step in which the legs of either side move in unison. Others are such "collected" gaits as the rack and the slow canter, in which the horse is literally gathered up, shortened fore and aft under a carefully gauged rein, and held in a stiff high-stepping gait, when his inclination might be to slow to a walk or break into a faster clip. True, families of horses have been developed which have an inbred tendency to all of these "unnatural" gaits, but their execution still must be developed through long and patient training.

Of the natural gaits, even the walk must be disciplined so that the horse will pick up his feet neatly and not shamble along loosely. The walk should be an even, four-beat gait, slow enough

Cutting horse's ability to react swiftly, often without guidance, demonstrates extent to which equine intelligence can be developed.

so that the animal does not appear to be waddling, which occurs when the walk is too quick.

The trot is a metrically rhythmical gait in which the front and rear legs of the diagonal sides strike the ground in unison. A trot can be a slow and easy way for a rider to cover ground, the "strong," or quick, stylish trot of the show ring, or the all-out, thirty-mile-an-hour gait of the top trotting racer. The horse that trots correctly lifts his legs crisply but without exaggeration and throws the hoofs of his forelegs in front of him as he goes.

The uneven, three-beat gallop ranges from the canter, which is a slow gallop, all the way up to the furious running gait of the racing Thoroughbred. On a left lead—that is, a sequence of stride that begins on the left foreleg—the second foot to strike the ground will be the right hind leg, followed by the left hind and right fore in that order. In a slow, collected canter, there are short intervals when three feet are on the ground at the same time. In the race horse's fully extended gallop there is one phase in which all four feet are tucked under his body as he momentarily sails through the air.

The degree of ability which can be developed in a horse to race, jump, perform in the show ring, or execute a task lies only partly in the hands of the human instructor, however. The horse must himself have willingness—or "generosity," as horsemen usually call it—a quality that may be stimulated through proper training but may be soured by bad handling. It is also a capacity that would seem to have a relationship to intelligence.

Professor George Gaylord Simpson, of Harvard, an eminent historian of the horse, once observed that "The horse is both intelligent enough and stupid enough to do what we demand of him." To this it might be added that he also has superb physical equipment to do it with. He is, in fact, exceptionally well designed for man's use. His sensory system is far better balanced than that of most animals. His vision is extraordinary;

without moving his eyeballs he can see nearly as far to the rear as he can ahead. His hearing and sense of smell are highly developed. He is blessed with sharp reflexes and motor coordination that is generally considered superior to man's.

But the subject of the horse's intelligence, or lack of it, has always been a matter of hot debate between his sentimental admirers and skeptical detractors. Actually, it is also Dr. Simpson's opinion that the thought processes of the horse are "almost unrecognizably different from those of men," which, if true, would make comparisons of human and equine intellect fairly pointless. For it then becomes logical to ask whether our intelligence enables us to understand the horse any better than he does us.

In one facet of what we know as "intelligence" the horse is quite strong. He does have latent memory powers that can be strengthened to an astonishing degree. On the negative side, he rarely forgets a bad scare and can be counted on to react violently if similar circumstances recur.

More positively, an excellent instance of horse memory is the long and intricate routine performed by the Lipizzan stallions of the Spanish Riding School in Vienna. In some ways, exhibitions of the well-drilled stock horse's skill in cutting cattle are even more impressive. In these events, the horse, without any direction or "body cue" from the rider, must pick a designated steer from a herd and move it quickly to a selected location. The movements of the steer are often swift and always unpredictable, so that the horse must rely entirely on what he has been taught in meeting the contingencies that arise.

It is safer to evaluate the horse in terms of his personality than of his mental equipment. Anyone familiar with horses is aware that they vary considerably from one breed to another, and that there are great differences in personality among individual horses. There is a basic, inborn character in each horse, which, if deficient in quality, cannot be improved later by human masters, however skilled in horsemanship they may be.

Celebrated Lipizzaners of the Spanish Riding School in Vienna perform exacting routines during appearance at New York's Madison Square Garden. Stallions at right maneuver in unison.

Like human beings, horses can be charming or dull, energetic or listless. They can be as "dead game" as a great race horse striving to win on a shattered leg. And they can be plain, no-good bums. William Steinkraus, captain of the United States Equestrian Team, has called this kind of horse "a congenital rogue"—not simply "the spoiled horse, the high-strung horse, or the horse who is frightened because of past abuse," but the horse who is "fundamentally dishonest in the sense that he will try to cheat you if he can."

(The horse is not by nature a brave animal. Courage in the face of danger is something he is taught by man. It is true that horses can become vicious through bad treatment—and even, in certain rare and inexplicable instances, under good treatment. It is also true that a stallion, either in domestic stud or in a wild state, can be extremely hostile, particularly toward males of his own species.* But generally the horse inclines to timidity, which must be overcome if he is to be a useful, sociable animal.)

* In some parts of the world, the cruel but ancient practice of stallion fighting is perpetuated. Placed in an enclosure together, the horses bite each other and slash with their hoofs until one is killed, or maimed and helpless.

After man has done all he can, it remains for the individual horse to decide how much he is willing to give.

The evolution of the horse was a process that lasted some sixty million years. But to find the earliest ancestor of horses—or men either, for that matter—it is necessary to go back to the Jurassic period, the great age of the dinosaurs, one hundred and sixty million years ago. It was at this time that the first warm-blooded, furred creatures who bore their young live slowly emerged to become the common ancestors of all modern mammals. These were furtive little animals. Existence was a precarious affair in a world ruled by such rapacious predators as Tyrannosaurus rex and the eagle-eyed, flying pterodactyl. But survive they did, and as the era of the giant reptiles drew to an end some seventy-five million years ago, the mammals had become larger and a definite pattern of type differentiation had been established. At this time the ancestors of man and horse began to follow divergent paths.

Among the many predecessors of the horse was the now-extinct biological order of five-toed mammals, called condylarths, which was prevalent over the earth, save in Australia. Condylarths were thick-bodied, short-legged, inoffensive creatures. Scientific restorations of their skeletal remains remind one oddly of the animals young children draw. These rather nondescript beasts were to father the entire modern order of Perissodactyla, or "odd-toed," mammals to which the family of Equidae—the horse, the zebra, the ass, and the onager—belongs. (More distantly related to the horse within the order Perissodactyla are the rhinoceros and the tapir.)

Many of the condylarth's descendants never made it all the way up the evolutionary ladder. One was the terrifying two-horned titanothere. A specimen of this bully, a female not thought to be fully grown, was uncovered in South Dakota. It measured fourteen feet long, eight feet high, and four feet wide, and its outsized mandibles contained about eight pounds of teeth. The titan-

othere passed from the picture about thirty million years ago. Another evolutionary dropout in the clan was a tall, loutish beast, called the chalicothere, which sported long, curved hoofs and did not leave the scene until about a million years ago.

A much less impressive, though more durable, family descended from condylarthra was a mild-mannered tribe of leaf browsers called Hyracotherium. Fossil remains indicate it was quite common in the Paleocene epoch, which ended sixty million years ago. Ranging from ten to twenty inches in height, the Hyracotherium bore small resemblance to the modern horse except in one important respect: the feet showed signs of becoming hoofs.

Most Hyracotherium had four toes, the first digit having shrunk to a vestigial "splint," but one variety, a smallish chap about the size of a fox terrier, was somewhat more advanced in hoof evolution in that his hind feet had but three working toes. This was eohippus, the so-called "dawn horse." His fossilized remains have turned up in

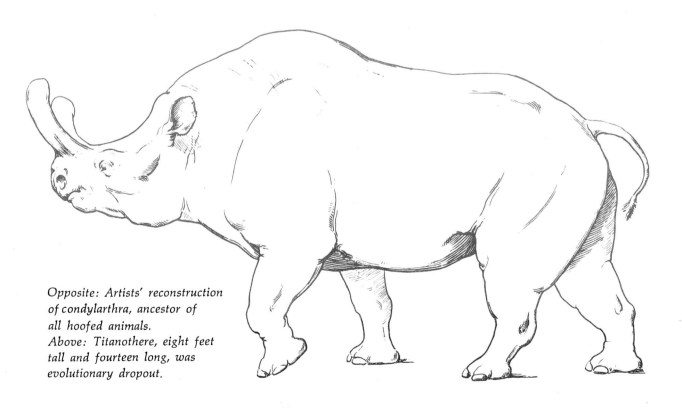

Opposite: Artists' reconstruction of condylarthra, ancestor of all hoofed animals.
Above: Titanothere, eight feet tall and fourteen long, was evolutionary dropout.

The Eohippus

Wyoming and New Mexico. Paleontologists have successfully linked eohippus to the modern horse.

Although there remains the remote possibility that there was a parallel development of Hyracotherium to horse in Eastern Asia, the evidence now seems to indicate that the horse is of purely North American origin. How early equine prototypes came to appear in other widely removed parts of the world will be seen shortly.

The steps by which the horse ascended in North America have been well recorded by fossils found in the corresponding strata of each geological epoch. The various evolutionary stages along the way are marked primarily by increases in height and progressive changes in the development of the mouth and hoof.

Many intermediary levels could be included here, but there are five principal milestones standing along the evolutionary route that brought the horse to his present-day state. The first is shy little eohippus himself, who is still properly classified as Hyracotherium. The feet, as noted earlier, show an inclination to become hoofs, particularly in the central digit which is becoming enlarged at the expense of its neighbors. This development is owing to the fact that defenseless eohippus went about almost constantly on the tips of his toes, alert to take flight at the approach of danger. His mouth was small and the crowns of the cheek teeth were low. There are the beginnings only of what will become molars. Restorations show him to be a charming little animal, but one which authorities like Simpson believe to have been excessively stupid. In geological time, he belongs to the late Paleocene epoch of perhaps sixty-five million years ago.

The Eocene epoch which ensued was a period when many modern orders of mammals emerged. The horse plods through these twenty million years in a series of minor transformations until he reaches a stage called the Mesohippus. This took place in the Oligocene epoch (forty million years ago). Mesohippus, of rather deerlike appearance, was about the size of a sheep and has

OF THE HORSE

The Mesohippus

The Pliohippus

The Merychippus

Two of horse's close relatives.
Burchell's Zebra (some horses have vestigial
striping) and Mongolian Wild Ass (right).

been pinpointed around South Dakota. He had three principal toes on each foot, with the central digit now showing considerable enlargement. The two side toes still touched the ground though they were probably of little use. The splint of the first toe was gone and that of the fifth was vestigial. His jaws were better developed and the teeth had higher crowns. Like Eohippus, he was a forest creature and subsisted on the leaves of trees.

In his study, *The Evolution of the Horse in Nature*, W. D. Matthews points out that the later development of the horse went hand in hand with the evolution of the great western plains. Before a gradually increasing flow of cooler and drier air from the north, the densely forested lands of the West were giving way to the less opulent vegetation of the plains. In Miocene time, which ended about ten million years ago, the horse's forebears were converted from munching leaves to grazing on grass. The open expanses also afforded less concealment from predatory foes and demanded more speed for self-protection. (It may be an unromantic way to look at it, but when a great Thoroughbred pounds so willingly down the homestretch, he is displaying nothing

more than an instinct his ancestors developed when running for their lives.)

The change in the horse family's environment brought corresponding anatomical developments. Merychippus, typical of the Miocene period, was about the size of a Shetland pony. His neck was somewhat lengthened since he had to stretch down and crop his food from the ground. His teeth, as adapted to the function of grinding up coarse grass, approximated those of the modern horse. Two side toes remained, but they no longer touched the ground and were on their way to becoming the splints of the present-day animal.

The Miocene epoch gave way to the Pliocene, which lasted until a mere million years ago. In equine history, this was the period of Pliohippus, numerous skeletal remains of which have turned up in Nebraska and in the Texas Panhandle. Pliohippus was a true miniature horse, about the size of a donkey. His hoof was thoroughly developed and the useless side toes had disappeared.

The stage is now set for Equus, the horse of today, whose evolution took place in the final million years of geological time, the epoch called the Pleistocene, in which we now live. Fossil

Two of horse's more distant relations.
Tapirs (left) at Rangoon Zoo, in Burma,
and Indian Rhinoceros.

specimens of this true wild horse, so like the modern animal in all respects save for a few man-made refinements, are found in profusion all over the American Southwest. Evidence points to their presence on this continent less than ten thousand years ago. This was long after man himself had arrived from Asia, though there is not a shred of evidence that horse had any relationship to man at this time except, possibly, as food.

Why were there no horses of any kind remaining in the New World when the Spaniards first set foot on the North American continent? And if the horse is truly an animal of North American origin, what accounts for the existence of fossil remains of the horse, in various states of evolution, in Asia, Europe, and South America?

The answer to the first question is not known. Famine, pestilence, the rigors of the ice age, and possibly an assist from the human hunter as well —all these factors may have combined to drive the horse from his native American heath.

Why he appeared on other continents during his evolutionary process is somewhat more easily answered. During this sixty-million-year period of growth, from Hyracotherium to Equus, it ap-

pears certain that at various times the evolving horse clan used the land bridge to Asia now washed by the Bering Strait in a series of migrations to the Old World. The same route was followed in the emigration of other animals of North American origin, like the camel and the pig, and in the immigration of such Old World mammals as the bison, the now-extinct mastodon, and eventually man himself. Expeditions of horse types from the New to the Old World may have begun as long as fifty million years ago. Other invasions of Asia, Europe, and Africa by progressively developing horse varieties took place in Miocene times—that is, between ten and twenty million years ago—and in the beginning of the Pliocene epoch, perhaps nine million years back.

None of these early migrants, however, survived to establish anything more than interesting, and often confusing, fossil beds. Only the fully developed Equus, which emigrated over the Bering route to Asia, and thence to the rest of the Old World, lived on to be domesticated by man. Surprisingly, this took place only ten thousand years or so ago, at about the same time the species vanished from North America.

2 A RIDE

I t is not known just where and when the first confrontation of man and horse took place. What probably happened on this encounter has been succinctly described by Dr. Simpson: "Equus undoubtedly eyed strange and clumsy Homo with apprehension, and this apprehension was well-justified because to Homo, Equus looked like food."

Primitive man was a hunter. He ate vegetables, but evidently meat suited him better for he undertook considerable risk in slaying some rather fearsome creatures: the bison, which still abounded in the Old World; the rhinoceros, a North American immigrant; and the now-extinct mammoth. From the beginning, men tended to be gregarious. Like wolves and coyotes, they hunted in packs. Their first crude settlements were camps of short duration established in areas where game abounded. The discovery of fire made these gathering places more comfortable and hence more permanent. The warmth of man's fires (and the enticing odor of his garbage heaps) also attracted an inquisitive little camp follower, the dog, whose aid in the hunt man enlisted at a very early period in history.

Human diet is revealed in the fossil debris man left in profusion around his campsites. Study of these ancient remains discloses that he enjoyed a wide variety of fish, fowl, and animal meat and that he had a particular liking for that of the horse. The rubbish pile around the site of a Cro-Magnon camp at Solutre, France, attests to this. Surrounding the camp, author-artist Pers Crowell tells us, there have been found "the remains of not less than one hundred thousand horses." And, he adds, there is no evidence the camp's inhabitants "either bred or raised any of these animals; it seems they pursued them only for food."

With the aid of the dog, man turned gradually from hunting to herding. Sheep, goats, and somewhat later cattle and pigs entered his pens at a distant date in prehistory. The establishment of stationary herds transformed the nomadic camps into settlements and, as the first shelters went up,

a need arose for beasts of burden to haul the heavier materials required for construction. And so man broke the ox, the onager, and the ass to his service.

The horse is believed to have been the last of the important animals to be domesticated. Most authorities doubt that he was ever herded to any great extent for food. Bigger and stronger than the ass, faster than the ox, and more susceptible to training than any beast yet encountered, the horse was soon recognized as too valuable to slaughter for food, hence the very early primitive taboos against eating horseflesh.

The usually accepted estimate that the domestication of the horse took place some four thousand years ago seems to be based on factual evidence that horses were in use in the Middle East around that time. Since 1950, when scientists began using carbon isotopes to determine the ages of ancient objects, the date has been fixed more precisely as considerably earlier. Investigation of the remains of a very early settlement named Sialk, on the western edge of the Persian desert, reveals the existence of a fairly sophisticated farming community employing horses of the sturdy desert type about six thousand years ago.

Another generally accepted though probably invalid cliche is that man drove the horse before he rode on his back. This appears to be based on a belief that ancient horses were too small to bear a man's weight. The best-informed authorities today say this is poppycock. The horses whose remains were uncovered in early human settlements were just as large as, and quite similar to, modern Arab horses, and a sound Arab can go all day with a two-hundred-pound rider in the saddle. Besides, they point out, it is hard to believe, on the basis of everything that is known about our curious and athletic ancestors, that they could have resisted the obvious temptation to climb on these horses' backs.

Certain it is, however, that the development of wheeled, horse-drawn vehicles had a far more drastic effect on the course of early civilization

Preceding pages: Rosa Bonheur's "Horse Fair" is famous representation of man-and-horse relationship. Opposite: Egyptian version of Hittite chariots.

than did the art of riding. Like such later inventions as the airplane and rocket, this invention had a double potential for good and evil. On the credit side, it registered a marked growth in commerce and industry, but in red ink it spelled war. And while the wagon of the merchant and the chariot of the soldier evolved side by side, it is the latter that dominates much of ancient history.

Military historians divide the chronology of warfare into three general phases: primitive war, the intertribal feuding of prehistoric man; historic war, which commences with discovery of the arts of horsemanship and writing; and modern war, the period which begins with the innovations of gunnery and printing. Primitive war seldom, if ever, arose from economic reasons, because man had no valuables to seize or defend. But given the mobility of the horse and his other servant animals, and the material advantages which accompanied a transportation culture, man began

to turn a greedy eye on the accumulating possessions of his neighbors. With improving communications, tribes grew larger and more cohesive, and finally turned into embryonic nations with common obsessions of conquest and of survival.

Such a people were the ambitious and warlike Hittites, who arose from somewhere in the general area of Sialk. Historians of the horse attach great importance to the early Hittites, because for many years the development of the superior Arabian horse was credited to them. They certainly were the most expert horsemen of their time. However, from the translation of a set of ancient Hittite tablets it now appears that they learned the equestrian arts from another people, their neighbors to the southeast. These were the Mitanni, linguistically an Aryan group with cultural ties to India.

The tablets contain instructions given to the

Hittites by a Mitanni named Kikkuli, who apparently served as a master of horse to the Hittite rulers. They prescribe a lengthy and highly detailed training routine for horses so like that employed in conditioning modern harness racers as to provoke incredulity in veteran trainers. They explain how horses are to be exercised daily at varying distances and speeds, then cooled out and rubbed, just as they are today. They even specify the use of warm water to wash down the animal after a workout, and the exact amount of fodder it should get (a sensible mixture of hay and barley), and when. They suggest a knowledge of horsemanship that could have come only from many centuries of experience, and the possibility of an even earlier date for the domestication of the horse, perhaps in India.

In about 1750 B.C., the Hittites exploded into the then rather serene land of Egypt, their light, horse-drawn chariots carrying all before them, and established the Hyksos (shepherd) dynasty of pharaohs that kept that nation under its heel for five centuries. Hittite men and horses also scored notable triumphs against Babylon and Assyria. Chariotry had existed long before this, but the Hittite chariot, with its six-spoked wheels and fighting crew of three men, was incomparably faster and more effective than the older, solid-wheeled cars. In *The Hittites*, O. R. Gurney writes: "It created a revolution in the nature of warfare: Henceforward speed was to be the determining factor in the battle."

The highly mobile Hittite troops, operating usually on the wide expanses of the North Afri-

Above: Frieze of Parthenon shows Greek cavalry, which was brought to peak of excellence under Philip of Macedon, and brilliantly used by Alexander the Great (opposite).

can and Near Eastern deserts, proved the marked superiority of equestrian forces over the traditional, tightly packed infantry phalanx in this sort of terrain. As a rule, the Hittites used infantry only to guard their command posts and baggage trains. In other places, notably Greece, there was rugged mountain country to contend with and here the infantry persisted. So it was partly because of topographical differences and partly because the desert peoples had access to more and better animals that ancient war in western Asia was horse-dominated, while that of Europe relied more heavily on foot soldiers. Effective use of the cavalry-infantry team was yet to come.

In 490 B.C., Greece was invaded by a vast force of Persians whose principal striking arm was comprised of numerous horse troops of excellent quality. This army deployed for battle on the plain of Marathon, where its great mobility would set the Greek foot soldiers at a disadvantage. But Miltiades, the Greek commander, wisely refrained from engaging the Persians on their own terms. He kept his foot troops concealed in the hills bordering the flat plain until his intelligence informed him that the Persian horses had been taken off to be watered. At this point, the Greeks came streaming from the hills to rout the inferior Persian infantry.

Philip of Macedon, who welded the Hellenic city-states into a nation a century and a half later, was the earliest commander to integrate horse and foot troops into a coordinated fighting force. He also expanded the role of his cavalry to add the functions of reconnaissance, maneuver, and pursuit to that of simple attack. Philip specialized his horse troops into three distinct types: one was heavily armed for the purpose of direct assault; another more lightly armed and mobile group was used in scouting and skirmishing. The third was a unit of dragoons, equipped to fight either afoot or ahorse.

Philip was assassinated in 336 B.C. and was succeeded by his son Alexander, who built the most efficient military machine the world had

yet seen and invented tactics that are still in use today. Of the several classically brilliant victories Alexander won while assembling his empire, that of Jhelum in 326 B.C. is thought to be outstanding. This engagement, fought in what is now the disputed state of Kashmir, pitted the young emperor against a wily general named Porus, who commanded some fifty-five thousand well-trained troops supported by nearly one hundred and fifty elephants, counterparts of today's tanks.

Alexander's first move was to lull his adversary into a false sense of security as he prepared for battle. This he did by sending out foraging parties to lay up vast supplies of provisions and thus give the enemy the impression he was preparing for a siege. Prior to crossing the Hydaspes river, he sent small detachments of cavalry up and down its banks, creating a great clamor at widely separated points. In each instance, Porus thought Alexander was about to cross in force and moved large bodies of troops up to meet him. The continual forced marching wearied his men,

strike the enemy rear. Total disorganization, which nullified Porus' attempt to use his elephants, resulted when Alexander's infantry hit from the opposite side and rolled up Porus' left flank. In the eight-hour battle, some twelve thousand Indian troops were slain. Alexander's losses numbered less than a thousand.

That Alexander was a master tactician is clear, but it is also observable in the histories of the ancient empires, including Alexander's, that the quality, as well as the quantity, of horses used had much to do with deciding the fortunes of war. In a detailed study published some forty years ago in *The Thoroughbred Record*, entitled "The Horse Called Arabian," Marguerite Farlee Bayliss took cognizance of the fact that every successful empire, from the Hittite through the Roman, depended on the fine desert stock of North Africa and the Middle East. Some of Mrs. Bayliss' conclusions, of which more will be said later, are inexact in the light of more recent historical evidence (though they still provide food for speculation), but this particular one is fundamentally correct.

At first, the Romans had inferior cavalry, mainly because their supply of good horses was inadequate. They learned a bitter lesson from the Carthaginian general Hannibal at the Battle of Cannae in 216 B.C. This encounter, which is given in detail in every modern textbook on tactics, saw Hannibal, who was slightly outnumbered but had more and better cavalry, send his horse troops from both flanks of his infantry center into a complete encirclement of the Roman legions, which were then annihilated.

After this debacle, Rome bent every effort to secure the better Eastern stock and to raise the proficiency of her mounted soldiers. In the end, it was the Roman cavalry that prevailed over Hannibal in his defeat at the hands of Scipio Africanus.

In time, Rome, too, fell before cavalry—the superbly mounted barbarians who swept over the borders of the Empire in the fourth century.

while the body of Alexander's force remained resting in camp.

When he felt he had Porus thoroughly confused, Alexander took a picked detachment of men, including about five thousand horse, well to the north of the enemy's base and rafted it across the river. To deceive his foe further, he left the bulk of his army in its original position, so that Porus would take his present maneuver to be a diversion. The ruse succeeded. Porus reacted by sending an inadequate force of some three thousand men to meet Alexander. This unit was quickly cut down as Alexander knifed southward toward Porus' lightly guarded right wing. Proceeding according to plan, the main body of Alexander's men now commenced crossing the river in a frontal assault. After parrying a thrust of cavalry which had been dispatched by Porus to defend his right wing, Alexander sent a fast unit of crack horsemen around to

Above: Not until Romans secured fine horses were they able to defeat Hannibal. Opposite: As medieval armor got heavier, horses grew bigger.

The weakness of Roman horse troops was clearly demonstrated in the crucial Battle of Adrianople in 378 A.D., in which they suffered a crushing defeat at the hands of the Goths.

For a good part of the dark ages which followed the collapse of the Roman Empire, "armies" consisted mainly of small forces of mounted aristocracy, or chivalry—a term deriving from "cheval," the French word for horse. The infantry in most cases had degenerated to little better than a rabble of looters which followed in the wake of the chevaliers. Warfare of those days has been described as "socially trivial" in that only a handful of the population was involved in, or even greatly affected by, its outcome.

The nature of combat in this period brought about a change in the kind of horses employed. Breastplates and helmets had been in use since ancient times, but the requirements of combat in the Middle Ages forced the knights to wear progressively heavier and more cumbersome armor. As a result, bigger and stronger horses had to be developed to carry not only the weight of the fully accomplished knight, but also the jointed steel skirting devised to protect the animal itself. The so-called "heavy breeds" of horses, predominantly cold-blooded in background, were "bred up" in size to meet this need. Later, when the cannon and musket ended the age of medieval warfare, these horses found useful work as farm and draft animals.

War was the medieval gentleman's way of life. A strong military flavor even permeated his sports, chief of which was the joust. Certainly the knight and his majestic steed, in the elaborately decorated armor they wore in the tournament, must have cut singularly heroic figures. Stephen V. Grancsay, former curator of arms and armor of New York's Metropolitan Museum of Art, describes the picture in these words: "No hero of any age ever surpassed the magnificence of the medieval knight when he entered the lists to display his prowess. Even his horse was enveloped in brilliant trappings. . . . Everything

about the games was attended by much chivalrous ceremony. Before the combats, the squires carried their masters' crested helms to the hall, where the king-at-arms judged each blazon, and where visitors—especially ladies—examined them with a critical eye."

Those faraway medieval years were witness to widespread ignorance and bigotry, and great oppression of the poor and unfortunate. Nevertheless, the crash of gunfire that ended the age of chivalry swept away rather admirable standards of nobility, as well—a code of courtly behavior expressed in the tests of knightly worthiness, the zeal of the early Crusades, the spirit of the joust, and the valor of the lone cavalier journeying abroad to fulfill a vow of honor. The bullet and cannon shot could not distinguish the hero from the coward, however, and a good part of the element of personal courage and skill at arms perished with it as the era came to a close.

The horse himself was generally relegated to a somewhat lesser role with the advent of gunpowder, though many engagements still lay ahead in which cavalry would play an important, even a decisive, part. Gustavus Adolphus's victories at Breitenfeld and Lutzen, Marlborough's success at Blenheim, and Frederick the Great's triumphs at Rossbach and Zorndorf were all won through well-executed cavalry movements. Again, in the American Civil War, the skillful employment of cavalry at such engagements as Chancellorsville and in the daring Confederate raids in the Shenandoah Valley gave the South the upper hand for the early part of the conflict. And, ultimately, it was the highly mobile cavalry force under General Philip Sheridan that contributed greatly to the collapse of the Confederacy. But no longer did the army consist mainly of horse to which the infantry was but an appendage.

Finally, in the middle of the nineteenth century, the perfection of long-range, rapid-firing weapons ended the effectiveness of the cavalry charge, as was disastrously proved by the Light Brigade at Balaklava. Thereafter, the role of the cavalry would be that of reconnaissance and liaison. It was a tragic anachronism, indeed, at the start of World War II, when a force of gallant Polish cavalry rode out to meet the Panzer divisions of the Nazis.

In view of the fact that the horse, through the centuries, has served his human master well in the pursuits of peace and war, it is not at all surprising that in the lore and letters of past ages, he is accorded a place of honor.

The Greeks had a special affection for horses, and, in the legends from which their epic literature is fashioned, he almost invariably appears as a symbol of the gods' munificence toward men, as opposed to reptiles, vultures, dogs, and goats, which often are represented in loathsome and monstrous forms dangerous to mankind's heroes.

Thomas Bulfinch takes note of the ancients' attitude in commenting on the half-man, half-horse centaurs. The Greeks, he says, were "too fond of a horse to consider the union of his nature with that of man as forming a very degraded compound, and, accordingly, the centaur is the only one of the fancied monsters of antiquity to which any good traits are assigned." It was in fact the most famous of the centaurs, Chiron, who was said to have brought men the skills of medicine, music, and the hunt, and to have taught the art of prophecy to the first sages.

The horse enters Greek mythology soon after Zeus, Poseidon, and Hades cast lots for the domains of earth, sea, and underworld. Poseidon, to whom fell the oceans, was, like his brother Zeus, plagued with a harridan for a wife—not without some justification, however, for the sea lord himself was of a grumpy, unpredictable nature and much given to dalliance with nymphs and goddesses.

Indeed, it was in lustful pursuit of his sister, the goddess Demeter, that he came to father the first horse. Demeter at this time was sorrowfully seeking her daughter, Persephone, who had been carried to the nether region as the unwilling bride of Hades. Not in a mood to gratify Poseidon, she changed herself into a mare. Poseidon was not deceived by the disguise and, transforming himself into a stallion, covered her as she grazed by the riverside. The wild horse, Arion, later to become the steed of Hercules, resulted from this union.

Of all the Grecian deities Poseidon was the one most concerned with horses. The stables of his stately underwater castle near Aegae were stocked with white stallions who drew his chariot through the waves as tritons and dolphins sported around them. Mythology also credits him with inventing horse racing.

Sometime after fathering Arion, Poseidon sired another horse. This took place one night as he lay with Medusa, who at that time was a beautiful maiden. Unexpectedly, the couple received a most unwelcome visit from Athena, who was in a rage because they had picked one of her tem-

Artillery ended era of chivalry.
Military horses hereafter would be lighter,
faster than those of Dark Ages.

ples to defile with their passion. Powerless to punish her lewd old uncle, Poseidon, Athena vented her spleen on the Gorgon maid by turning her into a hideous, winged monster with a lolling tongue, a coiffure of wriggling serpents, and a pair of burning eyes whose gaze turned men to stone. Later, when Perseus slew Medusa, the winged horse, Pegasus of the Wells, bounded from her womb.

Unruly Pegasus was gentled by Athena and given into the care of the Muses, who dwelled on Mount Helicon. Later, the hero Bellerophon, on the advice of a seer, sought the aid of the winged horse in destroying the fire-breathing monster, Chimera. With Athena's aid he bridled Pegasus, and in what surely must rank as the first convincing demonstration of the superiority of air power he flew over the Chimera, riddling its hide with arrows. After this and other notable deeds, Bellerophon was given the hand of Philonöe, daughter of King Iobantes of Lycia.

But now success so turned Bellerophon's head that the company of mere mortals palled. Saddling Pegasus once more, he set out on a heavenward flight to visit the gods on Olympus. Zeus was so irritated at this presumption that he dispatched a gadfly to sting Pegasus under the tail. The winged horse reeled in the sky, throwing Bellerophon back to earth where he landed painfully in a hedge of thorns. The fall left him lame and blind. Accursed by the gods who once befriended him, he wandered the earth, an object lesson to mortals who aspired to intimacy with the Olympians. Pegasus remained thereafter in the care of Zeus for whom he carried thunderbolts through the skies.

In mythology, as in religion, the horse frequently is assigned the honorable role of bearing heroic or divine persons to paradise. The Scandinavians believed that heroes slain in combat went to the great hall of Valhalla on the horses of the Valkyries. Mahomet is said to have ascended to heaven on a winged horse named Al Barak and described as a "fine-limbed, high-standing horse,

strong in frame, and with a coat glossy as marble."

From earliest recorded history to comparatively modern times, certain peoples have been favored from time to time by the intervention of divine horses and riders. Among them were the early Israelites. In II Kings vii, when the Jews are about to be annihilated by a huge force of Syrians, it is related: "For the Lord made the host of the Syrians to hear a noise of chariots, and a noise of horses, even the noise of a great host . . . putting them to flight."

In the battle of Lake Regillus, in 496 B.C., the celebrated equestrian gods, Castor and Pollux, came to the aid of the beleaguered Romans and helped them overcome the Latins. Much later than that, Saint James, the patron of horsemen, appeared on horseback on several occasions to help the Spanish battle the Moors. A mounted Archangel Michael led the French when they drove the English from Tournelles, in 1429.

Sometimes the hero and his horse are a symbol of hope for an oppressed people—for instance, King Marko and his steed Sharatz who encouraged the Serbians when they were in the thrall of Turkey, and later of other nations. Sharatz was a Piebald or Paint-type horse who trampled Turkish cavalrymen into the ground, contemptuously biting off the ears of their horses as he went. It was said he could leap four lance-lengths forward and three into the air. King Marko, the Serbs believe, is not dead, but slumbers in a cavern under the peak of Mount Urvina. With him Sharatz patiently waits. As he sleeps, King Marko's sword is slowly rising from the summit of the mountain. When it finally emerges, King Marko will ride out on Sharatz to deliver Serbia.

The horse of the hero or monarch has himself frequently been the object of veneration. Alexander the Great's horse, Bucephalus, so fiery that no one except his youthful master had been able to tame him, was buried in an alabaster tomb, and the young emperor built and named the city of Bucephala in his memory. The emperor Caligula of Rome appointed his horse, Incitatus, to the senate and was in fact about to elevate the animal to a consulship when he was himself assassinated.

El Morazillo, the horse ridden by Hernan Cortes in the conquest of Mexico, earned such reverence from the Indians that they essayed to feast him on chicken and fruit. When he failed to survive on this fare, they deified him and carved his likeness in stone, which image they and their descendants worshipped until it was finally smashed

some two centuries later by a Spanish priest.

In the United States, the hero's horse is not uncommonly revered. Robert E. Lee's beloved gray Traveler was ceremoniously buried on the campus of Washington and Lee University, where a monument stands to this day. General Philip Sheridan's black Morgan horse, Rienzi, on whose back he arrived just in time to rally his troops and win the battle of Cedar Creek, was stuffed after death and placed on exhibition at the Smithsonian Institution. Unfortunately his glistening ebony coat has faded to a pale yellow.

And sometimes, of course, the horse's fame far eclipses that of the master. Impressive monuments mark the last resting spots of such mighty Thoroughbred race horses as Man O' War, Exterminator, and Seabiscuit, the immortal bull-dogging mare Baby Doll, and the wicked rodeo bucker Midnight. The farm in Ohio where Dan Patch, the most celebrated harness racer of all time, spent his last days is now a museum.

Even horses and horsemen of whom little or nothing is really known, and who in some cases may never have existed at all, are deeply interwoven in the folklore and literature of the people of many lands. English highwayman Dick Turpin's whirlwind ride to London on his mare Black Bess, to establish an alibi, actually never happened. But Harrison Ainsworth drew upon this folk source for his popular novel, *Rookwood.* American writers have similarly tapped an abundant folklore to produce such classics as Washington Irving's "Legend of Sleepy Hollow," and Ambrose Bierce's "Horseman in the Sky." Though mythical in content, such literary works often reflect the atmosphere of an era better than historical fact. How aptly, for example, Irving captures the feeling of the wild and misty Catskills with his tale of a phantom rider, and how well Bierce reflects the melancholy of the Civil War South with his ghostly, brooding cavalryman!

The lore of the American West is mainly concerned with men and their horses—sometimes just with horses. One insistently recurring legend is that of the White Pacing Stallion, an elusive wild horse to whom supernatural powers were ascribed by Indians and frontiersmen alike. According to most accounts, which go back to the 1840's, he never was observed trotting or galloping, but always pacing and at a speed which defied all efforts to capture him.

Most incredible, and perhaps most popular, is the story of the White Stallion's adventure with a little immigrant German girl, who is usually named Gretchen. This child, about eight years old, was traveling west with her mother and father and numerous brothers and sisters. She had been tied securely to some meal sacks on the back of an old pack mare and had fallen asleep. A wheel on the family's wagon broke and, as it was being repaired, the mare wandered off. When Gretchen awoke the old pack animal was trotting along briskly in the wake of a prancing white horse. Toward dusk, they caught up with a numerous band of brood mares who found the meal in the sacks much to their liking, so much so that in their eager nipping at the bags they also nibbled the child's legs. The White Stallion is said to have run off the mares, chewed through the cords binding the little girl, and grabbing the collar of her dress in his teeth, he set her gently on the ground.

All the following day she was left alone, but on the ensuing morning she awoke to find the old mare had returned. Too small to get on the creature's back, she was in tearful despair until she heard the swift beat of the White Stallion's hoofs approaching. The stallion picked her up, set her on the mare's back, and shooed the beast off. Eventually the child and mare found their way back to the broken wagon. The child lived to be an old woman and, it is said, she often "proved" the veracity of her story by showing the scars on her legs where the mares had nipped her.

The horse plays an equally large role in the realm of painting and sculpture. As Geoffrey Grigson says: "The horse is admirably formed for the artist. He does not only symbolize power and rank and strength and speed, as the swiftest creature of the plains; he is made as it were to be drawn or carved. . . . His neck curves, his tail streams out, head, legs, body combine volume and delicacy."

Man has been painting and carving horses for a very long time, indeed. Credit for the discovery of some of the earliest known painting belongs to a sharp-eyed five-year-old girl, the daughter of a Spanish engineer and archaeology buff named Marcelino de Sautuola, who lived in Santander, near the French border. In 1879, following a trip to the Paris International Exposition, where his interest in primitive artifacts had been whetted by exhibits of prehistoric tools found in southern France, he visited a cave in the mountains nearby, accompanied by his small daughter, Maria. He was elated to discover a clutter of animal bones and stone implements, which he was busily attempting to classify when he heard Maria cry out: "Bulls! Look at the bulls!" The child pointed toward the ceiling. Flashing his lamp in that direction, de Sautuola made out a myriad of beautifully sketched figures of animals, some one hundred and fifty in all, including goats, boar, deer, bison (that Maria had thought were bulls), and horses. This was the now-famous Altamira cave, whose drawings are ascribed to a period between 30,000 and 10,000 B.C.

The art of the ancient cultures of North Africa and the Middle East—particulary Persia—is replete with horses, and as the arts reached their peak in the Golden Age of Greece, some of the most magnificent equine statuary of all time, such as the "living marble" of the Parthenon frieze, was produced. Rome, which slavishly imitated the Greeks in cultural matters, added some examples which are noteworthy, although they fall far short of the best produced in Greece.

In his book, *The Horse in Art*, David Livingstone – Learmonth says: "One may group paint-

Michelangelo da Caravaggio's
celebrated "Conversion of Saint Paul" is
considered a classic in equine art.

ers of horses roughly into three categories: those who put art before the horse; those who are determined to produce a work of art as well as a faithful representation of horses; and those of whom there have unfortunately been quite a number . . . who definitely put the horse before art."

Most of the great masters of painting included horses in their work with varying success. Leonardo da Vinci, for example, made magnificent sketches of horses, but tended to minimize them in the over-all design of his finished work. Paolo Uccello's dramatic and justly famous "Rout of San Romano" is marred, in the opinion of many critics, by two most unlikely looking horses which appear prominently in the foreground. Michelangelo da Caravaggio's "Conversion of Saint Paul," however, is a masterly blend of artistry and skill in representing a completely believable horse.

Rembrandt and Rubens shone in equestrian subjects, as did Velazquez. The Spaniard's celebrated equestrian portrait of the five-year-old Infante Baltasar Carlos, however, has probably stirred up more controversy than any horse picture before the invention of the photo-finish camera. Allowing for the bulging distortion in

the animal's barrel— an intentional effect because the picture was designed to be viewed from below —its severer critics, like Livingstone-Learmonth, noting that the painting was a royal commission, comment that the artist "hands out impossible flattery in a manner so convincing that one forgets it is flattery." It is, Livingstone-Learmonth says, "as though someone painted Mussolini winning the Derby or Hitler coming over the final fence before winning the Grand National." Defending the portrait, Werner Schmalenbach, in *The Noble Horse*, sees it as combining "the official business of a court portrait" with "the unofficial pleasure of a Baroque painter grasping a fleeting moment." It is, moreover, he says, "a delightful piece of painting, no longer involved in the study of details, but enjoying its own freedom."

The artist who has probably won most praise for his treatment of equestrian subjects is the German Albrecht Durer, whose "The Knight, Death and the Devil," is a classic depiction of the hero faced with the eternal problems of death or dishonor. Note that the horse of Death is jaded almost to the point of foundering, while that of the knight expresses resolution. The animal's step is confident, his head is held smartly, and the

Upper: Polo scene from Persian manuscript. Lower: Fifteenth-century Florentine horse race. Right: Belles Heures of Jean, Duc de Berry, depicts the Duke setting forth on journey.

Damuien   Nuam was ta

ears are alertly cocked to peril. Indeed, the knight appears to be drawing his own strength of purpose from the courage of his steed.

Notable artists of more recent vintage have also found in the horse an engaging subject for brush and chisel. Outstanding have been Goya, David, Delacroix, Degas, Manet, and Toulouse-Lautrec; and, later still, Rouault, Chagall, Braque, and Picasso.

In the meticulous but utterly simple style that characterizes the art of the East, the painters and sculptors of Persia, India, and China left behind them a treasury of equestrian art. The Chinese, who so greatly admired beautiful horses that they sent embassies to secure the prize stock of the desert, were especially adept at representing these animals in artistic forms. Li Lung-mien, of the Sung Dynasty in the late eleventh century, and Chao Meng-fu, of a hundred or so years later, are among the Eastern artists well remembered for their exquisite scroll paintings of horses.

Almost entirely within the world of horsemen and the "hunt set," there arose, mainly in Britain, a school of specialization in art which produced a profusion of "sporting prints," without a set of which no country pub or squire's den was complete. Of these, the English critic John Cadfryn-Roberts notes: "The artistic merit of the sporting print has often been questioned....But the English sporting print has an invaluable position in the field of art. At worst it is a unique record of a unique period in sport with its detail and often its humor, conscious or unconscious. And at best the quality of some of the leading artists and painters—Stubbs and Marshall, Morland and Alken, Pollard and Turner to name but a few—can only be described as superlative...."

The period in which these men worked was the Golden Age of racing and fox hunting in England. Exaggerated decorum was the order of the day, when even an insult would be prefaced by a courteous, "By your leave, sir." The amusing combination of pomposity and pratfall comedy innate in hunting did not escape the notice of artists like Henry Alken, whose work so frequently depicts dandified riders sprawled on the ground while the backsides of their horses stick up from the far side of a hedge or fence. When fox ap-

*Right: Durer's "The Knight,
Death and the Devil" is sublime equine art.
Above: Horse on medieval amulet.*

*Above: Odd proportions of Velazquez'
equestrian portrait of Infante Baltasar Carlos
stirred controversy. Right: Stubbs' painting of
Willman family with Eclipse.*

pears in the picture he is likely to be flying as fast as his four legs will carry him, but his face almost invariably wears a sly and lecherous smirk of so human a character that it suggests he is about to circulate a scandalous rumor or, perhaps, crack an off-color joke.

The times surely cried out for caricature and the response was a large and often brilliant band of satirical artists like Gillray, Cruikshank, Tenniel, Daumier, and Thomas Rowlandson, who gave particular attention to the more ridiculous aspects of the hunt.

In the nineteenth century, horse racing had taken a firm hold on public fancy in England and continental Europe, and in America, as well. The equine stars of the turf became noted personalities and, as such, fit subjects for formal portraiture. In the poorer examples of horse portraits (even today; for they are still much in demand by proud owners), there is often considerable un-

intentional humor. It is reflected in the overly haughty bearing of the subject and in the flattering camouflage of his minor defects.

The best horse portraiture, however, must rank as painting of real worth. Of George Stubbs, one of the best horse portraitists, Grigson writes: "The connoisseur may be irritated because too few of his countrymen value [him] for his painting; too many for painting horses." Rosa Bonheur, a French specialist in animal painting, also executed many outstanding portraits of race horses of the period, as did the English-born Edward Troye in America.

The British author and eminent amateur jockey John Hislop speaks of this as an "era of great horses and great men, of progress, development, and change." But, with the advent of the steam locomotive, it also became the period in which the horse himself changed from a creature of necessity to an item of luxury.

3 HORSES OF

THE BLOOD

The history of hunting and racing is so intertwined that it is difficult to dissociate them. This has come about through the people who participated in these sports, as well as through the kinds of horses they employed. While each of these diversions is usually thought of as a development of the past two and a half centuries or so—those years which reflect the impact of the Thoroughbred horse on mounted sports—both actually have taproots deep in classical history.

The first known race involving mounted riders appears in the records of the Olympic Games of 642 B.C., when a "woman of well-rounded domestic skills" (and doubtless other virtues of like description) was put up as a trophy for the winner. Hunting on horseback and to hounds was also a popular pastime of the Greek aristocracy. "It makes the body healthy, improves the sight and hearing, and keeps men from growing old," wrote Xenophon in the fifth century B.C. Many fox-hunting "widows" today might add that it keeps them from growing up at all.

Both hunting and racing were brought to Britain by the Romans, who had acquired them—as they acquired so much else—from the Greeks. There is evidence that the earliest races there took place on Salisbury Plain, near Stonehenge, and it is known that racing and hunting flourished throughout the six centuries of Roman occupation and the Anglo-Saxon period which followed.

When William the Conqueror established Norman rule in 1066, the character of all sport assumed an aristocratic flavor. Racing became the affair of the nobles. Richard I, in fact, offered the first known "purse money" to a group of his knights who raced over a three-mile course. History does not record the victor, but the prize was £40 in gold. The hunt became even more a prerogative of nobility when vast tracts of prime forestland were set aside as royal hunting parks for the exclusive use of the sovereign and his court.

Lady Viola Apsley, in "Bridleways Through History," has noted that in Britain "a passion for Hunting" appeared to be a "characteristic that most of our ancestors shared in common—a taste which has defied the passage of time and adjusted itself in a remarkable manner to the exigencies of each period in our history."

"Most particularly," she continues, "has Hunting appealed to that type of mind and character fated to be in the forefront of the action of the times." She might well have added racing as another preoccupation of England's leading public figures over the years, its patrons in many cases being the same persons who followed the hunt with such zeal.

Hunting and racing have enraptured an almost unbroken succession of British rulers from the Conqueror until the present day. Queens as well as kings. Good Queen Bess pursued the stag from the age of five until she was quite old. Queen Anne followed the hounds until she became too fat to sit a horse. Queen Victoria enjoyed the hunt, as does that fine horsewoman, Queen Elizabeth II. All of these ladies were also extremely active in racing. The colors of the current monarch are a familiar sight to all who follow the British turf.

Until the Stuart era, hunting in England was a crude, hell-for-leather sport. In France, however, where the chase was so refined it even had patron saints (Saint Hubert and Saint Eustace), it was far more orderly and in every way technically superior. When James I ascended the British throne, one of his first acts was to summon huntsmen from across the Channel to teach his subjects better hunting manners and methods. To this day, hunting in England and America is patterned after the French mode.

The impact that James I and succeeding Stuarts had upon racing was even greater than it had been upon hunting. James, in association with George Villiers, the Duke of Buckingham, established regular race meets at Croydon and Enfield, and encouraged the breeding of fleet Eastern-type blood horses for racing purposes. James I's

Preceding pages: Thoroughbreds break from gate at New York's Aqueduct racecourse.

running stable and his racing stud at Tutbury were inherited by Charles I, a somewhat less avid horseman. Upon Charles' death and the interregnum of the puritanical "Roundheads," racing was banned as immoral, although Oliver Cromwell was a great lover of fine horseflesh and managed secretly to acquire several of the royal horses for himself. The Stuart Restoration, which enthroned Charles II in 1660, marked the return of racing, on a far vaster scale than before.

Charles, often called "the Father of the British Turf," was devoted both to racing and to the pleasures of the hunting field. His extravagances had the exchequer in a continual turmoil, even as his affairs of the heart kept a succession of mistresses in maternity garb, but his contributions to the progress of racing and hunting cannot be minimized. Once in power, he reestablished the Royal Stud and took over the small racecourse at Newmarket, started by James I, and made it the center of British racing. (It remains an important hub of racing to this day.) Charles often rode in races himself, and in this way helped popularize the sport among his courtiers and the public at large. By the time he died, in 1685, the foundation of modern horse racing had been laid.

It was not long after Charles' death that a British Army officer, one Captain Byerly, brought to England a horse of desert blood which he had acquired in Turkey. This horse, which we know today as the Byerly Turk, was the first of three such "horses of the blood" from which all modern Thoroughbreds are said to be descended. The Byerly Turk was followed in 1704 by the Darley Arabian, a stallion bought in Syria by a certain Thomas Darley. Some twenty-five years after that, the third appeared. This was the Godolphin Barb, so named because he stood in the stud of the Earl of Godolphin.

Throughout the entire formative period in Thoroughbred history there is considerable confusion over the use of the designations "Barb," "Turk," and "Arabian." Correctly, the appellation "Barb" means a horse whose breeding is of the blood of the Barbary region of North Africa. A "Turk" is a horse of Turkish descent and, similarly, an "Arabian" is of Arabian stock. All too often the terms were used to indicate the places where horses had been acquired, rather than their true breeding. Thus, if a Barb was purchased in Turkey or Arabia the animal would become incorrectly known as a Turk, or an Arabian. Whatever the mistakes of nomenclature, the three breeds originally were derived from the same hot-blooded desert strain, although the Arabian was unquestionably more refined because of the greater care exercised by his breeders.

The three Eastern progenitors were sires of exceptional prepotency. Standing 15 hands or so—small compared to the modern Thoroughbred but taller than the average Arab of today—they were able to reproduce through three of their linear descendants, the foundation sires of the Thoroughbred dynasty, such exceptional qualities of speed and stamina that the British General Stud Book excluded all other bloodlines on the male line at the turn of the nineteenth century.

The three descendants of these Eastern stallions which founded the Thoroughbred family were: Matchem, foaled in 1748, a grandson of the Godolphin; Herod, in 1758, a great-great-grandson of the Byerly Turk; and Eclipse, in 1764, a great-great-grandson of the Darley Arabian. Each of these horses enjoyed a spectacular racing career, which, taken together with the quality of their offspring, led to their being designated the Thoroughbred foundation sires. Matchem, who ran in the silks of one William Fenwick, of North Cumberland, began racing at the age of five and was not defeated for several seasons thereafter. His two most famous wins were earned against the celebrated runner Trajan, at Newmarket, over a course of four and a quarter miles. Throughout a lengthy racing career he was rarely defeated and, after winning his last race at the age of fifteen, he retired to an equally successful term at stud. His rather slender modern line of descendance includes the American

Fair Play family, whence sprang Man O' War, still considered by many to have been the United States' greatest race horse.

Herod, bearing the colors of the Duke of Cumberland, also entered racing at the age of five (this was the customary age in those times) and went undefeated for more than two years. Thereafter, he was plagued by a circulatory injury, but in 1780, at age thirteen, he climaxed his running career by defeating the good horse Ascham, an animal which, incidentally, had been the first to defeat him five years before. Herod's male line of descendance is perhaps the least impressive of the three, but through a large number of crosses on the distaff side his blood is the most widely diffused.

Eclipse also was bred by the Duke of Cumberland, who died shortly thereafter. The colt then passed through the hands of a sheep dealer named Wildman and to a swaggering Irish officer, Captain Denis O'Kelley. Legend has it that Eclipse was so named because he was foaled during a total eclipse of the sun, and, to the extent that there was indeed a solar eclipse in the year of his birth, history supports this bit of folklore. But even if it was no more than coincidence, the big chestnut horse lived up to his name by eclipsing every horse to face him. His strenuous career lasted only a year and a half, but was so overwhelmingly successful that it gave birth to a long-lived turf cliche: "Eclipse first, the rest nowhere." The same could be said of his progeny down the male side, which far outstrips that of the other two founding sires.

All modern Thoroughbreds, it is claimed, are descended in the male line from these three stallions. While records of the earlier years—those which predate the appearance of the British General Stud Book—are not well enough validated to make this assertion one hundred per cent ironclad, it can be accepted at its face value, as far as any important influence on breeding is concerned.

It is also maintained that the mares to which

Charles II, called "Father of the British Turf," established big-league racing in England; often rode races himself.

54

August 24 1684.
The last Horse Race
Run before
CHARLES the Second of
Blessed Memory
By Dorsett Ferry
near
Windsor Castle.

these stallions and their direct descendants were bred were also of pure, or very nearly pure, Eastern background. This is questionable. It is true that many of these brood mares did have strong ancestral ties to the desert stock. Some were, in fact, imported directly from the Near East and North Africa. There is, however, no documentary proof that the pedigrees of all were so overwhelmingly Oriental that the influence of other strains is wholly inconsequential. There is, in fact, much evidence to the contrary.

Horses of Eastern background had been in Britain since the days of the Romans, who for centuries had exacted these animals as tribute from Roman vassal states in Syria, Arabia, and North Africa and had then scattered them to the far corners of the Empire. Later, the Crusades to the Holy Lands resulted in a steady stream of desert-type horses to England. After these military expeditions to the Near East were halted, other Arabians, Barbs, and Turks were imported —most notably by Henry VIII. Still another wave immigrated into Britain through Spain as a result of Charles I's projected engagement to the Spanish Infanta. All of this would appear to support the contention that today's Thoroughbred is to all intents and purposes a horse of impeccable Eastern descent on both sides.

But if that is true, what accounts for the very marked differences between modern Thoroughbreds and modern Arabians? Contemporary Thoroughbreds are tall, rangy in build, and the swiftest-known breed afoot. The Arabian is considerably smaller and more compact. And, while he is the most durable of the light-horse breeds, he is anything but speedy. There are important anatomical and conformational differences, too. The Arabian, for example, has one less vertebra than the Thoroughbred. A good-looking Thoroughbred is said to have an "Oriental head," but this feature at its best does not approach the classical quality of the Arabian head. In brief, these are two quite dissimilar horses.

It has been argued that the fine pasturage and vigorous climate of England has been mainly responsible for the differences. There is a very slight bit of truth in this statement, because it is a fact that over a long span of years the Thoroughbred did increase a bit in average height. But the horse is an animal of extremely slow evolution; it took him sixty million years to reach his present estate. So the environmental factor in no way explains how the 15-hand Godolphin Barb (some records say he was even smaller) in two generations could have produced the 16.3-hand Matchem, a horse who in every particular resembled the Thoroughbred of today.

Two theories are offered to explain the differences between the modern breeds of Arabians and Thoroughbreds. There may well be some truth to both. The first is that offered by Mrs. Bayliss in "The Horse Called Arabian." While in no way minimizing the virtues of the modern Arab, Mrs. Bayliss here sets forth the contention that today's Thoroughbred is descended from an entirely different strain of desert horse, one much larger and swifter than the Eastern horses of today. She takes care to distinguish between horses that should properly be called "Arabs" for the geographical reason that they were bred in that part of the world, and those which she calls "Arabians," as being biologically "of the blood," i.e., of Thoroughbred ancestors. Writing in 1926, she stated flatly that "if the *Arabian* horse is not extinct in Arabia, it is surely very nearly so. It is said that at the close of the Middle Ages there were not six hundred horses of the blood left in Arabia Deserta but since then we have withdrawn the cream for the formation of our racing Arabian breed."

Mrs. Bayliss may have been a highly provocative writer but, as authoress of the meticulously compiled *Matriarchy of the American Turf*, her credentials are very much in order. Some substantiation of her belief appears in a number of works written during the formative

J. N. Sartorius portrait of Darley Arabian, whose line of descent, through Eclipse, is largest of founding sires'.

The Darley Arabian

57

Thoroughbreds at great Bluegrass
breeding farms. Mares and foals (opposite,
top and bottom) graze at A. B. "Bull"
Hancock's Claiborne Farm, Paris, Kentucky.
Foal of a few days (below) finds
the "milk bar" at Leslie Combs II's Spendthrift
Farm, Lexington, also home of successful
sire Dark Star (bottom, left), 1953 Derby winner.
Brood mares (bottom, right) are of John W.
Galbreath's Darby Dan Farm, Lexington.

years of the Thoroughbred clan. As late as 1771, Richard Berenger, master of horse to the British crown, for example, describes the Barbary horse, which he says was then common in Europe, as having "withers standing high and fine." Its gallop, he said, was "very rapid." The Arab of today is characterized by low, flat withers and, as noted, a gallop that can scarcely be called "very rapid."

The other explanation, and one which unquestionably has much foundation in fact, is that during all the years when Eastern horses were being brought to England prior to the arrival of the Byerly, the Darley, and the Godolphin, there had been a considerable amount of crossing of these desert types with the so-called Great Horses of chivalry. It is known, for example, that there is a good deal of Arabian blood in the background of the big Percheron. All this leads us to the inescapable conclusion that the early so-called "taproot" mares were not all so "Eastern" as some historians would like us to believe. And it is probably the breeding influence of the distaff side that accounts for most of the differences between the Thoroughbred and the Arab.

The emergence of the Thoroughbred in the early 1800's had a tremendous effect on the English sporting scene. Horse racing took a strong grip on the public fancy. The passion swelled rapidly throughout the eighteenth century with the wholehearted support of the British crown, first through Queen Anne, a ruler whose historical influence upon English racing ranks next in importance only to Charles II's. "Herself an enthusiastic owner," writes John Hislop, "she founded Ascot races, and the Royal Meeting of the present day appropriately opens with the Queen Anne stakes."

During this period, Hislop points out, "the practice of 'match' races, pitting just two horses against each other, gave way to larger fields of several horses." The idea of handicapping was introduced, though the method of that time of adding weight for inches of height was later to be supplanted by the weight-for-age system of today.* In 1750, the British Jockey Club was founded and its powers gradually expanded until it became the governing body of the sport in England. Around the very end of the century, the General Stud Book, the first accurate registry of pedigrees, appeared.

Queen Anne and the succeeding Georges were also great patrons of the hunt, where not only the speed but the "fencing" ability of the Thoroughbred was soon felt. It was during this time that fox hunting came into its own. Fox was not widely hunted until around the start of the century. Until then, the stag, the boar, and the hare were still the principal objects of the chase, while fox were destroyed as vermin and without ceremony. Much of this earlier hunting was in dense woodland and the tempo of the hunt was usually very slow. The increasingly large areas being cleared for agriculture and the consequent shrinking of the forests brought about the switch to fox. Fox was not only better suited to open-field hunting, but his destruction was justifiable on the grounds that he was a nuisance to the farmer. A good democratic relationship thereby grew up between the rural aristocracy and its farm tenantry. (A rather excessive instance of this cordiality is recorded by a contemporary writer who happened to attend a dinner proffered by Lord Yarborough to the tenants whose fields he hunted —a customary sort of affair to this day in hunting circles everywhere. On this occasion, an after-dinner speaker remarked in a most complimentary way: "What astonishes me is where Lord Yarborough gets his tenants," whereupon a stout farmer spoke up at once and said: "I'll tell you, sir, his lordship breeds 'em.")

In 1730, the Belvoir became the first hunt devoted exclusively to the pursuit of fox. It was followed shortly thereafter by a succession of great hunts many of which, like the Quorn, are in existence to this day. But England is a coun-

---

* In early American racing, handicapping was effected by giving the lesser horse a head start.

*Saddling up for a point-to-point, the annual
Grand National at Butler, Maryland.*

try where traditions die hard and the new-fangled sport of fox hunting did not find immediate acceptance among more serious elements in the community. Much foolery and many drunken antics marked the sport in its earlier days. In *The Fable of the Bees,* written by Bernard de Mandeville in 1714, the author notes that "Fox hunters who have all day long tried in vain to break their necks, join at night in a second attempt on their lives by drinking." Alexander Pope wrote in a similarly caustic vein. In a letter to a friend he describes the fox hunter as pursuing "with eagerness and hazard something not worth the catching." Another writer of the times added that "among the educated classes a fox hunter passed for, if not a fool, a clown." There is also no question that the early low repute in which fox hunting was held accounts for the abundance of caricature of the time, poking fun at the sport.

But by the end of the eighteenth century, fox hunting was firmly entrenched, and by the mid-nineteenth it had become a national rage. The American authoress Harriet Beecher Stowe, visiting in England at this time, recalled one evening while dining with Earl Russell and some friends that "the conversation turned on hunting." She expressed her astonishment that "in the height of British civilization this vestige of the savage state should remain." But, she said, "they only laughed and told more hunting stories." Perhaps Mrs. Stowe chose to overlook the fact that fox hunting was even then almost as old and well-established in America as it was in England, the first pack of hounds having arrived in Maryland in 1650 with a colonist named Robert Brooke, following which the sport spread rapidly.

The great facility with which the Thoroughbred horse negotiated fences, walls, banks, and streams was not only a great contributing factor in the rise of fox hunting's popularity, but also helped to promote steeplechasing, which is actually horse racing under simulated hunt condi-tions. These began as so-called "point-to-point," or here-to-there, events contested in open country, which were popular throughout colonial America, particularly in the Tidewater South where they flourish to this day. Not infrequently the second "point" was a faraway steeple—hence, the "steeple chase." England's Grand National, at Aintree, and the American Maryland Hunt Cup, at Glyndon, Maryland, are popular modern-day events descended from these informal beginnings.

In America, racing "on the flat" got its start in the towns and villages themselves. Many early settlements in Pennsylvania and the southeastern states had a straight thoroughfare designated as "Race Street" and not a few retain streets of that name to this day.

Similar races were conducted on straightaways cut through the thick woodland which covered much of the East in colonial times. Sometimes these early racecourses were nothing more than improved Indian trails. The distances were short and horses were bred for terrific speed for short intervals of time. Since few colonists could afford horses that did nothing for their keep except race, these animals had also to be good all-around workaday performers. In this way, the famous American breed of Quarter Horses—horses that had speed for the customary quarter-mile races of the time—came into being. Later, when Thoroughbreds became established as America's flat-racing breed, quite a number of these stout animals went west. Their qualities mixed well with those of the better grade of Spanish mustangs and the result was the modern Quarter Horse, without question the finest horse ever developed for handling livestock and one that knows no peer in kindness and amenability to training for complicated chores.

Tracks for flat racing evolved from the early straightaways to the oval, or "end-to-end," track. The first of these was laid out on Long Island in 1665. Richard Nicolls, the first En-

Above: Governor Nicolls institutes formal horse racing on Long Island. Below: Match race between American Eclipse and Sir Henry.

Great Match Race

Between the North and the South
New Union Course, L.I. May 27th 1823

Between Eclipse and Sir Henry
Heats Four Miles
Purse $20,000

Good race horses are both born and made. Right: D. M. "Mike" Smithwick schools steeplechaser over brush on Long Island estate of Ogden Phipps. Jump-racers learn first on longe line, without rider. Below, left: Early step in breaking Thoroughbred race horse. At Miss Judy Johnson's Blarney Farm outside Baltimore, Maryland, one handler circles yearling on a longe, while the other taps horse with light bamboo pole to propel him forward. Below, right: First time out on training track. Miss Johnson, seasoned breaker of yearling Thoroughbreds, rides mature, quiet horse between two youngsters to set them an example of track deportment.

glish governor of New York after the colony was seized from the Dutch, established a course at a spot called Salisbury Plain, not far from where the modern racing center, Belmont Park, stands today. Nicolls, a great racing fan in his homeland, named the course "Newmarket" in honor of the racing plant that Charles II had established a quarter century earlier in England. The horses raced at Salisbury Plain were not Thoroughbreds. This was almost a century before the first Thoroughbred sire was foaled. It is believed these animals were mainly a type called "Dutch" horses, a strain imported from Holland and bred in the valleys of the Hudson and Connecticut rivers. The breed was chunky and durable and its blood figures importantly in the development of such American breeds as the Morgan and the Standardbred.

Even though the word "Thoroughbred" had yet to be coined, there are frequent mentions of "bred" horses in the English and colonial American records of most of the eighteenth century. The references were to animals of outstanding Eastern parentage. The first such "bred" stallion to come to North America was Bulle Rocke, a son of the Darley Arabian, who arrived in Virginia in 1730.

During the Revolutionary War, New York was virtually the only place where racing continued to operate, albeit on a restricted basis and mainly for the amusement of the British soldiery stationed there. The Revolution featured no cavalry engagements of any note. The heavily forested character of the countryside was a complete deterrent to the cavalry charge, and thereby acted as an ally of the Americans, for the British army had superb cavalry it could not bring to bear on the rebels. Nevertheless, horses were in heavy demand as officers' mounts, and for hauling artillery and baggage trains, so that the conflict greatly depleted the new country's equine stock. Heavy fighting drove much of the breeding activity out of Tidewater Virginia and Maryland and into Ken-

tucky (then actually a part of Virginia). When the war ended, the citizens of the new republic had to look to the mother country for new breeding stock.

The first postwar imports were led by a smallish gray stallion named Medley, in 1784. He was followed by Shark, a horse with a brilliant racing record in England, then by Messenger, and finally by Diomed. Messenger and Diomed are of particular interest. Messenger not only appears in the bloodlines of many outstanding Thoroughbreds of today, including those of the notable Kelso, but, through his great-grandson, Rysdyck's Hambletonian, he also founded the Standardbred harness-racing family.* Diomed had been the winner of the very first Epsom Derby, in which he carried the silks of Sir Charles Bunbury, one of the noted and influential figures of British turf history. He was a venerable twenty-one years of age when he arrived in the United States. For some reason, his reputation in the breeding shed had, in later years, greatly deterioriated in his home country. He was so notorious as a "bad foal-getter" that his stud fee had dropped to a paltry $10 when he was purchased by Colonel John Hoomes, of Bowling Green, Virginia, for $250. Diomed's poor repute in the stud preceded him to America, but William Ransom Johnson, a handsome North Carolinian who was the leading racing man in post-Revolutionary America, nevertheless bred several mares to him.

Running in Johnson's silks, Diomed's son, Sir Archy, mowed down all opposition and retired to become the first important native-bred stallion. Other early descendants of Diomed were his grandchildren, American Eclipse, the standout horse of his generation, and the fabulous filly, Haynie's Maria.

Maria occupies a unique niche in history, as William H. P. Robertson has noted in his excellent and comprehensive *History of Thoroughbred Racing in America*. According to Robertson, Haynie's Maria was the only living creature ever to

---

* Messenger's sire, Mambrino, had a penchant for offspring of mannered gaits. He figures importantly also in the ancestry of the English Hackney and American Saddle Horse.

defy successfully the iron will of General Andrew Jackson. Jackson, like many prominent early Americans, was an ardent follower of the turf. In the first years of the nineteenth century, Jackson established an important center of racing at Nashville, Tennessee. Hither, in 1806, came a well-known trainer of the day named Green Berry Williams—familiarly "Uncle Berry." The very first horse Williams entered in the races there was soundly beaten by a horse from General Jackson's stable. For some reason, Williams was outraged. Although a friend and admirer of "Old Hickory," he vowed he would never lose another race to him. In beating Jackson's horses thirteen consecutive times, Williams—to use Robertson's words—employed Haynie's Maria as "his principal instrument of torture." No matter what the conditions of the race—four-mile heat race, two-mile dash, even a half-mile sprint —Maria methodically humiliated the general's best entries. To defeat her became an obsession with Jackson. Even during the War of 1812, when he was directing the New Orleans campaign, he periodically sent dispatches home ordering his stable to buy something, regardless of price, that could overtake this flying mare. Always the word came back down the Mississippi that he had been trounced again.

"In later years," Robertson writes, "when Jackson was asked whether he ever in his life had failed in any undertaking, he replied: 'Nothing that I can remember except Haynie's Maria; I could not beat her.'"

During the period between the Revolution and the Civil War, racing in the United States expanded greatly in scope and popularity. What had once been the pastime of country gentlemen, with few onlookers, progressed rapidly toward being the major spectator attraction it is today.

Before the outbreak of the Civil War, major racing centers had been established at many metropolitan communities in the United States, scattered throughout the East, the South, and the Midwest. In New York alone there were racecourses on Long Island, and in what today are uptown Manhattan, Greenwich Village, and Harlem. It was at Harlem that what was probably the first important match race in North America was staged just before the Revolution. This was the encounter between the imported Old England, and the Maryland-bred True Briton, in which the latter upheld the good name of American breeding by thrashing the British horse roundly. There already were hard feelings in colonial America between loyalists and separatists, and the outcome of the race was eminently satisfactory to the latter.

Ill feeling, this time of a regional nature, also preceded the great match race of 1823 which pitted the Southern horse, Sir Henry, property of the redoubtable William Ransom Johnson, and the son of his great Sir Archy, against American Eclipse, owned by the Northern sportsman, Cornelius van Ranst. Since the event was contested at Union Race Course, on Long Island, American Eclipse's hard-won victory was immensely popular with the local backers, who had turned out forty thousand strong to cheer the home-town horse. (Partisan sentiment ran so high that an estimated twenty thousand additional spectators journeyed up from all parts of the South to witness the contest.) Thirteen years later, Johnson and van Ranst bumped noses a second time at the same racecourse. This time the Southerner was victorious when his John Bascombe defeated the Northern entry, Post Boy.

Of all the matches that preceded the Civil War, probably none attracted more attention than the race between Boston, a Virginia horse who was thought to be the greatest runner of his time, and the Northern-owned mare, Fashion, in 1842. Estimates of the crowd which mobbed Union Race Course to see this event run as high as one hundred thousand. It was, moreover, a disorderly group of spectators which edged onto the track itself, leaving only a narrow strip of running room for the contestants. Fashion's rather unexpected triumph in this race

Thoroughbreds generally race
in the afternoon, but working day
around the track begins early as horses
are exercised, then carefully cooled out
before returning to stalls.
Above: At historic Saratoga
horses that have completed
"works" are slowly led around barn area
under blankets, or "coolers."
Center, left: Ready to return
to his Saratoga quarters is
mighty Kelso, recently retired
winner of nearly $2,000,000.
Below: Exercise boys stand in
irons to pull up horses after workout
at Santa Anita, Arcadia, California.
Exercise boys are required
to give horse a quiet, soothing ride,
unlike jockeys, who must hustle
their mounts, yelling as
though pursued by fiends.
Opposite: Close-up of exercise
boy breezing his charge down stretch at
New York's famous Belmont Park.

again brought glee to the local rooters. She is commemorated in New York to this day in the important Fashion Stakes, held annually at Aqueduct race track.

As a brood mare, Fashion was little more than adequate, but Boston went on to a glorious career, leaving among his brilliant progeny the great race horse Lexington, who, in the Great State Post Stake, held in New Orleans in the spring of 1854, defeated the highly regarded Lecomte, another of Boston's offspring.

All of these celebrated contests, and many more, were conducted under the old system of running each event in a series of the best of three heats, each often as long as four miles. Under these conditions, horses frequently had to run twelve miles to decide the outcome of a single race. "Dead heats," or ties, were much more

Above: Mural at Aqueduct, by Pierre Bellocq, depicts notables of "Golden Age" of American turf. (1) Jim McLaughlin, (2) Leonard Jerome, (3) George Lorillard, (4) Fred Taral, (5) August Belmont, (6) Tod Sloan, (7) George Odom, (8) J. R. Keene, (9) Snapper Garrison, (10) Isaac Murphy, (11) "Father Bill" Daly, (12) William C. Whitney, (13) David Holland. Opposite: Ogden Phipps, chairman of The Jockey Club, Inc.

frequent in the days before the invention of the photo-finish camera, and there were instances of horses running twenty miles before a winner could be established. Naturally, in such grueling tests, horses could not be fully extended in every heat and the result was often a rather listless galloping contest in which the animals were taken under a tight hold. This factor was undesirable, since it was more possible to cheat and "throw" a race with a horse held in check than with one running all out.

The English, under the prompting of Bunbury and other notables of the British turf, had long since abandoned heat racing in favor of the more exciting shorter single dashes. And as America's Civil War drew on, this type of racing became more and more popular here too.

The Civil War disrupted racing almost completely. What had remained of the post-Revolutionary breeding establishment in the Southeast was wiped out. Kentucky, too, was ravaged. The Confederates appropriated many fine horses for use as officers' mounts, in which they doubtless had the compliance of the many Southern sympathizers in that border state. Valuable breeding records were irretrievably lost. But Kentucky's famous Bluegrass breeding center survived better than the rest of the South, and upon the cessation of hostilities, the rich farmlands surrounding Lexington became truly the heart of the Thoroughbred breeding industry. It remains so to this day, although Florida and California have risen to a challenging position, and many other states, such as Maryland, Virginia, and New Jersey, which were important in colonial days, have staged strong comebacks.

Prior to the Civil War, the Old South, where, generally speaking, the best horses and horsemen in early American history were to be found, was not only the most important stronghold of breeding, but also of racing. Williamsburg, Virginia, and Charleston, South Carolina, contend for the honor of being the first community to establish racing in America, and the sport was soon popu-

lar in North Carolina, Georgia, Alabama, Tennessee, Maryland, and Louisiana as well. In the Northeast, while New York was a racing center of consequence, elsewhere the sport was in disfavor in many places where today it flourishes, most notably New England. (Today only Connecticut does not have racing.)

The years that followed the conflict saw a reversal of positions. In the impoverished South, a new moralistic approach inspired by the rise of strict religious sects brought an end to racing everywhere except in Maryland and Louisiana—both states where the more tolerant Roman Catholic tradition was stronger.* Conversely, racing in the prosperous North became far more acceptable in the years following the war—a trend which was greatly favored by the huge immigra-

---

* In this the Roman Catholic Church can be compared with the old Church of England of colonial days, which not only tolerated racing but actively encouraged it through the lively participation of the many "sporting parsons" of that period. In fact, one of the most powerful figures in pre-Revolutionary racing was The Right Reverend James Blair, Bishop of Williamsburg and a founder of its Jockey Club.

Upper: Santa Anita post parade
is colorful sight as riders in bright owners'
silks pass stands before race.
Lower: Riders maneuver for position immediately
after start at Aqueduct. Opposite:
Samuel D. Riddle's great Man O' War.

tion of the horse-loving, racegoing Irish.

It was, in fact, an upstate New York Irishman, John Morissey, at one time a bare-knuckle pugilist of considerable note, a successful gaming-house operator, and briefly a congressman,* who played perhaps the most important role in establishing today's oldest, most tradition-laden racecourse. This was Saratoga, opened in 1864. Morissey's partners in this venture were the socially prominent Gothamites John Hunter and William B. Travers.

Saratoga, whose famous springs were used for medicinal purposes by the Indians before the first paleface was seen on the continent, had been for years a popular watering place among the fashionable and well-to-do. Harness racing had already made a successful start there. With the establishment of the Thoroughbred track, it was to become one of America's most glittering resorts. At its gambling tables and at trackside the biggest names in society were seen with such flamboyant figures as "Bet-a-Million" Gates and "Diamond Jim" Brady. Gambling, illicitly conducted, lasted at Saratoga until quite recent times. Today it is gone, but the old "Spa City" remains a mecca for the nation's socially prominent stable owners, many of whom maintain large mansions, quaintly referred to as "cottages," for their use during the August race meeting.

In Maryland, as in New York State, racing returned in the post-Civil War years with new vigor. In 1870, Pimlico—the nation's second-oldest racing plant—was built near Baltimore. Today Pimlico is the scene of the famed Preakness Stakes, the second gem of racing's Triple Crown. In 1872, New Orleans opened the Fair Grounds track. Three years after that, Churchill Downs—and with it the Kentucky Derby, where Triple Crown honors begin—came into operation at Louisville. Chicago soon became the focal point of Midwestern racing. On the West Coast, the sport developed rapidly around the older cities like San Francisco.

But New York State by now had become what

it is today: the "big apple" of Thoroughbred racing. The Travers, inaugurated at Saratoga in 1864, remains the United States' oldest stakes event. In 1867, the Belmont Stakes, named in honor of August Belmont, the aristocratic arbiter of racing in the Empire State, came into being. Run at a mile and a half, this race is today considered the sternest test of three-year-old campaigners and, appropriately, it is the final accolade of Triple Crown greatness.

Many stout horses grace the so-called "Golden Age" of American racing—the years between the Civil War and the dawn of the twentieth century. In this era are recorded the names of such equine stars as the great filly Ruthless, winner of the inaugural Nursery and Belmont stakes, as well as many other rich events including the Travers; unbeaten Norfolk; Kentucky, Longfellow, and Henry Bassett. These latter two met in a historic renewal of the old North-South rivalry in a match race at Monmouth Park, New Jersey. In this clash, the Kentuckian Longfellow, a giant of a Thoroughbred, walloped the Northern contender, Henry Bassett, with a smashing forty-length win to return the intersectional laurels to the South. In the later years of the Golden Age, racing was adorned by the names of Hindoo,

* As a congressman, Robertson records, Morissey's "legislative impact was negligible." However, he did achieve a sort of immortality in a congressional speech in which he offered to "lick any man in the House."

Domino, Ben Brush, and a long list of other standouts, who not only won honors at the track but improved the quality of American Thoroughbred stock by the luster of their progeny.

But in the stud, none emerges with the stature of a stallion who dominated the first years following the war. This was Lexington. For eighteen years, commencing in 1861, this great son of Boston was virtually unbeatable in the racing abilities of his offspring. In sixteen of these years he was the leading stallion in the country, and fourteen of those years were in succession. Horses sired by Lexington won three of the first five Travers, nine of the first fifteen Belmont Stakes. Many other fine sires like Hanover and Broomstick, and in later years Bull Lea and Nasrullah, have "improved the breed" in America. But none ever approached Lexington's record in the stud.

Toward the turn of the century, racing became so widespread and unregulated that abuses such as doping horses and fixing races flourished. The "sport of kings" acquired a reputation of being the "sport of crooks."

A wave of repressive legislation rose against the sport. In the first decade of the twentieth century, the game was banished in all important centers except Maryland and Kentucky. It took a machine—and a face cleaning—to restore its prestige. The machine was the totalizator, a mechanical odds-making device perfected earlier in France, but generally ignored in America, where wagering was handled exclusively through trackside bookmakers. But in 1908, the mayor of Louisville, on the very eve of the Kentucky Derby, was pressured by reform politicians to enforce an old "blue law" which outlawed public bookmaking. The resourceful Matt Winn, who then ran Churchill Downs, dusted off some old pari-mutuel equipment that had been tried once before, but without attracting much enthusiasm from the fans.

Not only was the 1908 Derby thereby salvaged, but so was all racing. The installation of pari-mutuels, a system in which the trackgoers actually establish the odds by the varying amounts they bet on each entry, gave lawmakers an opportunity they were quick to recognize.

This was to "license" the sport by tapping a small percentage of each betting "pool" as a fee. This new-found source of governmental revenue looked highly appetizing to legislators in other states, and soon politicians who had found the game morally objectionable decided that it wasn't so injurious to the public interest after all.

But racing also had to do a lot on its own to clean up its public image. Its comeback was accomplished under the careful supervision of the various state racing commissions with the invaluable assistance of The Jockey Club, a nationwide organization of sportsmen, headquartered in New York, which keeps breeding records of all American Thoroughbreds and maintains liaison with similar foreign organizations.

Its faith in racing restored, the public returned to the track with new zest and in the twenty years that followed World War I the sport was rendered more attractive through the perfection of the mechanical starting gate, which ended the time-consuming process of getting a field of nervous horses and riders lined up at a tape, and the photo-finish camera, which can separate horses in a finish the eye is incapable of judging.

A large company of good horses parades through the years prior to World War II: the celebrated "chocolate soldier," Equipoise; Regret, the only filly ever to win the Kentucky Derby; Zev, who won international recognition for the American turf by trouncing the British Derby winner, Papyrus, in a special match race; Gallant Fox, the only Triple Crown winner in history to have a son, Omaha, who would share that honor with him; these and many more fine runners, too numerous to list here, provided racing's big comeback with an over-all high quality of animal that had not before (and has not since) been matched. Two must be singled out, however, as dominating even this fine field of champions. One is Samuel D. Riddle's peerless Man O' War, who lost but a single decision, and that through bad racing luck, and retired to become one of the most important modern sires in America; the other, Willis Sharpe Kilmer's "galloping hatrack," Exterminator, whose amazing eight-year career included one hundred races, of which he won fifty and was unplaced in but sixteen. The careers of these two, in the late teens and early twenties, overlapped briefly and a match was once proposed between them. But Riddle declined it as Man O' War was about to be retired into the stud, and he wished to take no further chances with the horse. It has remained to this day a matter of hot debate between the partisans of "Big Red" and those of Kilmer's bony old gelding, Exterminator, as to which would have copped the honors in this dream race of all time.

World War II brought a lull to racing activity in some parts of the country, but total track

Contemporary racing figures. Top, left to right: Elizabeth Arden Graham; Winston Guest, Mrs. Guest, John W. Hanes; beloved trainer, the late James "Sunny Jim" Fitzsimmons; jockey John Sellers, Mrs. C. V. Whitney, trainer E. Barry Ryan. Bottom: Eddie Arcaro and Marshall Cassidy, noted official; jockey Manuel Ycaza; John Hay Whitney, trainer John Gaver; the late Ambrose "Mr. Brose" Clark.

attendance actually increased during the war years. The wartime period also was productive of two Triple Crown winners, Calumet Farm's exciting Whirlaway, in 1943, and Mrs. John D. Hertz's Count Fleet, who, after easily winning the Derby and the Preakness, really put his jockey, John Longden, in the driver's seat when he romped off with the Belmont in a twenty-five length win. The immediate postwar years, 1946 and 1948, were productive of two more winners of the three-part honors, King Ranch's Assault and Calumet's Citation, respectively. There has been none since.

The growth of racing attendance since 1945 has almost doubled, from twenty-four million to more than forty-seven million, making it the largest spectator sport in the country. Its rapid rate of expansion is reminiscent of the great boom in the Thoroughbred game of the past century, which led to abuses so grave that it nearly put itself out of business. In guarding against the recurrence of such evil practices the Thoroughbred Racing Association, an organization to which most leading tracks belong, has been of great assistance. Through its investigative and enforcement agency, the Thoroughbred Racing Protective Bureau, which is staffed by men with extensive backgrounds in criminal investigation, racing is policed more rigidly than any other sport in this country, and with such success that many sportswriters call this once highly suspect game a shining example of integrity.

If a criticism can be inferred from the perhaps too rapid postwar growth of racing, it is that the over-all quality of the horses themselves is diluted by the demands of more than one hundred

tracks and the ever-lengthening racing schedules being allotted by revenue-hungry state governments. Certainly the postwar years have been productive of an array of great race horses, the likes of Native Dancer, Swaps, Round Table, Nashua, Stymie, and Tom Fool, and, of course, Mrs. Richard C. duPont's Kelso, who, long before his career was over, rightfully assured himself of a place in that special category of immortals like Man O' War and Exterminator. These years, nevertheless, have also produced a disproportionately large number of "cheap horses," and in the opinion of many turf veterans have weakened the general character of American racing. It is true that in international competition the United States more than holds its own—a fact dramatically demonstrated when the American Jay Trump in 1964 captured England's Grand Na-

tional steeplechase, which, at four and a half miles over thirty jumps, is considered by most authorities as the most grueling event in all racing. But, on the other hand, the United States produces more Thoroughbreds than the rest of the world combined and from an annual "crop" of more than fifteen thousand yearlings it would be strange, and ominous, indeed, if there were not a few "good ones" in that number.

Actually, the problems of physical unsoundness, rather than the lack of breeding quality, are probably responsible for the fact that so few good two-year-olds ever make it to the Triple Crown classics. To understand the reason for this, it is necessary first to explain the colossal financial stake an owner has in a horse before he ever reaches the track at all. If bought as a yearling (a year-old horse—all horses celebrate their first birthday on New Year's Eve of the year after their birth) the very well bred youngster may have carried a price tag of $30,000 or $40,000, or even more. In 1964, for example, a record high of $170,000 was paid for a Bold Ruler colt at the Keeneland yearling sales in Kentucky. Then there are the costs of breaking the young animal and schooling him to race. Just to keep a horse in racing form costs about $6,000 a year. To these costs must be added the nominating fees plus the additional sums that are required to keep a horse eligible for the big stakes events. Clearly, before he ever appears in his first post parade, a two-year-old of the top category

Two scenes from important Rolling Rock point-to-point, held near Ligonier, Pennsylvania. Above: Horses go to post. Left: Thoroughbred goes over last jump before crossing finish line.

79

may represent an investment of six figures.

It is only human that owners—particularly less affluent owners—are anxious to see some return on this investment as quickly as possible. To this end, many big-city tracks offer extremely rich stakes for two-year-old horses. Now, the Thoroughbred race horse is the most fragile of the entire equine clan, and at two years of age he is far from having attained his full physical growth. This is particularly true of his delicately made underpinning. As a result of overwork, many of the most promising young horses break down before they reach the age of three. This is probably the unhappy reason why racing has seen no Triple Crown winner since Citation nearly twenty years ago.

The breaking and training of a young race horse is a task that begins almost as soon as he sees light at his dam's side. A good healthy foal is often afoot an hour or so after he is thrown by the mare. Shortly thereafter he is fitted with a small hempen halter and learns to be led on a shank. Thus he becomes accustomed early to being handled by human beings. Foaled usually in early or mid-spring, the infant horse remains with the dam until fall when, as a suckling foal, he is weaned and placed in a paddock with others of his sex. When the animal is big and strong enough to carry a man's weight, the training process begins in earnest. The halter is replaced by a bridle and bit which are attached to a long leather strap called a longe (pronounced lunge) on which he learns to circle his handler at an easy jog. A saddle and reins are added and often the yearling will stand for a period of time each day in his stall getting used to the feel of these unfamiliar trappings. Then a man will gently mount his back or drape himself, belly down, across the saddle. The young horse will be walked around inside the barn accustoming himself to the human burden. This stage is followed by his first appearance on the training track with a rider up and in the company of mature horses. Gradually the tempo is stepped up from a slow walk to the pounding gait of the running horse.

Around the time he reaches his second birthday, he may be sent to the track and handed over to his future trainer to be schooled to the starting gate and worked against the stop watch until he is deemed ready to run in races against others of his age and relative quality.

The breeding and training of race horses at the top level is big business, indeed, as is the operation of such large plants as New York's Aqueduct, Miami's Hialeah, Chicago's Washington Park, and Los Angeles' Santa Anita and Hollywood Park. Every mechanical adjunct associated with big business, including the most up-to-date computers and other data-processing equipment, is used both in breeding and in track operation. On the scientific front there are some eighteen colleges and universities offering degrees in veterinarian medicine, graduating nearly a thousand new vets every year. A large proportion of these find their way to the race tracks and breeding centers (there are some thirty-three horse specialists in Lexington, Kentucky, alone). A number of research centers, like that operated by the University of Pennsylvania, at Kennett Square, and the Grayson Foundation in Lexington, do advanced work in equine health.

How strange, then, that despite this supermodern approach to Thoroughbred racing, many of the largest and most scientifically operated farms still resort to breeding "by the sign," that is, in a favorable phase of the Zodiac. How anachronistic that to this day, even at such space-age racing plants as New York's Aqueduct, where tote tickets are dispensed through a duplex computer system, horses are still summoned to the track by a red-coated bugler sounding the call of "boots and saddle," just as they have been called since before Charles II.

Tradition is the name of the game in Thoroughbred racing and real sportsmanship is its handmaiden. Attesting to this is the fact that only a very tiny percentage of all racing stables operate at a profit and only a few more even have profit as a principal objective. From the rolling green paddocks of the breeding farms to the colorful post parade before each race, racing's opulence is everywhere manifest. As in England, where the racing stable is traditional to the crown and the peerage, so in America the "Sport of Kings" is the heritage of such prominent old families as the Vanderbilts, the Whitneys, the Woodwards, and the Wideners. And so, to many, it has come to have the connotation of a "social" sport. But snob appeal is not the real lure to the many new owners, successful businessmen for the most part, who are joining the ranks of the older stable masters every year. Rather, it is the irresistible challenge that a man who has made his mark in other fields feels when the tangibles of his skill and knowledge are pitted against the intangibles of breeding luck, training luck, racing luck, and just plain luck. Briefly—that's what racing is all about.

The race is over. Jockeys rise in stirrups seconds after Thoroughbreds cross finish line at Aqueduct racecourse.

HOUNDS

The hunter is not a breed. He is, strictly speaking, any mount which may be used effectively in the hunting field. More than a few horsemen would vow that the best ride they ever had was on that animal usually thought of as a delicate, pampered, hothouse creature—the American Saddle Horse. Occasionally, one hears of eccentric individuals who have delighted in hunting on mules and some who have ridden mounts of a more spectacular variety, for instance, an Englishman named Mr. Hirst who hunted at Badsworth on an enormous, foul-tempered bull—"the very bull which served him for a shooting-pony when he shot partridges over his team of pointing pigs."

Exceptions and eccentrics notwithstanding, the sport has for more than two hundred years imposed certain demands which some horse types could fulfill better than others. And as man became increasingly knowledgeable in breeding horses to meet specific requirements, he soon developed criteria by which he could judge the horse best suited to the hunt.

If the eighteenth century is looked upon as the period when hunting in its modern form originated, it is because it introduced an important new dimension to an age-old sport. This was speed—which thereafter dictated the type of horse to be used in the field. In earlier centuries, the chase was a leisurely diversion, partly because the fox had not yet become the customary quarry, and partly because the pursuit of larger game took the rider into dense woodlands and bosky retreats which slowed the pace. Also contributing to a relaxed atmosphere was the fact that the hunt was appreciated for its aesthetic rewards as much as for its action and excitement. Color and pageantry were emphasized, and the riders even took time to stop and feast along the way. Serious attention was paid not only to the skill with which the hounds tracked the game, but also to the melodiousness of their baying. Listeners were distressed if the chorus

contained too much bass, or the high "notes" were not suitably mellifluous. How well Milton observed in L'Allegro:

Of listening to the hounds and horn
Cheerily rouse the slumbering morn
From the side of some hoar hill,
Through the high wood, echoing shrill.

The favored pace averaged about two miles an hour, and the gallop was not a traditional part of the chase. In fact, on one occasion, when a royal duke lit off down a hill and over a fence, it was suggested that his lordship had been run away with by his mount.

Three hundred years ago these customs were changed by the advent of the Thoroughbred, which supplied the new and pleasurable element of speed in hunting. Once the Thoroughbred evolved as a breed, it became the source of speed blood in all horse types.

Today, centuries after the Godolphin, the Byerly, and the Darley, hunting remains one of the most exacting tests of speed, stamina, and sense that a horse can face. And it still is Thoroughbred blood which is the primary influence in the pedigree of most of the horses used to meet this challenge. The modern hunt generally covers some thirty or forty miles and lasts an average of four or five hours. The terrain is uneven, and dotted with such hazards as high fences, stone walls, streams, ditches, and fallen trees. Sometimes there are hidden dangers to contend with, for the pasture that seems safe for an open run may be peppered with treacherous woodchuck holes.

A variety of conditions, ranging from weather to outright luck, will affect the pace of the hunt. If the atmosphere is dry or a strong wind prevails, the hounds will have difficulty picking up the scent and cause long delays. A moist and reasonably temperate climate, such as that found in England, makes ideal hunting country. Occasionally there are days when the weather cooperates, but every varmint in the country seems to have moved elsewhere. And then there

Preceding pages: New Jersey's
well-known Essex Hounds meet for day's sport.
Opposite: Meadow Brook Hunt of 1886 met
at Teddy Roosevelt's Long Island home.

are the golden days. The field is off at a dead run moments after setting out, racing toward the horizon without slackening for thirty minutes or more, then pausing just long enough for the pack to check the scent, before resuming the breakneck pace over countless jumps, pushing on and on until the fields stretch into miles and the miles into hours.

Such extremes of good and bad fortune as these, however, are not likely to occur more than two or three times in the course of an entire season. A typical day in the field combines periods in which progress is slow and hesitant with sudden, exhilarating runs of fifteen or twenty minutes, when the pack is close on the scent and there is no letup in the pace. Five or six such all-out gallops up hill and down, covering perhaps forty or fifty jumps, is enough to tax most ordinary horses, but for the hunter

they are a normal Saturday's or Sunday's work during the five months (October to February) of the hunting season. There is always the possibility that the following week he will have to run twice as much, and clearly any horse without a lion's share of courage will falter in the task. It is these grueling demands of speed and heart that prompt hunting men to rely on Thoroughbreds, or at the least on horses with a high proportion of Thoroughbred blood.

Allied as they are by blood and background, the racing Thoroughbred and the hunting Thoroughbred should logically be exact duplicates of one another. The fact is, however, that while they share the common denominator of swiftness, the differences in the nature of their work causes subtle but visible differences in their conformation. Indeed, the very fact that there are differences in their uses explains why it is not always necessary or advisable for the hunter to be of absolutely pure Thoroughbred ancestry.

The racing Thoroughbred is bred and conditioned to go at his highest speed, to shave seconds off the clock under the most favorable conditions possible. For this he has been fined down to a lithe slenderness, with the lean, extended look reminiscent of his canine counterpart, the greyhound. The long legs which will send him breezing past a hunter will also be his most fragile points, vulnerable to injury.

The hunter contends with many elements, but the time clock is not among them. Even a minute matters little in the course of several hours, as long as the horse is able to stay with the hounds. Far more essential to a hunter's success is what

horsemen call "substance"—that is, the solidity of bone and firmness of muscle that enable the horse to carry a full-sized adult over rigorous countryside, absorbing the shock of constant pounding on ground that may be frozen, of hard landings over steep jumps, or of a stiff rap on the legs from the top rail of a fence.

The structure of the racing horse is so streamlined to meet the pressures of split-second timing that he cannot be expected to function under these circumstances, but the hunting Thoroughbred is suited to them because his tendencies to fuller, thicker proportions are encouraged. His muscles are inclined to be rounded and less attenuated, providing the spring required for jumping rather than the reach needed in the

racing stride. His legs are ever so slightly denser, shorter, and less delicate, giving him the support that is needed in fencing. And through the neck, shoulder, and barrel, he presents a more solid appearance, while still conforming to the sleek, rangy build of the Thoroughbred.

Since they share the same ancestry and belong to the same breed, the degree to which these two Thoroughbred types can diverge is naturally limited. Training, of course, tends to emphasize the differences. If the running horse were schooled over jumps it is certain that he would begin to develop the musculature of the hunter, and if the hunting Thoroughbred were trained in the manner of the racer, he would assume a closer physical resemblance. As it is, the training of the two types is entirely different not only in content, but in timing. A hunter must be brought along slowly, for he should not be jumped too hard before his bones have set. Hunters are rarely used in the field before they are five years old, an age at which many race horses have already broken down and been turned out for breeding. But even training can go only so far, and there are many hunting men who feel that the pure Thoroughbred is so geared to the purposes of racing that even the

Left: J. F. Herring print shows fox breaking cover, an early stage of the chase. Hunt breakfast, pictured above, awaits riders on their return.

sturdiest of them do not have enough substance for hunting. In the British Isles, particularly, where hunting is held in even higher esteem than in the United States, it is felt that the horses most suitable for the field are not Thoroughbreds but crossbreds—the offspring of blooded horses crossed with colder strains to produce more solid, heavier-boned foals. Draft-horse types, notably the Percheron, are commonly used in these matings. Wild ponies native to the land also serve to give qualities of hardiness and durability to the hunter. Ireland, famed the world over for its fine hunters, has not achieved this reputation by amassing the best Thoroughbreds, but by skillfully breeding blooded horses to its excellent ponies and native animals.

In addition to substance, the hunter must have a reasonably reliable temperament and a certain measure of common sense. No rider, regardless of how expert, can gauge every jump with infallible precision and the good hunter needs enough judgment to be able to get himself over a sticky hurdle without disaster. Nor should the horse be disposed to nervousness and excitability, since these qualities are only aggravated by the noise and action of the chase. Hunt whips crack, hounds bay, horns sound, other horses approach at a gallop from every direction, and creatures of the field dart from nowhere. The hunter must be able to take it all in stride, either because he has inherited a measure of calmness from the docile nature of a cold-blooded ancestor, or because he remembers the patient lessons the wise owner included as part of his training. This unexcitable disposition, combined with a suitability for cross-country runs, makes the hunter an ideal mount for pleasure riding as well as for following the hounds.

If the present-day hunter requires courage to spur his drive and speed, horses used in ancient times needed another form of fearlessness because of the different methods of hunting and different species of prey. From pre-Christian times until the eighteenth century, the fox was considered too insignificant to be a worthy quarry. Only in recent centuries has the hunting man appreciated his wiliness and subtle maneuvers, and come to consider him the most challenging of all game.

Before the advent of swift horses and the decline of larger game combined to help hunting people "discover" the fox, such animals as the stag, the fallow, and the roe, and such fierce beasts as the boar, the bear, and the lion were the usual quarry. A bas-relief dating from the time of the Assyrian Empire, illustrating the sporting feats of Ashurbanipal (669-626 B.C.), reveals methods of hunting which did not change significantly for two thousand years thereafter. Like the French and British monarchs many centuries later, the king, in addition to hunting in open country, sported in parks and preserves adjacent to the palace. Game was not dispatched by the hounds, as in today's sport—because it frequently supplied food for the table, any ravaging by the pack was to be avoided. Instead, if the quarry was not captured in pits or nets, the horsemen made the kill with their spears or arrows. Obviously, then, the mounts used in these hunts needed to be of sufficient boldness to approach within spearing distance such dangerous animals as the cornered boar or lion.

The works of Oppian, a young sportsman and poet, offer one of the earliest descriptions of the ideal horse for the cornering of such fearsome animals. Oppian wrote four books on hunting called Cynegeticon, which were so highly prized by the Emperor Caracalla that he awarded the author a gold piece for every line they contained. Oppian suggests that a rider determine the suitability of a horse by examining its eye. A mount with a blue-gray eye "would look unflinching on the black-maned monster [probably a wild bull or water buffalo] who dies grimly, a javelin through his loins. . . ." A gray-eyed charger "would dare close enough to the catamount to enable his master to thrust once more and finally." And the parti-colored horse with a yel-

At this point in its evolution hunting was brought to America. There, devotees of the sport soon included such prominent figures as George Washington, who ran down a fox or two almost daily on his favorite hunter, Blueskin.

As noted in the previous chapter, the first pack arrived here in 1650. The sport became popular immediately and by the 1730's many packs existed in Maryland and Virginia. The first hunt club, the Gloucester, was formed in 1766 and is the ancestor of today's famed Rose Tree Fox Hunting Club founded in 1859. Another early hunt that is still among America's most distinguished and prosperous is the Myopia in Massachusetts, originally comprised of gentlemen who wore spectacles.

As might be expected, fox hunting first took hold in the colonies whose nature and climate were most like those of England. Today, although hunting is increasing in the West, chiefly in California and around Denver, Colorado, the great centers are still Virginia, with its exceptionally fine Middleburg Hunt; New Jersey, with its superb Essex Hounds; the three R's in Pennsylvania—Radnor, Rolling Rock, and Rose Tree; and the splendid old Myopia among the many New England hunts. The Masters of Foxhounds Association of America recognizes over a hundred hunts, all of which practice the sport with traditional eighteenth-century style and vigor.

In the majority of sports, the newcomer who wishes to participate is first obliged to learn the

rules and regulations that apply to the game. Hunting, however, is governed by one rule alone —courtesy. Throughout the finding, pursuing, and killing of the fox, the field is subject to no written laws and to no form of policing. A hunt assumes that its members are honorable people who behave with the utmost consideration for their horses and their companions, and, as a result, the hunt's followers are far more affected by a stern word from the Master of Foxhounds than by a formal penalty.

Courtesy in the field is also encouraged by the fact that the hunting devotee cares for more than the speed and excitement of the chase. A large part of his enjoyment lies in watching a good pack of hounds at work and this requires patience and discipline from all the riders. The horseman who is simply out to race or to take as many jumps as he can belongs not on a hunt but on a challenging cross-country ride.

The courtesy and spirit of hunting will, per-

haps, be best understood by following along on an imaginary chase. Suppose that we are setting forth on a clear October morning in New England; the sky is scattered with blue-gray clouds, the still air, chill and faintly moist, brings a glow to the cheeks.

The riders assemble at a spot called "the meet"; the hunt members are informed of its location and time in notices, or "fixture cards," sent out during the week. It is customary to arrive at least a half hour early to attend to last-minute details without delaying the start of the hunt. At this time guests who are not regular members of the hunt pay the small fee charged for the privilege of the ride, called a "capping fee" from the days when these monies were collected in a hat.

Already present is the foremost personage of the hunt—the Master of Foxhounds. He is the man who assumes the ultimate responsibility for the success or failure of the season and whose

Whipper-in, disciplining one of his charges, scolds stray hound back to the pack.

94

word is law. The initials M.F.H. after a sporting man's name identify him as an all-around leader who has proved his skill in the field, and who is trustworthy, diplomatic, and gracious. He oversees the kennels and stables, decides what terrain shall be hunted and when, and deals persuasively with farmers whose land the hunt may cross, assuring them that they will be recompensed for any damages. The M.F.H. is the hunt's social organizer as well—it is from him that the esprit de corps of any hunt stems. He considers it an obligation to see that his field enjoys the best of sport. It is de rigueur to greet the Master at the start of the day—gentlemen tip their hats—and to thank him afterwards for the pleasure of the hunt.

In some instances the Master will choose to work the hounds himself. In other cases, as in the hunt described here, they will be handled by a professional huntsman. The huntsman is never concerned with the riders in the field. His total attention is on the pack, which looks to him for affection and instruction. He knows each of the hounds by name, and, from their individual mannerisms, can tell just which one has at last caught the scent. Out in the field, the huntsman rides first and controls the strategy of the hunt, guiding the hounds with his horn and his voice.

Other hunt officials congregated at the meet are the Field Master, who is responsible for the followers riding in the field, and the Whippers-in, or Whips, who assist the huntsman in controlling the hounds and urging strays to join the pack.

Milling around together, playful and frisky, are the hounds—which are always referred to as hounds, never as dogs. The whole pack is counted in couples, that is, in pairs—a tradition originating in ancient times when they were leashed in twos. If the total number is twenty-four hounds, the pack is said to consist of twelve couples. If there are thirty-three hounds, then the pack has sixteen and a half couples.

When it is time for the hunt to ride off, the huntsman sounds his horn and shepherds the pack down a winding trail, heading for a likely spot for a fox to be in hiding. The field follows behind, novices remaining politely to the rear, always careful to keep out of the way and to defer to more experienced members.

Soon the riders come to a gate across the path. An eager youngster is yearning to jump it, but the experienced hunting man knows that he must conserve every ounce of his horse's strength for the critical moment. Only a dilettante takes unnecessary fences, which is called "larking."

The Field Master opens the gate and closes it after everyone has passed through so that any livestock enclosed within will not escape. After about ten minutes the riders begin a trot to limber up the spirited horses. Suddenly the cry, "Ware hole!" is heard, and this warning of a dangerous hole up ahead echoes and re-echoes as it is dutifully passed on to those behind. Hunting men must be on the lookout for such perils as holes and wire, and those who sight the dangers always relay the word, calling "Ware hole" or "Ware wire."

In time the field emerges onto more open terrain, a rough clearing with clumps of thickets and brambles, called "coverts," that would provide a fox with perfect hiding. The hounds fan out, searching for a scent—"casting." As they seek to flush the fox from his lair they are said to be "drawing covert."

At first there seems to be little progress, for the hounds are relatively quiet as they dart hither and yon with their "sterns feathering" (tails wagging), poking into every thicket and clambering over and about a nearby stone wall. But the riders are quiet and attentive lest they distract the pack from its work. Any undue disturbance will surely meet with a reprimand from the M.F.H.

Suddenly one of the hounds shows signs of special interest. He begins to bark in short yips, to "give tongue." The huntsman takes note and rides to him, sounding his horn and calling the other hounds, "Hark to Biscuit! Get to him,

boys!" The whole pack converges, and, giving tongue, heads north toward a large post-and-rail fence. The field moves off behind the pack, slowly at first, trotting and jogging so as not to "override," or pass, the hounds. The hounds skip through the rails of the fence, and the riders wait until the entire pack is clear of the obstacle before breaking into a canter and taking the jump. No one wants to be a "thruster," an inconsiderate rider who risks injuring the hounds by jumping before the pack is safely away from the hurdle. Indeed, a rider should never let his horse intrude among the pack.

The field continues at a moderate pace, down a slope through tall grasses, over a stone wall, a hedge, and a ditch. At another huge stone wall a fat gentleman has trouble with his horse and "comes a cropper"—falls off. Several riders rush to his aid, another catches his horse. The man is unhurt and quickly remounts. At another post-and-rail fence a lady's horse refuses. Politely she lets the riders behind her proceed before making another attempt, for a hunt is no place to school a horse and hold up the entire field. In fact, any rider who actually cannot control his mount should return to the stable to avoid being a nuisance.

Soon the pack arrives at a stream. Here the fox has obviously tried to use the water to con-fuse the hounds, for they are having trouble keeping to the track. They pause and scurry around, "checking" for the scent. After some delay, one of the hounds begins to give tongue, moving off to the west. The huntsman encourages the others with horn and voice and the pack moves off into a wood where the riders must follow a narrow trail. One of the hounds is found to have strayed and a Whip backtracks to look for the missing animal. The cry, "Whip, please," is passed down the line and each of the riders halts and backs his horse off the path, head toward the trail, so the Whip may ride through without danger of being kicked.

Several fallen logs are jumped, and, even on this narrow trail, the pace begins to quicken, for up ahead the pack is starting to bay strongly, indicating that they are "hot on the line"—close on the trail of fox.

Abruptly the trail opens onto a meadow of fenced pastureland. The hounds race ahead in "full cry," baying keenly, an indication that they are on the right track. The entire hunt surges up a steep bank and over a panel fence at the top. Then, at the top of the rise, the magical call is heard: "Tallyho!" At last the fox has been sighted! A rider to the left yells, "Gone away!" and points his horse to the south, indicating that the quarry is in the open and running all out.

Caldecott sketch (above) shows hunt in full cry, while Alken (right) captures final moment. Animals are exhausted, riders triumphant, and Charley Fox has feasted on his last ill-gotten chicken.

The field cheers. The huntsman shouts "halloos" to his pack, calling them to his side and setting them on the fox's new line, then "blows them out" with quarter and half-quarter notes from his horn. The pack is off at full speed, the entire field of followers stretched out behind, galloping hard—the fox is in sight, bounding, sprinting, leaping on ahead in fear of the pack closing in at his heels.

No one can guess how long the chase will con-tinue—perhaps minutes, perhaps hours. But sooner or later the fox will be run down, and to those who are first at the kill will go the treas-ures that signify the day's success—the "mask" (face) or the "brush" (tail) or the "pads" (paws) of luckless Charley Fox. No reward is more highly prized by the hunting man than these, and for every mask decorating his trophy room he will have a story to tell of color and high ex-citement, true to the spirit of the chase.

OF THE WEST

Only the sketchiest account can be given of the antecedents of the horses the Spanish conquistadors brought with them to the New World. It is known that horses existed on the Iberian Peninsula many centuries before recorded history. The cave paintings executed by Stone Age people at Santander show unmistakable wild horses among the many beasts depicted with such admirable fidelity. But how the horses got to Spain in the first place is a matter of conjecture. The most popular theory is that they migrated from Scandinavia and were of the cold-blooded Norse variety.

In the seventh and sixth centuries B.C., Spain was overrun by Celts from the north. It is generally accepted that by this time the Iberians had mastered the art of horsemanship, but that the Celtic newcomers brought with them fresh infusions of cold-blooded equine breeding stock. A breed of horse called the *Vilana* resulted from the mating of these horses with the native strain. It would later play an important part in the development of Spanish horses.

Spain became the object of Carthage's attention in the middle of the third century B.C., after the Carthaginians were driven from Sicily by the Romans in the first Punic War, and it was through Iberia that Hannibal's legions marched, not many years later, en route to a daring but futile attack on Rome. The Carthaginians brought along many fine Eastern stallions which were bred to the *Vilanas,* and the result was a horse so superior in speed and strength that, after Carthage's defeat and Spain's occupation by the Romans, it was exported to every corner of the Roman Empire.

Rome's rule in Spain persisted until the fifth century A.D., when it fell under ever-increasing pressure from the Visigoths. Toward the close of the century the Visigoths acquired control of the entire peninsula, which they continued to exercise in an increasingly lax manner until the Moorish invasion of 711. The Visigoths neglected the arts of cavalry to such an extent that when King Roderick's legions were set upon by Moorish horsemen splendidly mounted on North African Barbs, they were thrown into total disarray.

During the nearly eight centuries that Spain was under Moorish rule, the Spanish horses were interbred with the hardy desert stock of the Moors to produce an animal that in those times knew no peer in performance.

To combat the Moors successfully during their long war of liberation the Spaniards needed horses with as much spirit and endurance as those of their adversaries. Mobility was the key to the conflict and for this reason the Spaniards did not bother with the huge, plodding war animals that were being developed elsewhere in Europe to carry the heavily accomplished knights of the period. Instead, they depended on a durable breed called the Andalusian with a heavy infusion of Barb in its background.

The final defeat of the Moors by the partnership of Castile and Aragon occurred in 1492. In the century that followed, soldiers, missionaries, and settlers from Spain fanned out through the Americas as far south as the pampas of Argentina and over much of what is now the southwestern part of the United States. To them the horse was indispensable. To travel the sweeping plains and prairies of the West, they imported horses by the thousands. In fact, the size and scope of the Hispanic explorations in the western world produced such a drain on the homeland's stock of horses that in 1520 King Charles V issued an edict forbidding their further export to the colonies.

Most of the Spanish horses that came to the New World were Andalusians of the type that had served so well against the Moors. It is also known that a number of pure-blooded Barb stallions were imported. After Spain cut off the flow of horses to her western possessions, Cuba became the principal source of horses for expeditions to the mainland. Here, according to Dr.

Preceding pages: Trail ponies scrounge meager repast among Rocky Mountains of Colorado. Right: Engraving shows "superb" Spanish horse famed in 18th-century Europe.

WELBECK.

Le Superbe Cheval De Seame.

C.van caukercken fecit.

101

Embarcadero de los Cavallos,

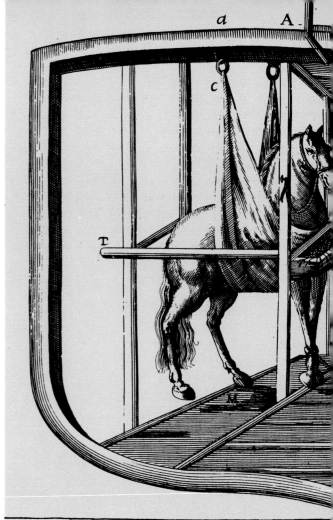

Como ba el Cauallo dentro de enbarcazion

George H. Conn, in his study of *The Arabian Horse in America*, a superior stud had been established. "It is said," he writes, "that all horses bred and raised in Cuba during the thirty-five years after the discovery of the New World were directly descended from the famous breed of Cordoba. The breed was formed during the Arab caliphate in Cordoba, Spain, from four sires brought from the Yemen or the Hejaz and crossed with native mares."

The horse gave the Spaniards an advantage in mobility in their first encounters with the mainland Indians. He also had a strong psychological effect upon the natives, who had never before beheld such a creature. Although the Spanish sought to perpetuate the natives' fear by spreading the falsehood that the animals were man-eaters, Indian superstitions about horses did not last long and their dread turned to hatred. The strange beasts were, in fact, easy marks for their

*Old engraving (left) shows horses
being loaded for shipment to Spain's New World.
Right: How horses were stowed in ship's hold.*

spears and arrows, and as mortal as their riders.

The Spanish did not permit the Indians to own horses or even to ride them. But as the natives were widely employed as slave labor around the stables, they were not long in learning the animal's ways. In due course the colonists noticed simultaneous disappearances of slaves and horses. Occasionally, Spanish officials were abducted and ransomed for horses. In other cases, Indians acquired horses by illegal barter with settlers.

It must be remembered that while Spain "conquered" vast regions of the New World in the sense that it was able to establish settlements and exploit the riches of the land, it did not subjugate a very substantial part of the native population. Spain's American empire actually consisted of a system of fortified points connected, for the most part, by primitive roads and trails upon which travel was extremely hazardous. Encroaching from every side of this spidery structure were

102

numerous tribes of hostile Indians.

At first, the Indian acquired horses at a very slow pace. But, as he obtained some, the process of getting more was simplified, because a mounted horse thief could ride into a range and run off several animals at once. Most authorities doubt that there were many mounted Indians in the Southwest much before the seventeenth century. But after that time they appear with increasing frequency. Just as the Indian was quick to lose his fear of the horse, so, too, he shed his fear of firearms, which at the outset had a value more psychological than physical. The common weapon of the Spanish soldiery was the clumsy, smooth-bored arquebus, which was replaced in the sixteenth century by the slightly improved musket. Both were matchlocks, inaccurate at any distance and painfully slow to reload. In European battles, arquebusiers formed in several ranks which fired in order, each repairing to the rear to reload while the next rank volleyed. In his *Horse of the Americas*, Robert M. Denhardt points out: "Once mounted, the Indian with his quiver of arrows was superior to the Spaniard with his single-shot arquebus. That the Spanish fear of mounted Indians was well-founded was later beautifully illustrated on the Great Plains. The great Spanish Empire was stopped short when it reached the Plains area where the natives had horses. The European nations were not even able to protect settlements within reach of the Plains Indians, much less subdue the natives themselves. The savages held the Great Plains until repeating rifles and revolvers were introduced."

Initially, the Indians learned horsemanship from the Spaniards. They copied the Spanish tack as best they could. As Frank Gilbert Roe notes in his comprehensive study, *The Indian and the Horse*, they also mounted from the right-hand side, a practice the Spaniards had inherited from the Moors and which prevails in parts of Spanish America. But to what they learned from the Spanish they were able to add much more from their own knowledge of animals.

Many of the tribes became more adept in horsemanship than the Europeans. Some tribes developed the technique of breaking horses by gentling them rather than brutalizing them into submission. They raced their horses as a pastime (the modern rodeo event of barrel racing evolved from the Indian stake race—the "stake" here meaning a pole stuck in the ground, not a sum wagered). They rode them into battle against their enemies, both white and Indian. Most importantly, they used them to hunt the buffalo, the Plains Indian's principal source of meat. The fleetest stallions were assigned to the hunters, while lesser horses were hitched to sledges. This greatly increased the tribes' ability to transport supplies of meat, hides, and family gear.

Some tribes, such as the Nez Perce of northern Idaho and northeastern Oregon, also became superior breeders, selecting stallions and mares with care and gelding inferior male animals. These Nez Perce horses have come down to us as today's highly popular Appaloosa breed. The neighboring Cayuse tribe also bred fine horses. It has been said that the Nez Perce and Cayuse horses were of such quality that other Indian tribes often chose to steal them—or, if necessary, to barter for them—in preference to Spanish horses. Meriwether Lewis encountered Nez Perce Indian horses in 1806 and noted in his journal: "Their horses appear to be of an excellent race; they are lofty, eligantly formed, active and durable; in short many of them look like fine English coarsers and would make a figure in any country."

One reason for the superior breeding practices of the Nez Perce and Cayuse was their location in the high mountain valleys, where peaceful pursuits could be carried on with greater security from attack by hostile tribes. Also, the forage in these areas was better than that of the Plains.

Among the first tribes of the Plains to have horses were the Apache, the Ute, the Kiowa, the Pawnee, and the Comanche. Of these, the Comanche were most renowned for their horseman-

ship, although the Pawnee were thought to have better horses. J. Frank Dobie, the eminent historian of the Southwest, states: "The dominance of the Comanches as horse people is unquestioned. Their horses varied widely in quality, but probably no more widely than the Spanish supply from which they constantly drew."

Dobie is alluding here to the increasingly bold and widespread raids the Plains tribes were perpetrating upon the Spanish settlements throughout the area which today comprises New Mexico and the Mexican states of Sonora and Sinaloa. A figure of one hundred thousand horses stolen in the single year of 1694 is considered a reliable, perhaps even a conservative, estimate.

None of the Plains tribes bred horses with anything like the care that the Cayuse and the Nez Perce did. Some were selective as to stallions and gelded the unfit, but little heed was paid by any of them to the mares. In many instances, horses were simply turned out on the open ranges where they bred as they chose. George Catlin, the artist-explorer, visited a Comanche encampment outside of which some three thousand horses and mules were ranging. He described the horses as a "medley group of all colors and sizes . . . generally small, of the wild breed, tough and serviceable."

Until disproved by recent studies, it was believed that the Indians got most of their horses by capturing and breaking the feral descendants of horses that strayed from the Spanish ranchos. This so-called "stray theory" also was supposed to account for the large bands of wild horses encountered by the frontiersmen arriving from the eastern United States in the 1850's

Logic would not seem to support the theory. A few stray horses, bred in captivity and conditioned by years of man's care, would have little chance of surviving on those arid plains or of propagating herds of thousands of animals.

The stolen or stray horses which fell into Indian hands, however, were mingled with the tribe's large, often semiferal herds and soon

Indians stole horses in wholesale lots
from Spaniards and soon became adept horsemen.
E. W. Deming here depicts Indian horse race.

learned how to shift for themselves. They became accustomed to slim rations and developed protective tactics against attack by predators. It is thought that the unique "pitching" movement of the mustang—the violent upthrusting of the hind legs that makes him such a fine bucking horse for rodeos—was developed through instinct as a means of driving off the wolves which prowled the fringes of Indian encampments.

Though the careless breeding procedures of the Plains Indians led to a deterioration in their horses' appearance, they also were toughened to a degree that allowed them to survive in wild herds. It is possible that some of these hardened stallions and their brood mares could have strayed from the Indian ranges. What is more likely, however, is that most of the wild herds were created when a large camp was suddenly attacked by a hostile tribe and either annihilated or put to horseless flight. Internecine warfare among Indians was constant before they were mounted and, from all evidence, was intensified afterwards.

Today, apart from the handful of Chincoteague ponies that lives as wards of the state in the salt marshes of Virginia's Eastern Shore, virtually the only wild horses in the nation are found on the desert of northern Nevada, southwestern Idaho, and southeastern Oregon. Romanticists love to spin tales about the nobility of the wild stallion, but there is little noble about the pitiful creatures found in this country. Shaggy, scrawny, and misshapen, they have degenerated to a point far down on the evolutionary ladder—eloquent, if sad, testimony to the fact that the horse more than any other creature owes his present-day quality to thousands of years of care and development by his human master.

As noted earlier, the horses with which Spain flooded its New World possessions were predominantly of the Andalusian strain. Within the Andalusian family, however, there was a number of sub-breeds. There were some spotted animals among a group of Andalusians which Philip II presented to his uncle, Ferdinand of Austria, in

1560, and which were incorporated into the famous stud at Lipizza. Spotted horses also were sent from Spain to the New World; there is even an indication that some came from Trieste, then an Austrian city, in which case they would in all likelihood have come directly from the nearby Lipizzano stables.

Paint horses, which the English call Piebald and the Spanish refer to as Pintos, and which are distinguished from spotted horses by the greater size of their markings, were also shipped from Spain, evidently in some quantity judging from the large number of varicolored animals in the big American mustang herds of later days.

Actually, both spotted and painted horses have

family trees whose roots are planted deep in antiquity. Many authorities believe that their unusual markings originally developed as protective coloration, or camouflage, to aid the horses in concealing themselves from predatory animals. Whatever their origin, however, or condition at the time of their importation, the haphazard breeding that took place when they were in Indian hands or running wild so thoroughly scrambled them that individual types became almost unrecognizable.

In recent years efforts have been made by dedicated groups of horsemen to sort these color types into definite families and upgrade them by crosses with Thoroughbred, Quarter Horse, Arabian, or other "improvement" stock. To this day, however, a male and female pair of spotted or painted horses cannot be relied on to produce offspring which are similarly marked. Such a mating quite often results in a solid bay, chestnut, or other color, a throwback to a cross perhaps many generations back. (A Paint mating with a Thoroughbred or Quarter Horse, however, stands a very good chance of producing a Paint offspring of high quality.)

Horse breeds like the Thoroughbred, which have been carefully developed through many generations of closely supervised selective breeding, grow ever more uniform over the years. A person closely associated with Thoroughbreds will see

Top: Toughened by exposure, Indian horses soon were able to survive in feral bands. Sketch at left by artist-explorer George Catlin shows brave acquiring mount. Right, top: Appaloosa stallion "Toby II's Patchy's Cochise." Below: Appaloosa handles stock skillfully.

differences between one horse and another that appear to him quite pronounced. To the less experienced eye, however, these points of distinction not only are nearly invisible but meaningless as well. With the color breeds, which are still in early stages of development—perhaps "redevelopment" or "re-establishment" would better describe the process—the distinctions between one animal and another are plain to see. The stud books of the Appaloosa, Paint, and Palomino registries are still open to sires of such breeds as will improve the stock. (By contrast, the Thoroughbred stud book has been closed for more than one hundred and fifty years.) As a result, a wide latitude in conformation is found in each of these breeds or types.

In judging a Thoroughbred's appearance, color is of no consequence, provided that it comes through brightly and that the coat is lustrous. The markings among the color breeds, on the other hand, are of very great importance. In fact, without them these horses would be common

range stock that no one would consider registering and "improving."

Each of the three principal color breeds merits a closer look. What is their background? What are their strong points? What are the aims of their breeders?

THE APPALOOSA

On October 5, 1877, Chief Joseph and a handful of weary Nez Perce braves capitulated to the U. S. Army. It was the sixth day of a siege following a surprise Army attack. The Nez Perce were outnumbered five to one, their supplies were gone, and they were unable to resist further.

Thus came to a pathetic end one of the proudest of the Indian peoples, a tribe hounded from the mountain fastnesses which for centuries had protected them from the fierce Blackfeet. With them they still had eleven hundred of their carefully bred spotted horses, which today are called

Above: Gold rush of '49 brought new wave of migrants to frontier country. Right: Appaloosa mare and foal, near Moscow, Idaho.

Appaloosas after the Palouse River that runs through the traditional land of the Nez Perce. (Some nine hundred other animals had been lost during the long retreat, while attempting to swim the flooded canyon of the Snake River.) The horses they surrendered to the Army were sold off to traders from the East. Many others, which had been on the open range at the start of the campaign, were corralled by white settlers under the Government's "finders-keepers" policy. Still others roamed in wild herds.

That the breed survived at all was due in no small part to the circuses and Wild West shows which found the gaudy appearance of the spotted animals to have special appeal. As a result, a few small breeders kept the strain alive. Even so, by the 1930's it verged on extinction.

Then, in 1937, Dr. Francis Haines, the leading authority on these horses, published an article in the *Western Horseman* called "The Appaloosa or Palouse Horse," which prompted an astonishing number of letters of inquiry. The following year the Appaloosa Horse Club was formed. It had six charter members. Little happened during the war years, but the growth of the organization—and the breed—after the war was nothing short of astounding. In September, 1947, the club established permanent headquarters at Moscow, Idaho, where it now maintains a central stud book and registry for Appaloosa foals. From the original half-dozen members it has grown to a present (1966) membership of more than ten thousand. Total horse registration is about thirty thousand and currently increasing at the rate of some eight thousand per year. The club's magazine, *Appaloosa News*, started before the war as a single-

Cowhands' ponies—the horses that won the West—came from good Spanish stock. Right: Young Appaloosa, owned by Carl Miles of Abilene, Texas, shows proficiency at jumping.

sheet newsletter, has expanded to a seventy-two page slick-paper monthly with more than twelve thousand subscribers. The club also sponsors a National Appaloosa Show. In 1964, when it was held in Albuquerque, New Mexico, it drew some five hundred entries and six hundred riders.

To serious students of horses perhaps the most interesting work fostered by the club has been the historical studies tracing the breed through history, from representations of the spotted horses in Chinese art as early as 500 B.C., through their appearance in Spain and Mexico, to their acquisition by the Nez Perce, about 1730. Research has

revealed the presence of the breed in Korea, Japan, India, and in Persia, whose literature refers to the mighty warrior Rustam as riding a polka-dot horse sired by a *dwi,* or devil. From these studies it can be inferred that the horses brought back from Persia and India by Alexander the Great's army in the fourth century B.C. eventually entered Europe via the Balkans. However, the presence of much older artifacts showing spotted horses have been found in Italy and suggest that the Appaloosa's forebears may have reached the European continent around 800 B.C., in an Etruscan migration from Asia Minor. Research of a

Opposite: TV star Jimmy Dean, a top horseman, flashes form on Palomino. Left: Dina DeLong of Tucson, Arizona, holds her handsome Palomino, Gypsy's Mist of Gold. Palomino coloring occurs in many light-horse breeds.

much later period, around the time of Spain's New World adventures, show the breed to be fairly well distributed throughout Europe and the British Isles. The romantic history of the spotted horse, ably publicized by the Appaloosa Horse Club, has been a factor in the animal's rise.

Appaloosas (and Appaloosa types) range in size from the little Pony of the Americas—a subbreed created by crossing Appaloosas with Shetland ponies—to something over 15 hands. In its *Show and Contest Manual*, the Appaloosa Horse Club, while establishing a minimum height of 14 hands, states specifically that there is no maximum height or weight restriction for showing the breed. A fairly stocky, deep-chested horse, the Appaloosa may weigh from 950 to nearly 1,200 pounds at maturity. Besides conformation, the color scheme is an important factor in show judging. The Appaloosa Horse Club states: "All Appaloosas have breed characteristics setting them apart from other breeds in the equine world. The eye is encircled by white the same as the human

eye. Skin of the Appaloosa is mottled, an irregular spotting of black and white, especially noticeable about the nostrils. The hooves are striped vertically black and white. Appaloosa coat pattern varies . . . most individuals will be white over the loin and hips with dark round or egg-shaped spots. Spots vary in size from specks to three or four inches in diameter. Some Appaloosas carry the spotting all over the body, but it is usually dominant over the hips. Others will show white over the hips without the dark spots in the white. Still others will appear mottled all over the body, or will show white specks or spots with dark background. *All, however, will have the white encircling the eye, the parti-colored skin and the parti-colored hooves.*"

Appaloosa fans have a remarkable-looking animal in their better specimens. They feel, too, that in the revived horse of the Nez Perce, they have an able, good-tempered, all-purpose mount suitable for rugged ranch work, as well as for showing and jumping in the ring.

THE PAINT HORSE (OR PINTO)

At least one of the horses that accompanied Hernan Cortes on his expedition to Mexico in 1519 was known to have been a Paint. This animal, the property of a settler from Bayama named Moron, was identified as a Pinto by no less a person than Father Bernal Diaz, the adventurous priest who accompanied the conquistador and chronicled his exploits. As noted earlier, quite some number must have followed.

Like the spotted horse, the Paint has a background of great antiquity. The type is known to have existed for many centuries in Tibet and the Himalayas. Egyptian tomb decorations depict Paint horses as far back as 3400 B.C. although they evidently lost favor, for later on in North Africa and the Near East only solid-color horses

Preceding pages: Paint stock horses move herd of cattle on Cross Plains, Texas, ranch of Mr. Horace L. King. Above: These Paints add a splash of color to brilliant Western scene near Flagstaff, Arizona, entrance to Grand Canyon Park. Right: Paint stallion owned by Mr. Hugh Lamb of Abilene, Texas.

were bred. As with the ancestors of the Appaloosa, there was a scattering of them in Europe at the time of the New World's discovery.

Among the buffalo-hunting tribes of America's Great Plains, Paints were enormously popular. Those fine horsemen, the Comanches, preferred Paint horses to any other kind. They found them speedy and tough, and in particular they liked their bright coloration—so much so, in fact, that when they found an animal with insufficient Paint markings, they got out the brush and added some more.

The cowboy of the early West is also known to have favored the Paints and often to have paid a premium of $50 or more to obtain one in preference to a horse of a solid color. But with the rise of such solid-color breed registries as the Thoroughbred, Arabian, Morgan, and Quarter Horse, "Old Paint" appeared to be headed

for the last roundup—as a fashionable breed.

In recent years, though, several newly founded organizations have come to his defense. One of the most recent of these is the American Paint Stock Association, founded in 1962, which now has its headquarters in Fort Worth, Texas. This group has undertaken a vigorous program for improving the breed and expanding its popularity as a cutting and racing specialist, as well as in the role of a general using horse.

Paint horses come in two general categories: the *overo* and the *tobiano*. The *overo* is a colored horse—roan, dun, sorrel, bay, brown, or black—with large, white, irregularly patterned markings. Tail and mane are dark or mixed, and the face is either white or bald. The *tobiano's* base color is white, with patterns of another color on his coat. The mane and tail are always the same color as the neck and the rump. Legs

usually are white, the head and face dark. The face may be marked with a snip, star, or similar decoration.

Although it is only recently that there has been an effort to organize a stud book and breed registry for show purposes, individual Paints have for years excelled as hunters and jumpers. Some are quite leggy and extremely fast. Many of the best "brush racing" horses who compete on private tracks in the Southwest, particularly in those states which have no pari-mutuel laws, are Paints. They can be very deft working with cattle. Several have also been standout polo ponies. No less a player than the late Tommy Hitchcock had a Paint in his string that he considered one of the best mounts he ever owned.

THE PALOMINO

Besides the Appaloosa and Paint horses, there is a third type commonly classified among the color breeds. This is the Palomino, the handsome horse with the golden-hued body and the blond mane and tail. There is some controversy as to whether Palominos can, or ever could, be called a "breed" in the strictest sense of the word. The coloration occurs in several breeds—often by pure accident, occasionally by design—although mating to produce a Palomino is a very uncertain process. (It is generally true that the breeding of one Palomino to another has less chance of producing a Palomino foal than does the cross of a Palomino with a golden chestnut.) There are those who allege the Palomino to be the descendant of a very old, pure breed whose genes are present in the various horse clans in which the type occurs. Others argue that, if so, then black, brown, gray, and all the other colors of the equine family must also have been separate breeds at one time. (Perhaps they were, but the point is academic.) Breed or type—take your choice. A Palomino bred from stock characterized by good conformation, like the Arabian, is one of the most beautiful of horses.

Palominos are much in demand as parade horses. Here Mardi Gras procession in New Orleans is escorted by posse mounted on Palominos.

119

The standard for acceptance as a Palomino horse by the Palomino Horse Registry is that the animal must not be more than three shades darker, nor more than three shades lighter, than a newly minted gold coin. Mane and tail must consist predominantly (at least eighty-five per cent) of white hairs. White markings on the face and legs are both permissible and common, but there must be no white on the rest of the body.

History has been dotted with horses filling this description and almost anyone who has seen a big parade like the Mardi Gras or Tournament of Roses will easily recognize the beautiful "golden horse."

In a brief history of the Palomino published in the March, 1963, issue of *Palomino Horses*, official journal of the Palomino Horse Breeders of America, Inc., which maintains the registry of these animals, Howard Grekel notes that the written use of the name "Palomino" is of recent origin—about 1920—and is believed to have been the fairly common Spanish surname of the owner of a golden horse in California.

Historically, Grekel sees possible allusions to golden horses in Homer's *Iliad* and a more positive identification in Virgil's *Georgics*, which constitutes a sort of paean to the joys of country life, in the words: "The bays and grays are nobles' beasts, the poorest color is yellow and white." Later opinion of the golden steed appears to have swung in his favor. The Bayeux tapestry, depicting William the Conqueror's campaign in Britain, is replete with horses of Palomino coloration. And Botticelli's "Adoration of the Magi," painted about 1481, displays several golden horses, one with a pronouncedly flaxen mane.

There seems no doubt that Palomino types were introduced to America by the Spaniards. One of the later Comanche chiefs, Quanah Parker, was photographed with one in the 1870's. Another Indian, Jose Bueno, a Navajo, was known to have two Palomino stallions and a band of thirty golden brood mares. That the red man did not have more was undoubtedly due to the fact

they were breeding accidents that rarely occurred in the strains of horse he used. Today, efforts to reproduce Palominos by intention are paying off with more success, but it still would appear to be a discouraging business. The peak registration of more than two thousand five hundred Palominos in 1947 has dwindled to about half that number today.

Palomino coloring turns up most frequently in

breeds with heavy backgrounds of Eastern blood —the American Saddle Horse, the Morgan, the Quarter Horse, and the Tennessee Walker. The Palomino registry itself establishes separate divisions for Palominos appearing in each of these breeds, and also for those resulting from matings with Thoroughbred and Arabian horses.

Of all of the breeds in which Palomino coloration appears, the highest proportion—about nine per cent—is among Quarter Horses. Generally, these are the best Palominos. Among quite a few outstanding animals, they number a world-champion racer, Paleo Pete, and a world-champion cutting horse, Cutter Bill.

Paints, once favorites of
Plains Indians, are popular today
on Western dude ranches.

6 THE AMERICAN

QUARTER HORSE

Although the Quarter Horse has come to be as closely associated with the American West as the longhorn steer, this chunky little speedster actually was created as a race horse in the colonial South. From the early 1800's on, however, the Quarter Horse breed pushed westward, out of Virginia and the Carolinas, through Kentucky, Tennessee, and Missouri, into the plains, the great Southwest, the Rockies, and beyond. It was among the vast cattle kingdoms of the frontier that the breed really took hold, for there his incredible, lightning-like sprints, his turn-on-a-dime maneuverability, and his sudden dead stops proved to be invaluable assets. What he could do, he could do better than any other breed, and, above all, his job on the range proved to be one that not even modern machinery could take over. Largely for this reason, he has more than endured. He has become by far the most numerous breed in America. In 1960 alone more than forty-six thousand Quarter Horses were registered—more than all the Thoroughbreds, Standardbreds, Appaloosas, Tennessee Walking Horses, American Saddle Horses, Arabians, and Morgans combined. As these figures suggest, the Quarter Horse offers a great deal more to the modern horseman than the dogged virtues of a good, hard-working cow horse. He is a first-rate conformation animal for showing in hand in halter classes, and the outstanding performer in rodeo and Western show events. He is also a big winner in the three-hundred- and four-hundred-yard races which in recent years have offered some of the richest purses in all of racing—including *the* richest, the $400,000-plus All-American Futurity at Ruidoso Downs, New Mexico.

Like the color breeds of the West, the Quarter Horse has ancestral ties with Spain. When, in 1539, DeSoto pressed northward from Florida and, in 1565, Pedro Menendez de Aviles established settlements and forts in Florida, South

Carolina, and Georgia, both expeditionary parties brought with them a number of horses of Spanish and Oriental breeding—Spanish Barbs. The European adventurers were scarcely welcomed by the neighboring Indian tribes and during the periodic hostilities the Chickasaws in particular made off with many of the Spanish mounts. Knowing nothing of the quality of the horses they now possessed, the Indians let them mate freely. Had the animals not been plentifully endowed with fine Oriental blood, the result might have been a dismal array of mangy scrub stock. Instead, there developed a strain of trim, agile, fleet little horses no more than 14 hands high, with a strong strain of excellent Barb blood, known as the Chickasaw horse. These animals formed many wild bands which spread north to the newly established English settlements. The colonists were attracted to the Chickasaw strain and mated them with their own admixture of English, French, Irish, and Scottish horses brought from across the sea. The Chickasaw horse was certainly the dominant influence in this haphazard breeding, but it is reasonable to assume that by the time blooded horses were being deliberately imported to America there existed in colonial Maryland and Virginia a potpourri of many European horse types blended into both the wild herds and the domesticated animals. From this melange, and principally from Chickasaw mares, early sporting citizens cultivated the short, sturdy-legged, excessively muscular little ball of fire that burned up the only "race courses" available—the main streets of the local village and abbreviated clearings in roads and paths. The usual distance was a quarter of a mile and the sprinters that competed in these races were referred to, first, as Quarter-Pathers, and later, as they began to make a name for themselves, as the Colonial Quarter-of-a-Mile Running Horse, and the Famous and Celebrated American Quarter Running Horse. Lest the informal conditions of these early races give the impression that they were insignificant affairs it

Preceding pages: Quarter Horses at Irving T. Alderson's Bones Brothers Ranch, Birney, Montana, are tops at handling livestock. Opposite: Show-stopping Quarter Horses of Ringling circus.

should be noted that owners of Quarter Horse winners are estimated to have collected, in purse and side wagers for a single race, more than $40,000 in gold, silver plate, tobacco, and cloth.

By the mid-eighteenth century, importations of Anglo-Oriental horses accelerated and it was to the mares of Quarter, or "short," Horse running stock that many of these blooded stallions were bred. Among sires of the time who are thought to have contributed generously to the Quarter Horse was a stallion named Fallower, who stood in South Carolina when Quarter racing was in its prime, and another named Flimnap, a great-grandson of the Godolphin Barb, and so highly favored as a stud in South Carolina that during the Revolution both armies battled to secure him for their own.

But the name that towers above all others in the formation of the Quarter Horse breed is Janus, and the very mention of it is often sufficient to inspire lengthy controversy among people who speculate about the beginnings of the Quarter Horse. One of the prevailing misconceptions is that Janus was a Thoroughbred. He was a thoroughbred only in the sense of the word without a capital "T"—a blooded horse of close Oriental descent; and he was sired by Old Janus, who was by the Godolphin Barb. But he is not of the Thoroughbred breed. He was born before the first crop of foals of Matchem, the first foundation sire. Furthermore, imported Janus arrived in America in 1752, thirty-nine years before the first edition of the British General Stud Book, a hundred and sixteen years before publication of Volume I of the American Stud Book, and conspicuously excluded today from the listings of both.

The controversy about Janus's background in no way diminishes his true value. He was, as the records have demonstrated, a superb runner who enjoyed an illustrious turf career. As a sire he was no less distinguished. Although himself a "stayer" capable of running in the killing four-mile heats of that time, his offspring all possessed

the sort of dazzling early speed that is the trademark of the Quarter Horse. He also passed on to his get his own distinctive conformation, which would eventually become characteristic of the breed. He was of low build (a fraction over 14 hands), very compact and rounded, and markedly broad and muscular through the quarters. Like him, the Quarter Horses of today are short—about 15 hands—but solidly built, weighing approximately 1,175 pounds, with a chunky, sturdy appearance. Through the shoulder and haunch they are exceptionally wide and strong. Through the barrel they are compact and close-coupled, with a sloping haunch and withers that do not rise high; they sometimes give the impression that they stand taller behind than in front, although experts insist that this is an illusion. The neck is not long, nor is it highly arched, which would be impractical in a hardy working animal. The head is not carried excessively high and retains the clean, "breedy" look that suggests both an Oriental heritage and Thoroughbred blood.

That Janus is the single stallion most responsible for the early growth of the Quarter Horse is indisputable, but it is also a misconception that he is the sole foundation sire of the more than five hundred thousand Quarter Horses now in existence. There are two great strains of Quarter Horse families to which he was in no way re-

lated: those established by Mark Anthony (1763-1788) and Brimmer (1766-1786). In addition, modern Quarter Horse blood may also incorporate that of horses originating in Mexico from stock landed by Cortez. Many of these animals of Barb origin, which were stolen by the Indians and eventually became wild, developed Quarter Horse characteristics they would later contribute to the breed. If their contribution is acknowledged, then it must be admitted that their Quarter Horse lines are not of Janus ancestry, for they never came in contact with Janus's blood until his eastern descendants arrived on the frontier.

Beyond cavil, however, Janus is the paterfamilias of the Quarter Horses. Two of the eleven founding families in early Quarter Horse history may not be related to him, but the remaining nine, according to research, certainly are. If he does not account for one hundred per cent of the present race of Quarter Horses, his influence nonetheless is so phenomenal as to make him one of America's great sires.

THE ELEVEN EARLY AMERICAN QUARTER HORSE FAMILIES

JANUS, 1752
Established by Janus, 1746-1780; by Old Janus—mare by Fox.

PEACOCK, 1764
Established by Old Peacock, 1760-1786; by Janus—Old Spain.

MARK ANTHONY, 1767
Established by Lee's Mark Anthony, 1763-1778.

BABRAM, 1770
Established by Goode's Babram, 1766-1781; by Janus—mare by Janus.

BACCHUS, 1778
Established by Old Bacchus, 1774-1789; by Goode's Babram—mare by Janus.

CELER, 1780
Established by Meade's Celer, 1776-1804; by Janus—Brandon—mare by Aristotle.

TWIGG, 1782
Established by Old Twigg, 1778-?; by Janus—Switch—mare by Janus.

BRIMMER, 1787
Established by Goode's Brimmer, 1776-1786; by Harris' Eclipse—Poll Glaxen.

PRINTER, 1804
Established by Printer, 1780-1828; by Janus.

WHIP, 1809
Established by Blackburn's Whip, 1805-1828; by Whip—Soeckleback, Randolph's Celer.

TIGER, 1816
Established by Tiger, 1812-1832; by Blackburn's Whip—Jane Hunt.

With the increasing importation of English Thoroughbreds to America, racing folk soon turned to distance running. The old Quarter-Pather, no longer the sporting favorite of the Atlantic seaboard, traveled west with the pioneers. The unsettled conditions and perils of frontier life prevented most owners from keeping accurate records of their horses' bloodlines, and those who did establish such accounts often relied on memories that were not entirely faultless, or intentions that were not always honorable. Hence there exist some vagaries of breeding details and dates in some of the later important Quarter Horse families. A great debt of appreciation is owed to Helen Michaelis, at one time secretary to the American Quarter Horse Association, whose energetic research revealed that the following strains have played a major role in the growth of the breed and who provided these additional names for its stud book:

COPPERBOTTOM, 1832
Established by Copperbottom, 1828-1860; by Sir Archy, T.B.—mare by Buzzard, T.B. (He traces to Janus on his dam's side).

SHILOH, 1848
Established by Shiloh, 1844-1869; by Union—Shiloa.

STEELDUST, 1849
Established by Steel Dust, 1845-1874; by Harry Bluff—cold-blooded mare.

BILLY, 1866
Established by Old Billy, 1860-1886; by Shiloh—Ram Cat, Steel Dust.

At Ruidoso Downs, New Mexico,
Quarter Horses run for racing's richest reward,
$400,000-plus All-American Futurity.

COLD DECK, 1876
Established by Old Cold Deck, 1868-1890; by Old Billy—Maudy (a Missouri mare).

ROAN DICK, 1883
Established by Roan Dick, 1879-1901; by Black Nick—mare by Greenstreet Boanerges.

RONDO, 1884
Established by Old Rondo (Lock's Rondo), 1880-1897; by Whalebone—Mittie Stephens, Shiloh, Jr.

TRAVELER, 1889
Established by Traveler, 1885-1910. Pedigree untraced. Perhaps bred in Kentucky, or perhaps sired by Traveler or Steel Dust.

SYKES, 1891
Established by Sykes Rondo, 1887-1907; by McCoy Billy—Grasshopper.

FRED, 1897
Established by Old Fred, 1893-1915; by Black Ball—mare by John Crowder.

PETER McCUE, 1899
Established by Peter McCue, 1895-1923; by Dan Tucker—Nor M., Voltigeur, T.B.

BLAKE, 1900
Established on Steeldust, Shiloh, and Brimmer lines.

JOE BAILEY, 1911
Established by Old Joe Bailey, 1907-1934; by Eureka—Susie McQuirter, Little Ben.

Perhaps the most impressive feature of the modern Quarter Horse is that he is not only adaptable for a general assortment of farm and ranch uses, but for sophisticated careers in top-level competitions as well. In fact, there probably is no other breed in existence that can lay claim to such a variety of pursuits.

In show-ring breeding classes, for example, stallions of top conformation are valued for exemplifying the typical Quarter Horse look. Here breeders may inspect for themselves the "model" stock that may sire new championship lines—great sires such as the famous King, who has come to be as influential to contemporary Quarter Horse breeding as Steel Dust and Traveler a century ago.

King, who until his death in 1958 was owned by the Texas breeder Jess Hankins, was the son of a Mexican horse named Zanaton, a legendary racer often called the Mexican Man O' War. But despite his racing laurels, Zanaton was deplorably mistreated throughout his life and, according to the Laredo rancher who brought him to the United States, was so weak and emaciated that, when he purchased him, the animal could scarcely walk. He had been starved nearly to death, continuously tied out in the hot sun, jogged for miles to get to the track, never properly cooled out, and raced by the owner's one-hundred-and-forty-pound son under a heavy stock saddle. Despite all this he could run three hundred yards in 15.4 seconds from a walking start, giving his all to the run and finishing in such a condition that you could count every one of his ribs.

Zanaton was a horse of incredible courage which was reinforced by superb bloodlines. He was by Little Joe, by Traveler, and his dam was Jeanette by Old Billy. Jeanette's dam, in turn, was by Sykes Rondo, as was Little Joe's dam. King's dam was Javalina, by Strait Horse, by Yellow Jacket, by Little Rondo. But unlike Zanaton, King was not destined to earn his laurels in the public arena. It was as a sire, and a sire of sires, that he asserted himself as a champion. Of the six hundred and eight registered foals by King, seventeen have become American Quarter Horse Association Champions, sixty-seven have qualified for the Register of Merit for their performances in the ring, and eleven have qualified for the racing Register of Merit. The most illustrious of the racers was a daughter called Squaw H, who ran unbeaten in her day and blazed across the two hundred and fifty yards at a Tucson track in a creditable 13.6 seconds. But the horse that has done most to enhance King's reputation is his son Poco Bueno, one of the most spectacular cutting horses of all time, who has sired a line of Poco's that includes the well-known Poco Dell and Poco Tivio.

Conformation breeders are, in a sense, purists interested chiefly in the Quarter Horse as a type, regardless of what he can do. It is from their emphasis on structure that the horse has continued to be stamped by a short, rather chunky build and width through the quarters, and the fact that distinct characteristics have been cultivated in the breed is certainly to be praised. It is from the breeders' own circle, however, that the most severe criticism has come. Many owners, far more concerned with the Quarter Horse as a working stock animal, rebelled against this preoccupation with looks, feeling that the abilities of the horse in stock-work performance was more vital. Their complaints were that the American Quarter Horse Association, founded in 1940, adhered too strictly to the breeding goals and modeled too much "beefiness" into the horse. To satisfy their own interests they split off into the National Quarter Horse Association, which now has been reabsorbed into the AQHA.

Racing enthusiasts were at even greater odds with the type breeders, maintaining that above all else speed should be considered the greatest attribute of the Quarter Horse and that looks are of far less importance. To accommodate their needs they organized the Quarter Horse Racing Association (now incorporated into the AQHA as its Racing Division) as a regulating body for matters pertaining to the turf. And to beget increasing speed they have infused an extraordinary degree of Thoroughbred blood into the lines, so that in conformation the racing Quarter Horse is a little speedball replica of what appears at Aqueduct and Saratoga. Hence, it is perfectly possible for large numbers of the breed to have the long, rangy look of the Thoroughbred, while fellow members of the breed retain the short, stocky look of the traditional Western cow horse.

The beliefs of racing Quarter Horse people are perhaps most forcefully expressed by breeder Ott Adams: "Speed can be bred in horses through the use of the right kind of pedigree, and it can be bred out of horses by using pedigrees which include blood never known to have been associated with speed. You don't have to use mongrel blood to reduce speed in the offspring; it is as easily reduced through the use of conformation horses whose background shows no speed, or inferior speed, or even speed bred down too short.

"Conformation itself, or the matter of pleasing looks, should cause no worry to the breeder versed in these elementary facts, for it comes of itself with the use of proper bloodlines. . . .

"Speed is the only thing worthwhile as a goal in the breeding of Quarter stock; it is the only thing that should worry you."

Another Quarter Horse authority, J. S. Holman, says of speed in the breed: "Without it he is just a horse that may win a prize in a horse show, and very little else." In quest of it he goes on to advise: "Don't be afraid to get Thoroughbred blood in your horses." In fact, Quarter racing people have shown little hesitation in doing precisely that, with Thoroughbreds such as Three Bars and Top Deck, who is descended from Himyar, now being magical names in the annals of short-horse running.

Whether or not speed is the primary virtue of the Quarter Horse is an argument best left to the owners, but what is certain is that activity on the turf is what has brought the breed into the realm of big business.

Before 1949, Quarter racing was a minor and scarcely noticed activity, but in that year parimutuel betting was legalized in California and William Kyne, then president of the Bay Meadows track at San Mateo, began using the Quarter race as a preliminary event before the regular racing. Purses were meager, about $400, and distances were from three hundred and thirty to four hundred and forty yards. But the blistering action and the close photo finishes, traditional excitements in a Quarter race since the field generally arrives at the wire as closely aligned as at the start, soon captivated the crowds. Since that time its popularity has swept the West like a flash flood. For example, in 1945 exactly twenty-five recognized races were run for Quarter Horses. Less than twenty years later,

in 1962, this number had skyrocketed to more than two thousand seven hundred. That same year the total distribution of purses was no less than $3,188,410 and the total pari-mutuel handle was $58,379,917. In 1961 Quarter Horses began running, dollar for distance, for the richest purse in history: the All-American Futurity in which the gross value of the prize was $202,425—compared to the $178,700 prize for the Preakness, $163,000 for the Kentucky Derby, and $148,650 for the Belmont Stakes of the same year. By 1963, the fifth running of the All-American Futurity, the money had been upped to $285,000. In 1965 it passed the $400,000 mark.

The horses, too, command impressive sums. Through 1960 the highest price paid for a Quarter runner was the $125,000 fetched by the great racing stallion Go Man Go. Since that time others are reported to have sold for as much as $150,000.

Quarter racing has been highly organized into a system of classification whereby the entries are graded according to their track time and ranked in divisions where they will compete against horses with similar records, which helps provide the hairsbreadth finishes that are so thrilling. The standard distances for races are: two hundred and twenty, two hundred and fifty, three hundred, three hundred and thirty, three hundred and fifty, four hundred, and four hundred and forty yards. The top classification is an "AAA" rating and the qualifying times for this are: 12.1 seconds for the two-hundred-and-twenty-yard distance, 13.6 for the two-fifty, 15.9 for the three hundred, 17.3 for the three-thirty, 18.3 for the three-fifty, 20.6 for the four hundred, and 22.5 for the four-forty. The ratings continue, with appropriate time standards, down through "AA," "A," and on to "D," where the time allotment is increased to 13.1 seconds for two hundred and twenty yards, for example, and 24.2 for the four-forty.

It is impossible to mention Quarter racing without paying homage to the great contemporary sires whose blood has given the sport the speed and excitement responsible for its popularity. Foremost among these is the incomparable Three Bars, a horse who was once sold for a mere $300 to a buyer who was so unimpressed that he gave the horse away. Today Three Bars' stud fee is $10,000, and some authorities say that not since Janus has any horse been so important to the course of Quarter racing. Three Bars has sired about three hundred and forty-eight foals, of which two hundred and fifty-eight have officially started in recognized races with cumulative earnings of $1,825,521. Among his prominent children are Pokey Bar, Tonto Bars Gill, Lightning Bar, Mister Bar None, and Bar Depth.

Three Bars' closest rival was a horse named Top Deck, whose children have earned $569,060 —a tidy sum, but still less than half the winnings of the get of Three Bars. Moon Deck, a son of Top Deck, and Go Man Go are other celebrated names in this favored national sport.

Speed may be what has put the Quarter Horse in sporting headlines, but this is not the crucial element for the working cowman, who holds this animal dearer than dividends, dearer than public acclaim, and almost dearer than his truest friend. If a man wants the "runningest" horse in the world, say the ranchers, he's better off with Thoroughbreds. That's what they've been born and bred for in the past three hundred years, and they had to be good to put the Quarter Horse out of business as they did in the East. But if a man wants the "doingest" horse in the world, he'll never in a lifetime find anything superior to the Quarter Horse.

Wherever there are cattle there have to be horses, and of those that work the herds the Quarter Horse is far and away the best. There are many areas in which he is a wizard—for instance, roping and bulldogging—but it is in cutting that he works with consummate skill.

The function of the cutting horse is to separate an indicated steer from the bunch and guide it to

Preceding pages: Quarter Horse racing at "Nebraska's Big Rodeo." Sport's popularity is spreading eastward. Opposite: Nimble and fleet, Quarter Horse is ideal barrel racer.

the spot desired by the rider, a devilish task since the instinct of the steer compels him to use every wile to get back with the herd. Yet the fine cutting horse carries out this delicate task with no instruction from the rider, relying on his own split-second anticipation of the quarry's next move—and on the ability to beat him to it.

It would be a misfortune for horsemen if the only opportunity to see cutting horses at work were at remote encampments on Western ranges. Luckily, cutting events are the main attractions of many rodeos and Western shows, where working conditions are simulated by bringing into the ring a small herd of steers from which a specific animal must be diverted. The reins are all but dropped on the horse's neck as, for a moment, the horse stands flat-footed and still, taking the measure of the cow. Suddenly, as the steer swerves, the horse bursts forward on his own initiative. He skids abruptly to a stop as the quarry feints a halt, then wheels in a standing pivot and charges in the opposite direction to keep abreast of a new lunge by the steer. He then reverses in midair, swirling at a forty-five-degree angle to the ground as the steer attempts another tack. It is a stunning display, and in the near-human calculation required of the horse, it constitutes probably the supreme demonstration of balance, speed, agility, and native intelligence that any horse can offer.

Quarter Horse skids to stop
as roper's line goes out. No known breed of
horse can start as quickly or stop as
fast as well-drilled working Quarter Horses.

Naturally, the high finish of such a performance is to a large degree the product of an inordinate amount of top-level training, and here again there is almost as much variety in the method as there is in the Quarter Horse himself. At the King Ranch, one of the country's largest and finest breeding plants, foals are gentled and halter-broken during the summer when they are two to three months old. By the time they are weanlings, this early training makes them thoroughly calm and used to being handled by man. They are turned out to pasture as yearlings, but during the fall and winter of their second year they are broken to saddle and ridden in the company of other horses. At four years they are working cattle, and, at six, mares of superior ability join the brood-mare band.

Each King Ranch horseman trains his own string of mounts and is given an incentive to do the best job possible, for every hand who schools a filly that becomes quality stock for the brood-mare band has first choice of the mare's foals.

A man of a different viewpoint, however, is top cutting-horse trainer Louis Cabrell of Tres Pinos, California, who doesn't touch a horse until he is four years old. In six months he turns out a usable cow horse and in one year a thoroughly accomplished roping or reining horse. A horse that requires more than this Cabrell regards as an unlikely bet for top competition.

Cabrell's methods are of a rough-and-ready nature, almost biblical in their rigidity, and one might easily find fault with them if he had not proven the worth of his routine with many top animals. For example, Cabrell halterbreaks his four-year-old subject in a single day. The next day he takes the starch out of him by tying the reins from headstall to tail on each side for one hour. The third day he mounts. For three sessions he rides the horse in an enclosure—and from then on it's out in open pasture among cattle.

Perhaps the method which offers the happiest combination of gentleness, thoroughness, and speed is that of Jack Elliott of San Benito County,

California, who has achieved fame as a specialist in cutting horses. Elliott begins working with his foals when they are at the tender age of two to three weeks. Initially they are halterbroken, then trained to stand tied and accustomed to general handling, which includes getting in and out of vans and trailers. Thus they are thoroughly tractable when, at age two, they undergo more intensive lessons, such as learning to drive in long lines with a snaffle bit and surcingle. In time the surcingle is replaced by a saddle, and when an Elliott youngster is ready to be mounted at two and a half, he is usually so well domesticated that only in rare instances does he explode under his first rider.

At three the horse begins his real cutting education. Using a hackamore, Elliott takes the colt into a ten-acre field, rather than a corral, and begins instructing his pupil in the agile skills of holding cattle in a corner, cutting out an indicated animal, and quietly running him the length of the field. Practice continues for one or two months, during which time the horse is also taught to head cattle—hustle a maverick back into the herd before it can dash away. This is a lesson the horse picks up rapidly, since he soon learns that if the calf escapes he must chase it all over creation to round it up again.

After this general warming-up period in the field, the Elliott cutting horse is taken into a ring roughly a quarter acre in size where he is schooled in working small groups of three or four cattle. He learns to drive the herd from the rear and to concentrate on cutting an individual cow when asked; he is never allowed to switch from one cow to another.

Elliott firmly believes that when a three year old shows promise he should be taken along slowly. He himself is gratified with the subtlest signs of a good move in the early weeks of the more advanced training of the colt. He limits intensive sessions to about a half an hour and rewards real progress and effort with a leisurely workout the next day, for he is fully aware that bringing a top performer along is a delicate business, and that a horse can easily go sour if drilled to boredom.

Throughout the training Elliott finds that "teaching the horse to maintain a constantly advantageous position is the most important single factor in the making of a cutting horse. The horse must always be in a position to head his cow and must be trained to drift with the critter in much the same manner as a pass-defender drifts with an eligible receiver on the football field."

Vital as training is to the ultimate perfection of the cutting horse, one cannot train what isn't there. Inborn in Thoroughbreds is speed. Inborn in Saddle Horses is beauty. And inborn in Quarter Horses is a knack, an instinct, a decided will to function in association with other livestock. When a horse has it to an uncommon degree it is called "cow savvy"—and this is what the Quarter Horse brings to school for the trainer to develop.

Part of the inherent trait may be due to the antiquity of the breed, for the Quarter Horse is old as contemporary strains go, and even as he was being raced by the colonists in the 1600's, he was also being used to work the livestock in their cowpens. Later, on the westward trek, there were always some few creatures to be herded, and in his nomadic life it may be that he became sufficiently accustomed to the chores to pass on an aptitude.

Then, too, it is a fact that Quarter Horses have a notably sunny and kindly disposition. They are quick learners and genuinely like to be around people and other animals. The cowboy's fabled love for his horse is not simply the result of a lonely life or a saccharine sentimentality. One has only to test the Quarter Horse, discover his truly giving nature, his eager desire to do his share in challenges that range from racing to roping—and one will dismount firmly convinced that the warm regard is well-earned and more than deserved.

7 RODEO

R odeo is a peculiarly American form of insanity. Unlike most sports, which have "seasons," the rodeo circuit winds up on the last day of one year and resumes in the first days of the next. In 1964, nine and one-half million people in forty states paid to see cowboy contestants heave down half-ton steers and hurtle from the backs of angry broncs and bulls—a figure which topped the year's attendance at American League baseball games.

What was the genesis of this madness? How and where did it all begin?

Although several Western cities lay claim to having staged the first rodeo, neither the place nor the time has been established with certainty. In fact, most historians are agreed that the rodeo did not begin in a town at all. Rather, it seems to have originated on the big cattle spreads of Texas, where cowboys engaged in simple, man-to-man contests in roping and horsemanship.

The first American stockmen went to Texas in the 1820's at the invitation of the Mexican Government. Mexico cherished the hope that the *yanquis* would somehow be able to "civilize" this immense, sparsely settled land and bring its roving bands of Indians under control, an objective which neither the fledgling Mexican Republic nor its Spanish predecessors had been able to realize.

These first American ranchers were unskilled in handling the great herds of unruly longhorns, descended from stock brought in by the Spaniards. Nor did they have any notion how to tame the wild mustang horses they would need as mounts. Some tricks they learned by experience, but most of the techniques of ranching were taught them by the Mexican cattlemen. Even today the terminology of Western horsemanship retains a strong Spanish accent in such words as "lasso" (*el lazo*), "lariat" (*la reata*), "mustang" (*mesteno*), and "bronc" (*broncho*). In fact, the word "rodeo" is itself derived from the Spanish verb "*rodear*"—to round up or encircle.

(The preferred American pronunciation is *ro*-deo. Ro-*day*-o is a second choice.)

In the 1830's and 1840's, little settlements began to spring up along the developing cattle routes. Here the cowhands, weary and bored from weeks and months on the trail, were willingly separated from their hard-won wages by the fancy toggeries, drinking establishments, and bawdy houses which fed upon the growing cattle trade. Informal races, roping contests, and bronc riding, all accompanied by substantial wagering, were prime diversions in the primitive but lusty life of these early outposts.

The geographic spread of rodeo and its growth in popularity following the Civil War paralleled the expanding cattle industry. In the great push westward that followed the Civil War, the pastime began to take on more of the form of the present-day sport. The first recorded rodeo, involving teams from more than one spread, took place in 1869 at Deer Trail, Colorado, between the cowpokes of the Hash Knife, Camp Stool, and Mill Iron ranches. Much bigger affairs were staged in Cheyenne, Wyoming, and in Winfield, Kansas, in 1872 and 1882, respectively. In 1883, the Texas town of Pecos staged a wild-steer-roping contest which, for the first time, offered prize money. And, in 1887, Denver opened the era of modern rodeo by charging the spectators admission fees.

All these events, however, took place some time before the day of bucking chutes and enclosed arenas. Rodeos of early times were staged in the courthouse squares and main streets of the towns. There were no time limits in the bucking contests. Either the rider was tossed or he rode until the horse was too weary to buck any longer. It was not an uncommon sight to see a crazily twisting bronc, with a rider clinging grimly to his back, careen through a porch rail or unexpectedly enter the town saloon by way of the plate-glass window.

Everything a cowboy did in rodeo was a demonstration of his skills in his everyday job:

Preceding pages: Bulldogger locks onto running steer at Burwell, Nebraska, rodeo. Right: Rodeo probably began on big cattle spreads. Artist Russell guesses how.

138

roping steers, tying calves, breaking wild horses. In those days the horses were indeed wild—or incorrigible. For the Western style of breaking horses to saddle was brutally direct. Instead of patiently training the young or wild horse to have no fear of men, the cowboy—often it was a specialist who traveled from ranch to ranch—would rope a likely-looking animal, throw a saddle on its back, and ride it into submission. Many "outlaw" horses, animals that refused to be bullied into obedience, resulted from this primitive method of breaking. Often they became the prize bucking stock of early rodeo.

The first truly modern rodeo was Cheyenne's "Frontier Days," founded in 1897, which laid the cornerstone for today's so-called "Big Four"— the major league of rodeo around which the modern circuit is built. (The other three are the Pendleton, Oregon, "Roundup," the Calgary, Alberta, "Stampede," and Salinas' "California Rodeo.")

From this beginning, rodeo rapidly developed a round-the-year schedule that includes such events as the great indoor rodeos at Fort Worth, Texas, and San Francisco, California, and the biggest of them all, the December National Finals, held in Los Angeles, where the top riders and ropers of the year are gathered to compete in what has become known as the "World Series" of rodeo. The rodeo loop in 1964 included nearly

Vicissitudes of bronc riders'
world are pictured at Sydney, Iowa, rodeo.
Top three photos are of saddle bronc
events, bottom two of bareback contests.
In both, cowboy must keep one hand
free and clear of his mount. If he touches
animal he will receive no score no matter
how well he rides. Bareback time limit
is eight seconds, saddle is ten.

six hundred events approved by the Rodeo Cowboys Association, the governing body of the sport. More than $3,500,000 in prize money was handed out, a figure which exceeds the total offered in professional golf.

Many of the larger rodeos have become spectacular, latter-day Roman circuses with all sorts of contests, such as stagecoach and chariot racing, team steer roping, wild-horse racing, and wild-cow milking. But the main events around which all rodeos are built are bareback riding, calf roping, steer wrestling (bulldogging), saddle-bronc riding, and bull riding. To these, most rodeos have added barrel racing for girl riders—competitions against the stop watch in which the horses are run in a clover-leaf pattern around a triangular course marked by barrels.

After each of the principal contests, there usually are specialty acts to divert the audience while livestock is being readied for the next event. These range from trained-animal acts and exhibitions of trick riding provided by modestly paid performers to appearances by top motion-picture and television stars, depending on the size of the rodeo's budget. Clowns, usually two in number, are fixtures at all rodeos and render vital service in distracting loose horses and bulls when a rider has fallen. They also entertain between the acts with comedy routines and rustic commentary on current events. (Hardly a rodeo

Unhappy ending for bareback rider at Pendleton, Oregon, rodeo. Medical costs are part of rodeo man's budget.

audience in the campaign year of 1964 escaped this gem: First Clown: "Hear Goldwater shot his horse." Second Clown: "How come?" First Clown: "Caught him eating Johnson grass.")

One of the vicissitudes of the modern rodeo rider's fortunes is the fact that his success is not wholly dependent on his own skill, but is achieved through the quality of the animal with which he competes. Calves and steers for the calf-roping and bulldogging events are selected by drawing lots in advance of the contest. Inevitably some calves turn out to be quicker and more elusive than others and, similarly, one steer will be harder to spill than another. Since both events are decided on a time basis, these differences mean precious seconds on the official clock.

In the riding events, the animal element can be even more important. All contests have time limits which the riders must meet in order to score at all. In bareback and bull riding, eight seconds constitute an "official ride." In saddle-bronc riding, it is ten seconds. However, points are awarded by the judges on the basis of the animal's performance as well as on that of the rider, and the eight or ten seconds spent on a wicked bucker will mean a better point total for the rider than the same time on a quieter mount.

The order in which the five main events on the card are presented will vary somewhat from rodeo to rodeo. All rodeos, however, start with the

Grand Entry. Led by the Rodeo Queen and her court, usually mounted on muscular Quarter Horses and attired in their brightest Western riding garb, and followed by the contestants, officials, and a legion of dignitaries, all on horseback, the Grand Entry pours into the arena where introductions are performed. Then the flag is planted by two riders crisscrossing the grounds with their horses going full tilt. The show is now ready to start.

The first event on most programs is bareback riding. The bucking horses are loaded into the narrow chutes where the riders slip aboard. As each contestant signals, his chute is opened. During the wild eight-second journey which follows, all the cowboy has to cling to is a hand grip on the leather band that encircles the horse's body just behind the withers. To further stimulate the horse's natural urge to buck, an uncomfortable flank strap binds him ahead of the hind legs.

The rules require the rider to spur his horse out once the chute is opened. Failure to do so will earn him a flat zero for the ride, regardless of how well he may perform. To turn in a really good performance, he must keep spurring throughout the trip. At all times he must keep one arm waving clear of the horse and his own body. He must not change hands on the grip.

As soon as he hears the toot of the "welcome horn," signaling the end of his ride, he looks for one of the expert pickup men to gallop alongside and swing him clear of the bronc. If he has been less fortunate he may have already been picked up by stretcher bearers. (Two deaths and nearly four hundred and fifty hospital cases were recorded in 1964.)

The same method of scoring is used for all riding events. There are two judges. Each is given a maximum of twenty-five points he can award to the rider and another twenty-five he can give to the horse or bull. The score for the ride is the total of the points awarded by both judges. Theoretically, therefore, perfection would be a score of one hundred. In practice, a ride in the seventies is considered phenomenal, one in the sixties extremely good.

After bareback riding comes calf roping. Here not only the rider's dexterity with the rope, but the training and quality of his horse are of great importance. In calf-roping competition, the calf must be allowed to cross the "score line" marked on the arena ground before the horse and rider emerge from the adjacent runway. To insure this a light rope barrier is stretched across the runway exit. One end of the barrier is attached to a pin. An exactly measured piece of twine leads from the pin to a loop around the calf's neck, so that when the calf scampers over the score line the pin is pulled and the barrier drops. There is a weak spot in the rope barrier which is easily

parted if an overeager contestant gets away to an unfair headstart. Breaking the barrier is a violation of the rules and is penalized by adding ten precious seconds to the roper's time.

The good roping horse must be trained, first of all, to take off at full speed the instant the barrier drops. The rider must carefully judge the calf's speed and direction, so that when he throws the rope he will catch the animal cleanly. The moment the loop falls over the calf's head, he releases the coiled-up slack in his line, and, as his horse applies the brakes, he steps off. With one hand running along the line, he moves swiftly to the calf's side to flip the three- or four-hundred-pound animal on its back. Then, taking the "piggin'" string he has been carrying between his teeth, he knots one foreleg and the two hind legs in a three-way hitch. Then he steps back and throws one arm up to signal the judges to stop the watch on his performance. The tie must hold for five seconds to be credited.

From the moment the rider dismounts, his horse must back off just enough to keep the line properly taut, so that the calf will be im-

mobilized. If the line is allowed to slacken, the calf will try to scramble away. If the horse pulls backward too hard, the calf will be dragged away from the roper. It is axiomatic among rodeo performers that no roper is better than his horse, and some of the greatest roping mounts, like champion Dean Oliver's Mickey, Ike Rude's Baldy, and Dale Smith's Poker Chip, have over the years become as well known around the circuit as their riders.

How fast can a good man-and-horse team chase down a calf and rope and tie him? With the help of a horse like Mickey, Dean Oliver, for example, can sometimes turn the trick in as little as twelve or thirteen seconds.

Saddle-bronc riding usually comes third and is considered the classic event, the one most deeply rooted in rodeo tradition. Although the objective of turning in the best possible ride on the most fractious possible horse is the same as in bareback riding, the two contests are otherwise quite different. As the rodeo artist-writer Sam Savitt states in his excellent study, *Rodeo Cowboys, Bulls and Broncos:* "The things that would seem to help the bronc rider—the stirrups, the saddle, and the rein denied to bareback riders— may make the business of sticking on the horse a little easier. But they also make it considerably more complicated." The rein, Savitt points out, is no great advantage since it is fastened to a plain halter instead of a bridle and bit. The stirrups, while they offer some help in balancing on the horse, present a problem: if the rider loses one in the course of his frenzied excursion, he is automatically disqualified. Then, too, there is the ever-present danger of being thrown with one foot stuck in the iron and being dragged by the wildly pitching bronc.

The saddle and tack used in saddle-bronc riding are all "regulation," conforming to standards set down by the Rodeo Cowboys Association. The only leeway permitted the contestant is that he has the option of removing the horn from his saddle to avoid being gouged should

Wild West shows, like Buffalo Bill's,
(left, above) helped popularize rodeo events.
Left: Team roping, by Charles Russell.

the bronc take a notion to roll. The horn is no good to a rider anyway, since grabbing it in the course of a ride—"pulling leather" in rodeo language—will disqualify him from the contest.

As in bareback riding, the cowboy is required to spur his horse out of the chute and to keep one hand free at all times. He is not allowed to wrap the hempen rein around his hand, but may only grasp it in his riding hand. As in bareback riding he cannot switch hands during the ride.

In bucking quality, saddle-bronc horses are generally superior to bareback mounts. This fact, coupled with the longer time requirement, accounts for the greater importance usually attached to saddle-bronc riding over bareback riding. Some riders compete in both forms of bronc busting, but they rarely excel in more than one. (A notable exception was the now-retired Casey Tibbs, a six-time saddle-bronc champion who was often called the "Babe Ruth of Rodeo." * In 1951, Tibbs won that title *and* the bareback crown, as well.)

Bulldogging, as it is still called despite the efforts of rodeo folk with more delicate sensibilities to change the name to "steer wrestling," is the fourth major rodeo event. The reason for the squeamishness about the name stems from its origin. The story goes that sometime around the turn of the century a Texas ranch hand named Bill Pickett became so enraged with a steer he had been unsuccessfully trying to pen that he jumped from his horse, pitched the steer on its back, and bit its lower lip severely, even as a bulldog traditionally attacks a bull. It has been seriously questioned whether Bill actually

* A national rodeo champion in any event is determined by the amount of his earnings for the year. The 1964 saddle-bronc title went to Marty Wood, a Canadian, with earnings of $22,148. In addition to a national champion in each principal rodeo event, an all-around champion cowboy—one who competes in more than one type of contest—is named. In 1964, the honor went to calf-roper/bulldogger Dean Oliver, of Idaho, with total earnings of $31,150.

145

*Right: Roper on speedy Quarter Horse
closes on fleeing calf. Cowboy holds "piggin'
string" between teeth as he swings his
rope for the "catch." The instant he alights
to make the tie, his horse will
tauten rope so that calf is held in place.
Below, right: The good roping horse knows just
how to proceed. Observe that this
roper's well-schooled mount jams on brakes
without any pressure on bit.
Calf has been cleanly caught; cowboy will
jump off to secure it in a tie that
must hold for five seconds or he will receive
"no time" for this event.
Left: Rider in foreground is a hazer
in a bulldogging contest. He rides on right-
hand side of contestant's steer
to keep it from veering away as cowboy makes
his jump. This picture, taken just after
steer crosses the barrier, shows top Quarter
Horse's powerful musculature.*

bit the steer, but the term "bulldogging" has been applied to the art of throwing steers ever since.

At any rate, word of Bill's violent deed spread and soon he was being asked to toss steers for pay at such touring Western shows as Buffalo Bill's and Annie Oakley's. Others took up the act and, as Wild West shows gave way to rodeo, it gradually became incorporated into the regular program of events. It is now a fixture.

In bulldogging the contestant has an assistant called a hazer, who rides on the right-hand side of the steer to keep it running straight. The steer is released like a calf in a roping contest. Similarly, too, there is a barrier which is dropped when the steer crosses the scoring line, and the same ten-second penalty for an illegal headstart.

A good dogging horse is essential to success in this event. The horse must know how to rate the steer's speed while maintaining an even distance from its side no matter which way it swerves. If the steer is overtaken on the left side, the bulldogger slips from his horse with his heels pointed at the ground, so that he is in the correct position to crook the steer's right horn in the elbow of his right arm while his left hand shoves the left horn earthward. If the move is correctly executed, the seven- or eight-hundred-pound animal is smoothly flipped on its side. If not, the luckless dogger is likely to find himself clutching nothing but the ground while the steer canters off, shaking its head. Incredible though it may seem, this feat is occasionally performed in less than five seconds.

No comment on bulldogging is complete without mention of Baby Doll, probably the most celebrated rodeo horse that ever lived. In her eight-year rodeo career, this tough little Quarter Horse mare was ridden by literally dozens of top doggers (it is common practice for the much-traveled rodeo contestant to borrow a roping or dogging horse in which case a percentage of any winnings goes to the animal's owner), and she rewarded them with a total of about half a million dollars in prize money.

The final major attraction of the rodeo card—bull riding—has nothing to do with horses, but it has become about the most exciting spectacle in rodeo. The bulls used are of Brahma and mixed-Brahma stock and have a particular aversion to being ridden. All the rider has to hang onto is a loose rope around the bull's middle. From the bottom of this rope hangs a cowbell which serves to show the judges that the rope is loose, as the rules require, and to warn absent-minded cowboys in the ring that a dangerous animal is nearby.

Bull riding has some special risks not associated with bareback and saddle-bronc riding, the greatest of these being inherent in the nature of the animal itself. The bucking horse can be full of hell with a rider on his back. But once the rider is off and his bucking flank strap is released, the horse quiets down. The bull, however, is thoroughly vicious. Unlike a horse, he will attack and try to gore a fallen rider. Since mounted pickup men cannot be used—the bull would charge them, too—it is up to the clowns to protect the rider, whether he is spilled or dismounts voluntarily from his enraged mount on completion of an eight-second ride. The clowns move in swiftly the instant a rider leaves a bull, taunting it with laugh-provoking but highly risky stunts to divert it from the fallen rider. Many a cowboy owes his life to a quick move by a clown, and many a clown has been seriously hurt while protecting a fallen contestant.

Bull riding, perilous as it is, does offer one important inducement that draws competitors from the top ranks of rodeo, namely that, as a rule, there is less chance of drawing a spiritless bull than there is of getting a listless bucking horse. The rider thus runs less risk of losing points on a poor showing by his mount than he does in the other riding events. No less a person than the five-time all-around cowboy champion Jim Shoulders included bull riding among his events and was, in fact, the title holder in that specialty seven times.

What is the special lure that draws men to this violent world of concussions and broken bones? The monetary inducements are few. The top men in each event may earn about $20,000 a year. Dean Oliver's $31,150 earned in 1964 included competition in two specialties. The all-time record, set by Jim Shoulders in 1956, was $43,381.

Outside of the top circle of contestants, few rodeo performers do much better than break even. Their expenses are relatively heavy. Unlike professional football, baseball, basketball, or hockey players, they pay their own room and board on the road, as well as the costs of traveling some seventy-five or eighty thousand miles a year. A good dogging or roping horse may cost as much as $3,000, and the horse must also be fed and stabled. Medical expenses constitute no small item in the rodeo performer's budget. He is paid nothing to compete, but must himself pay an entrance fee for each event in which he

participates. In the face of such odds, it is surprising that the Rodeo Cowboys Association numbers some three thousand active members—six times the number of players in both of baseball's major leagues.

Many reasons have been offered for rodeo's attraction. Not the least of these is the free-wheeling camaraderie which prevails around the rodeo loop, where few men have enemies and even a chance acquaintance is good for an emergency loan. Competitive as the sport is, there is hardly a man in the game who would not volunteer to another some riding tips on a bronc or a bull that he had drawn for himself in a previous rodeo.

By and large, rodeo men are a happy lot—a set of hopeful gamblers who play less for money stakes than for the thrill of beating the unbeatable. As such, they are not so far removed from the pioneers who first rodeoed for fun on the lonely trails of the Old West.

Bull riding (left) vs. bronc riding: either one is dangerous enough. Once the rider is thrown, however, the horse is no longer vicious, whereas bull will often go for fallen contestant.

149

8 THE

spirit in the Arab's proudly arched neck, but the shrewder judge also will note that the horse's windpipe is uncommonly large and, because of the width of the lower jaw, free of obstruction at the throat. This gives him greater lung capacity and unusual freedom from respiratory ailments. The harmony with which head and neck are joined is another feature highly prized by desert horsemen, who call this juncture the *mitbah*.

The neck is set deeply between well-muscled shoulders which slope well away from the body and are angled so perfectly that it is difficult to find a good Arab with rough gaits. The withers, however, do not cut high above the back, and frequently an Arab will appear to be taller at the croup than at the withers.

Through the barrel the Arab is solid and compact, and has well-sprung ribs. The compactness is owing to the fact that the Arab has a shorter spine and fewer ribs than other horses. The ordinary horse has six lumbar (ribless) vertebrae, nineteen pairs of ribs with accompanying vertebrae, and eighteen tail vertebrae. The Arab has only five lumbar vertebrae, eighteen, or often seventeen, pairs of ribs, and sixteen tail vertebrae.

With the exception of Saddle Horse fanciers who artificially treat horse's tails to ensure a spectacularly high, arched carriage, no one considers the tail to be vastly important: if it looks pretty, so much the better, but it doesn't really matter much, as horses go. Not so with the Arab, whose tail is carried high up on the croup and, without surgery or devices, flares in a spirited arch. The Arab's tail is exceptionally strong and undoubtedly contributes to the sturdiness of his back. There are many accounts of Arabians catching and supporting with their strong, arched tails heavy cloaks that have slipped from their rider's shoulders. Even more interesting is the fact that they actually use their tails as a rudder in turning.

The fact that the legs of the Arab are slender and small-boned, like a deer's, often leads hunting people, who cross Thoroughbreds with colder-blooded horses to get hunters with bigger bone, to

think they are fragile. On the contrary, the Arab's legs are lined with tendons like iron and supported by bone that is as dense and smooth as ivory, and not nearly as likely to break as the larger, more porous bones of seemingly more substantial horses. They also are remarkably free of diseases, such as ringbone, and are rarely given to puffing or bruising during shipping.

Under saddle the horse is definitely spirited, but around the stable he tends to be docile and friendly, perhaps because in Arabia he has always been treated like a member of the family. The Bedouin tribesman sleeps with his horse inside the tent at night, expects to be awakened by him at dawn, and interprets a show of nervousness as a sure sign of approaching danger.

The uncanny intelligence and devotion of the horse are celebrated in many desert tales which, surprisingly enough, are largely true. One situation that has occurred frequently and as frequently been verified concerns riders who have been wounded in battle and have fallen from the saddle. Their horses, instead of fleeing, remain by the master's side, turn him over with a hoof, and then lower themselves to the ground, so that the rider can remount.

This, then, is the Arabian as he has existed for thousands of years and contributed of his substance to the many breeds favored by modern man. He is almost entirely responsible for the formation of the Thoroughbred, since the Godolphin, the Darley Arabian, and the Byerly Turk are the endurance blood in Eclipse, Matchem, and Herod, the Thoroughbred foundation sires. But his importance to racing stock by no means ended there. For generations Thoroughbred sires continued to be crossed with mares of strong Arabian blood, and in America Arab horses were registered with The Jockey Club, along with Thoroughbreds, until as recently as 1943. In England, for more than one hundred and twenty-seven years about eighty-seven per cent of English Derby winners were descended from the Darley; the remaining thirteen per cent also were of Arabian heritage—descending principally from the Godolphin and a lesser-known stallion, the Alcock Arabian, who is responsible for the gray color of Thoroughbreds now in existence.

The Arab's contribution to stamina has, of course, not been limited to the running horse and Thoroughbreds. Imported Messenger, from whom Hambletonian 10 is traced, was a direct descendant of the Darley Arabian, and from him, with the help of numerous other Arabian crossings, an official Standardbred horse was evolved.

A lesser-known influence on American trotting was a post-Civil War horseman and breeder named Randolph Huntington, who wanted to develop a completely American "national" horse, to be arrived at by crossing more or less in-

digenous trotting stock with Arabian blood. He owned an extraordinary trotter named Henry Clay, a great-grandson of the imported Arabian Grand Bashaw. As a trotter he was never beaten, and for many years he held an endurance record for covering seventy-six miles in less than five hours while drawing a heavy, two-seated sur-

Right: Aahdin, Grand National Reserve champion stallion belonging to Mrs. George Rosenberg, of Abbeville, South Carolina. Below: Yearling Arabian fillies at Mrs. Hewitt's Friendship Farm. Far right: Head of Arabian yearling. The fine qualities of Arabian horses have been used to improve many other light-horse breeds.

rey. Huntington put Henry Clay to stud and crossed Clay daughters with pure Arabians, including Leopard and Linden Tree, two stallions imported in 1879 and given to President Grant. Unfortunately, before Huntington's experiments could be properly evaluated he fell into bankruptcy and his stock was sold off at auction. The Arabs he imported, however, are the ancestors of many Arabian horses now in America, and there is no doubt that much of their blood found its way into contemporary trotters and pacers.

The precise pedigree of little Justin Morgan is uncertain and often the subject of heated debate, but what is clear is that the foundation sire of the Morgan horse resulted from inbred Arabian crossings not far back in his line. One reconstruction of his ancestry shows a fairly close link with the Godolphin, and a host of other Arab names figures prominently farther back.

Blaze, foundation sire of the Hackney, is still another direct descendant of the Arabian.

Quarter Horses, through crossings with Thoroughbreds, can boast the presence of his blood, and even the wild horses of the western plains have a touch of it, since they descend from the stock of early Spanish conquistadors, whose horses were pronouncedly of Oriental breeding.

In short, there is simply no breed of light horse with class, quality, and speed that does not stem from the Arab.

One unusual event that strongly influenced the breeding of Arabians in America occurred at the Chicago World's Fair of 1893. For this world-famous exposition, the Turkish Government arranged to bring over forty-five Arab horses that were to be put on a dazzling show, a star midway attraction. All Turkey was astir with anticipation. Businessmen vied for the honor of sharing in the Hamidieh Hippodrome Co., as it was called, and underlings dickered for the privilege of traveling with the group. A special Cunard steamship was chartered for the transfer and in they trouped to Chicago—one hundred and twenty men, women, and children, forty-five horses, twelve camels,

donkeys, and fat-tailed sheep. Not only were they the weirdest entourage ever to grace the Windy City, but by the time they got there they were penniless. They put on one performance which raised $16 and thereafter the $3,000,000 show was in the hands of loan sharks who stripped the supposedly "wily" Middle Easterners of what little they had. Improperly clothed for the fierce Chicago cold, the band then burned for warmth the one and a half million tickets to the show they had printed in Turkey. Fire broke out and killed several of the horses. Then word got around that the animals were of scrub stock and impure breeding. In all, it was a fiasco, and one by one the company directors ran off, leaving the authorities to care for the starving troupers and arrange for the stock to be sold into receivership.

As it turned out, not all the horses were of uncertain bloodlines. Eight of them were of the purest desert strains, and a mare named Nejdme and a stallion called Obeyran became foundation animals in the Arabian registry in America. Later, others of the eight were registered. Today their descendants are found throughout the United States.

If the recent history of the Arabian can be detailed with some authority, his origins in antiquity are shrouded in myth and legend and are a basis for a good deal of contention. The Barb and the Turk, for example, are types closely associated with the Arabian. Purists argue as to whether the Turk, the Barb, and the Arabian are entirely distinct and separate breeds, or whether the Turk and the Barb are offshoots of the Arabian. Some maintain that all three breeds evolved from separate sources; others claim that they shared a common ancestor in the Libyan lion-hunting horse.

Most evidence suggests that the Turk and Barb are slightly larger and coarser cousins of the Arab, not originally breeds apart, and that the Arab himself is the purest descendant of the Libyan horse. Still the dispute exists between

Left: Costume events are feature of many Arabian horse shows, like this "All Arabian" affair at Quentin, Pennsylvania. Below: Arabians are often shown in Western classes. Notice that this mare, though small, carries a big man with ease.

those who contend that the horse arose from a wild race native to Arabia since prehistoric times, and those who believe he arrived through importation or migration. Currently prevailing is the theory that horses were brought to that general region by the Hittites, who gathered them from the East, and eventually filtered down into the Arabian peninsula.

The most consistent factor in the legends surrounding the Arab is that the breed is a specific result of the offspring of five great mares who founded five original Arabian strains, which then branched out into substrains. The five mares are sometimes referred to as the five blue mares and also as Al Khamseh—the five.

One bit of folklore credits Mohammed with having been the original owner of the five blue mares, but this is obviously pure nonsense since it has been proved that the breed existed for centuries before Mohammed's birth in 570 A.D. Another myth tells how Ishmael, about 2000 B.C., received a divine gift from heaven—a wild mare which had become crippled by being carried as a foal in a saddlebag on camelback. The mare gave birth to a colt that was named Benat el Ahwaj—"son of the crooked"—who is said to have sired the first strain of pure Arabians, the Kuhaylan. On the heels of this comes the legend of Kuhaylan Ajuz, the first of the blue mares. In this account, a sheik rode into battle on his favorite war mare who, in the heat of a melee, dropped her foal and then bravely went about the business of war, carrying her master to a thundering retreat many miles away. Later, as the caravan was recovering from the ravages of battle, the sheik was astounded to discover a visitor at the campsite—the weary and hungry, but very much alive, day-old filly that had trailed her dam through the desert. The filly was entrusted to the care of an old woman and came to be known as Kuhaylan Ajuz, meaning "the mare of the old woman."

Lady Wentworth discounts this version, which she claims is the result of faulty translation.

Kuhaylan or *Kehilan*, both stemming from *Kohlani*, actually mean purebred, she maintains, and *Ajuz* is simply the Arabic word for old. Hence, the phrase is really "the old purebred."

From another mistranslation develops the tangled account of how King Solomon owned Al Khamseh. Here Solomon was confused with Salaman, who lived about 1635 B.C. and to whom ownership was intended to be attributed. In this fable, the precise number of five, which has since been faithfully handed down, first becomes significant. According to the story, Salaman (also known as Faras, the horseman) had traveled with his herd of horses through the desert for many days without coming to water. Eventually they approached a stream and the animals rushed forward to quench their fierce thirst. Suddenly, Salaman sounded a call on his horn and from the herd, five mares resisted the water and returned at the call of their master. It was these five that Salaman selected to breed and produce the five great strains.

The final stage of Arabian horse lore is the fable stemming from the time of David and held to account for the contemporary Arabian. During the reign of David there lived a man named Rabiah al-Faras, whose father designated him as heir to the horses derived from Al Khamseh. These purebreds were subsequently passed on to Rabiah's grandson, Anazah. Anazah's tribes spread through the verdant areas of the Nejd in central Arabia, and to this day these people are said to breed the finest horses of their land, the prize strain still called the Kuhaylan of Anazah.

Traditionally, not only the five blue mares but all purebred Arabian mares have had an almost sacred importance to their desert owners. Contrary to European and American custom, the Bedouin traces the lineage of a horse through the dam side. It is his prize war mare that he rides into battle, and mare's milk with which he frequently nourishes himself. While the importation of stallions has not been significantly difficult to negotiate, the foreign acquisition of pure desert mares has been an all-but-impossible task until fairly recent times. Some did, of course, find their way out of Arabia, notably into the stables of Charles II of England and Catherine the Great of Russia, who had a large number of matched stallions and mares.

Of prime importance in the early development of the Arabian is a fact largely glossed over by those who contend that the Arabian must have had post-Christian origins and been imported to the desert, since he is a grazing animal and presumably could never have flourished in those trackless wastes. But Arabia was not always a desert. The Bible, as well as writings of a much later date, abounds with allusions to "the forests of Arabia," and, in addition, accurately predicts the withering suns, winds, and tribal warfare that would eventually plague it. Fossils of these forested areas have been uncovered, in addition to pit-marked rock that gives evidence of torrential rains. The section of lower Arabia called the Nejd was not only lush and fertile, but also underlain by limestone rock, like the famed Bluegrass country of Kentucky. Small wonder that even today some of the finest blooded horses come from the Bedouin breeders of this region.

In the contemporary world of horses, the Arabian is an animal of paradoxes. In the first place, after having been an historic influence, it has been his fate to be so overshadowed by his descendants that a majority of professional horsemen tend to consider him as simply a list of often unpronounceable names in an official stud book, or as the fair-haired child of a coterie of fanciers. Secondly, while modern horsemen are constantly modifying breed standards, the owners of Arabians are concerned with preserving the breed in all the purity that has existed for thousands of years and nothing on earth would get the conscientious man to tamper with his heritage beyond certain limits. These are not men given to the folly of admiring a "pretty horse," but ones who recognize that if time has tested anything, it has tested the Arabian and that over the centuries no other breed has equaled his endurance, his intelligence, and his adaptability.

Chief among the great breeding plants in the United States is the Pomona Ranch in California, founded by W. K. Kellogg, the breakfast-cereal manufacturer. Here are assembled more than eighty magnificent Arabians deriving largely from England's famed Crabbet Stud, a farm whose Anglo-Arab horses have won countless grueling steeplechases. Another fine center is the Lazy V.V. Ranch in Colorado, owned by Lynn Van Vleet, where Arabians are bred under more rugged conditions for stock-horse purposes—and superb cow horses they can be. They can eat everything or anything and still make an eighty-mile workday seem like child's play. In Australia a horse of Arab descent named Adonis sired the greatest stock horses ever known in Queensland. In America a fourteen-year-old Arabian named Shereyn was bought by a man named McCann, schooled for stock work, and after thirty-seven days of training won first prize in the lightweight class against top horses in San Francisco's Cow Palace. An almost incredible feat is the trek made by an Arab called Astraled who, at the age of twenty-two, traveled from Oregon to New Hampshire in twenty-one days, averaging one hundred and nineteen miles a day! But primarily the Arabian's use today is as a pleasure horse.

Thanks to the devotion of breeders such as Mrs. Bazy Tankersley, of Al Marah Farm, near Washington, D.C., and Mrs. William Hewitt, of Moline, Illinois, Arabians now number some twenty-five thousand, as opposed to the paltry seventy-six registered in 1908 when the Arabian Horse Club of America was formed, and the twenty-nine hundred in 1944. In 1950 the breed was recognized by the American Horse Shows Association as eligible for its shows. These are but a few of the signs that show every promise of a splendid renaissance so richly deserved by the little desert horse that has given every ounce of his heart and every aspect of his beauty to every horse that has crossed with his blood.

9 A GALLERY

OF PONIES

Of all the inhabitants of the equine world, the most beguiling is that small, sturdy, and sometimes mischievous creature known in England by his nickname "Sheltie," and in America as the Shetland pony. Traditionally a favorite children's pet, he is the most popular of all pony breeds, having about forty thousand purebreds in the American Shetland Pony Club registry.

The Shetland derives his name, of course, from the Shetland Islands off the coast of Scotland where the type originated and has existed for uncounted centuries. Proof of the Shetland's antiquity was furnished when an ancient Celtic relic called the Bressay Stone was found in Scotland in 1864. This is a slab of chloride slate engraved on both sides in bas-relief with early Celtic characters and accurate renderings of small horses and riders. Experts have identified the find as dating from the Celtic Christian period before the Norse invasion (c. 800 A.D.), indicating that the animals were there before the Norsemen arrived. Moreover, one of the regions where Shetlands flourished was called *Hrossey*—Horse Island—by the earliest Norse explorers, and while there are many references to the horses they found there, nothing suggests that the Norsemen brought them. Hence, it may be assumed that the Shetland existed, if possibly in a somewhat larger form, as early as 600 A.D. and perhaps even earlier.

According to legend, the Shetland Islands were visited centuries later by ships of the Spanish Armada, which landed with Arab horses, introducing desert blood to the native stock.

Throughout the ages the Shetland, like other wild ponies, has managed to survive the rigors of bad nourishment, rocky terrain, and bitter sea winds purely and simply by means of adaptation. With nothing but rough heather, seaweed, and salt-marsh grasses to feed on the animal has gradually reduced its size until it eventually became small enough to thrive on this meager fare.

The harsh landscape has taught the Shetland to be surefooted, and he resists the biting cold with a coat that consists of wool rather than hair until he is two years old. In winter, the ponies grow long, furry hair that provides a rainproof thatch. Of course, this protection is less luxuriant among domesticated Shetlands, who no longer have to face survival in the wild, but their coats continue to grow thick and furry in winter and they thrive best with the least coddling. Hay or grass, water, and a modest shed for shelter is all they require; in fact, adding anything more than a few handfuls of grain may make the frisky Shetland so energetic that he leaves his rider viewing the world from the ground up!

Today's purebred Shetland averages about forty-two inches in height. Forty-six inches is the top limit set by the American Shetland Pony Club; occasionally the ponies are as small as twenty-six inches. They come in a wide assortment of colors: mouse gray, black, bay, brown, chestnut, cream, gray, white, spotted, and many colors of dapple. In conformation they vary according to type. The Island type, traditionally used in the mines and coalpits of the British Isles, resembles a miniature draft horse, a tiny Belgian or Clydesdale. Its features, like those of cold-blooded breeds, are notably coarser, especially about the head. The American type, which is in great favor in the United States, has a structure of refinement and quality produced through careful selective breeding. It has tiny ears, emerging from an abundance of mane, an intelligent-looking face with a profile that is sometimes slightly dished, like the Arabian's. It has a compact, well-proportioned little body with a deep chest, heavily muscled back, and a round, well-sprung barrel. Its legs are very short and remarkably sound.

The Shetland can be ridden with equal pleasure in either Western rig or English tack, and can easily jump obstacles of two to three feet. In horse-show classes where ponies are required to jump, the events are usually divided according to the size of the animals. Ponies under 11:2 hands jump two feet; 11:2 to 13 hands jump two and one half feet; 13 to 14:2 hands jump three feet. Since Shetlands registered with the American Shetland Pony Club must not exceed 11:2 hands, these purebreds usually jump only the two-foot height in competitions.

Shetlands are also ideal in harness. In fact, some owners prefer driving to riding them, since their short legs do produce swift, choppy gaits—though children don't seem to mind this at all. At any rate, some of the most elegant little pony roadsters and fine-harness ponies are Shetlands, and their stylish appearance at horse shows, as they prance along at a splendid gait in full harness, is an almost incredible contrast to their rugged background. They are also used with sulkies in the growing sport of pony racing.

Far less popular than the Shetland as an all-around family pet, but highly favored among an increasing number of horsemen, is the Welsh pony. Strictly speaking, there are two types of Welsh pony: the Welsh Cob, which descends from the old Welsh cart horse, and the Welsh Mountain pony, which, like the Shetland, is a wild type native to the land and used for pulling and hauling in the coal mines of Wales. The Cob is larger and, whether a measure of trotting blood was infused in the line, or whether he developed the gait on his own, he is employed mainly as a driving animal. His trotting speed makes him celebrated as a roadster.

It is the Cob's mountain cousin, however, that has dazzled the eye of American horsemen in recent years. When one refers to a Welsh pony in the United States, this is the variety that is meant.

About a hundred years ago some Arab stallions were turned out to breed among Welsh pony mares. This desert cross has left its mark on the Welsh more than on any other pony type, as is clearly seen in the conformation of today's representatives. The delicately articulated face, the bold, low-set eyes, the small, pointed ears, the long, arched neck that fits deep

into the shoulders, all point directly to an Eastern influence. The back is short, well-coupled and strong, blending into loins that are broad and muscular. The tail is set high upon the croup and is carried gaily. In the shoulder, the Welsh is long and sloping. His legs are short and set square and, when in motion, reach forth with a free, sweeping, natural flexibility. Instead of a low, daisy-cutting stride, his action is elevated and proud, tempting many fine-harness fanciers to consider the Welsh pony as possible breeding stock. However, because by conformation, endurance, and spirit the animal is so ideally suited to be a children's riding pony, and is so exceptionally good in the hunting field, the Welsh

Pony Society of America discourages use of the breed in fine harness with the long hoofs and set tails required for showing. The Welsh may, of course, be driven for pleasure, hitched to a small sleigh in winter or to the family pony cart in summer, but since he exhibits an almost natural talent for jumping, it is under saddle that he is generally seen at his best.

The Welsh Mountain pony may be any solid color. In the United States grays, whites, and chestnuts seem to predominate. Spotted combinations are not usual and when they do occur a suspicious eye may be turned on the animal's breeding. In height, the Welsh runs measurably larger than the Shetland, the official upper limit being 12:2 hands. But, like the Shetland, he needs no undue pampering and can thrive on a minimal amount of care. There are now about six thousand Welsh ponies registered in America and importations are increasing rapidly.

From the west coast of Ireland, in the county of Galway, among the mountain clefts of Connemara, comes a pony of the same name—a type that is comparatively rare in the United States and consequently high-priced, but well worth the thousand dollars that may be asked for an animal of good breeding.

Of all the pony breeds the Connemara is the most nearly perfect natural hunter, and at his best resembles a fine miniature Thoroughbred. Actually, he is not all that miniature, for he is the largest of the pony breeds, the official regulations of measurement specifying limits of 13 to 14:2 hands. At birth the Connemara is given temporary registration, and at the age of two is inspected by a representative of the Connemara Pony Breeders Society in Ireland, or the American Connemara Society in the United States, to ensure that as the animal approaches maturity he has not grown over the standard height of 14:2. In color Connemaras generally run to duns with black points, creams, strawberry roans, grays which turn to white, and, more rarely, chestnuts and bays.

By nature the Connemara is an unusually gentle creature, so that, despite his taller size, he is a thoroughly safe mount for the youngest riders. He can be used for driving and is commonly seen drawing carts through the villages of western Ireland. In fact, Cannon Ball, the first foundation

sire of the Connemara stud book, was a famous trotter in his day. But the Connemara's talents do not basically lie in the direction of a fine-harness pony. He has the long, low, extended gaits of the Thoroughbred that all but cry out his suitability for hunting. In addition, he has an instinctive jumping ability that is phenomenal. A 14-hand Connemara can sail over jumps that will stop a horse two hands larger. One such pony, the fifty-four-inch Little Squire, won renown in the United States in the thirties as an open jumping champion, competing against horses that towered over him and carrying a full-grown man over fences of five and six feet. This potential makes Connemaras superb show ponies for children who ride well and want an animal they can keep and enjoy into adult years. On the other hand, size and gentleness make them a fine pet for the family wanting one mount that every member can ride.

In the field of harness ponies, one name stands above all others: the Hackney, developed from the Hackney horse which originated in England on the North Sea, in Norfolk and Lincoln. The foundation sire was Blaze, a fine trotter of eighteenth-century England, and much of the quality blood traces back to Norfolk trotters and stallions "of the blood," including the Godolphin, the Alcock, and the Darley, as well as the Gray Barb and the Byerly Turk. The name Hackney derives from the Norman *hacquenee*, a general term for horse.

Originally, Hackneys were ridden as well as used for coaching. They have exceptionally strong backs and, if put to the test, can sometimes become good jumpers. But the fact is that there are many more Hackney ponies than horses, and these are such flashy, proud, magnificent little show animals in harness that only rarely does an owner want to use the pony under saddle as well. Their action is taut and animated, their hoofs are worn long, and the flexing of their legs is so elevated that they seem to be reaching for the sky with every stride. Their necks are arched and

their heads held high, with a bold, nervous look about the eye. Their tails usually are docked to a short brush.

Most Hackney ponies are bay, but there are some browns, blacks, chestnuts, and, occasionally, grays and roans. In height they average from 12 to 13 hands.

The Hackney pony has been bred to be a noble, nervous, elegantly high-stepping and high-styled animal that offers all the showmanship anyone could ask. For this reason he is too sophisticated a type for most children and is best enjoyed by adults who have the educated taste to appreciate the regal splendor of his bearing.

Other imported breeds that have increasingly gained the interest of American horsemen are England's Dartmoor and Exmoor ponies and the Icelandic pony. Both the Dartmoor and Exmoor are wild races and bear a strong resemblance to the Welsh pony, except that the Dartmoor is somewhat stockier. Neither Dartmoor nor Exmoor moves with the elevation of the Welsh, but they have a more extended stride. They are spirited little fellows and a very good ride in the hunting field; in fact, many English breeders cross them with full-sized horses to produce valuable hunters. In size they should not exceed 12:2 hands and they run to solid colors of brown, bay, black, gray, with a few chestnuts and even fewer duns. There are no spotted purebreds. Indeed, with the exception of a white star or fleck upon the face, the purebreds have no white on them whatever. They are strong, rugged, handsome ponies which still live very much in the wild and therefore require training before being turned over to the neophyte rider. The more experienced young horsemen, however, will recognize them as animals of class and high courage and will enjoy the challenge of natives who say, "If you can ride an Exmoor, you can ride anything!"

Icelandic ponies descend from stock brought to the island by the Norsemen about 875 A.D., and were used extensively in farming until the introduction of the American Jeep. Like the Con-

*South Carolina Marsh Tackys
(left) and Chincoteagues both are feral
strains found on Atlantic coast.*

nemara, Icelandic ponies are a tall breed, averaging 13:2 hands, and similarly gentle and affectionate. Their color is generally red or chestnut, or a spotted chestnut and white. They are a very hardy type now used in their homeland for trekking, the popular Icelandic sport of cross-country camping. Since their importation to the United States has been fairly recent, it remains to be seen what particular direction their talents will take, though it is already a certainty that they are a pleasing, all-around family pet.

Although it might seem otherwise, the entire pony population of the United States does not derive from imported blood, nor is every one a purebred. There are a number of domestic strains, both wild and cultivated, but the curious truth is that, with one exception, none of the native types has yet been organized into stud books or an official registry, and are therefore technically re-

garded as crossbred ponies. One such pony—a cultivated strain—is the Kentucky Saddle Pony, which is not a distinct breed, but produced by crossing a pony mare or stallion with an American Saddle Horse. These little Kentucky Saddlers are small-scale replicas of the Saddle Horse, a riding pony which demonstrates a taut bearing, an extremely flexed, high-stepping action, and an arched neck and compact little body reminiscent of the Hackney in harness. They perform at the usual three gaits—walk, trot, and canter—and many of them are five-gaited, as well, adding the rack and slow-gait, and making them ideal show-ring mounts for the young saddle-seat rider.

The Chincoteague pony, made famous by Marguerite Henry's children's book, *Misty of Chincoteague*, is a wild race found off the coast of Virginia on the islands of Assateague and

167

Above & right: Donald Schooler of Fayette,
Indiana, trains his Shetland, Trigger, for show.
Like many American youngsters, Donald is
enrolled in local 4-H horse program.

Chincoteague. These ponies descend from partly Arab horses which swam there after surviving the shipwreck of a Spanish sailing vessel in the sixteenth century, and, like other wild types left to breed at will and survive on salt-marsh grasses and seaweed, gradually dwindled in size. Each year, at a gala Pony Penning day, the herds are rounded up to swim the channel from Assateague to Chincoteague where the foals are then auctioned off. There is no stud book, so the ponies are considered crossbreds, and little has been done to change them. Nevertheless, they make fine family pets and have the size, ranging from about 12:2 to 13:2, to make pleasing hunters. In color they run the equine spectrum; solid colors are usually the best indication of some fine original blood.

Another wild race of native American pony is the rarely heard-of Marsh Tacky from the Carolinas. These are said to have descended from bands of wild Thoroughbreds that roamed the area after the Civil War, and while they are far less publicized than the Chincoteague, they are a slightly more refined type and would make good as children's hunters.

The one domestic American pony that *is* a specific breed and *has* an official stud book is the Pony of the Americas, developed by a breeder named Leslie Boomhower of Mason City, Iowa, who crossed a Shetland stallion with an Appaloosa mare and was so pleased with the results that he determined to found a new breed. The Appaloosa horse is strictly a color breed and Mr. Boomhower's mare has passed on to the pony strain the distinctive Appaloosa color characteristics. In addition, all Ponies of the Americas have a dark coloration around the jowls, nose, mouth, and eyes, and under the tail. These are called "varnish" marks and vary from about one-half inch to an inch and a half in diameter. Mature ponies must be between 11:2 and 13 hands, and, while foals are granted a temporary registration at birth, they must later be inspected to see that they fulfill the height and color requirements

specified by the Pony of the Americas Club. This breed has found favor almost exclusively in the West, where it has proved to be a first-rate cow pony.

Some horsemen tend to think of ponies—especially the smaller types—as waspish little devils, inclined to be mean and stubborn. Actually, they are docile and affectionate. The trouble is that because of their size they often have to put up with annoyances that no one would dream of inflicting on, say, a Thoroughbred. Sometimes this simply taxes the limits of their inherent good nature, and they call a halt. Their intelligence and strength may also work to their disadvantage. A four-year-old Sheltie, for example, can carry a full-sized man, but since adults feel foolish on so tiny a beast, he usually is left in the hands of children, and the pony soon learns that it is easier to play than to work. Since the pony is stronger and often cleverer than the child, it is easy for bad habits to set in. If, however, the pony is properly handled and trained, misbehavior will not occur in the first place and the owner will be rewarded with a friend that is bright, loyal, and willing.

PLOWSHARES

The heavy horse of today combines his role as a willing laborer with the aura of a glamorous past. Though now greatly diminished in numbers by the advent of the tractor and other agricultural machinery, he is still occasionally found working in the fields, mud-spattered, knee-deep in the ploughed furrow, with his neck lowered and his shoulders plunged deep into the collar as he goes about the humble routine of farm labor. This has been his principal role for many years. Nevertheless, there is something majestic in his staunch bearing and deliberate movement that makes it impossible to forget his heroic performance as the steed of knighthood in the days of chivalry.

Over-all, he is a rough-hewn animal. His head is large and often Roman-nosed. By the standards of other horses, it could be called coarse, but it is not at all inappropriate to the heavy breeds. Though he stands in some instances as tall as 20 hands, his large-boned legs actually look short in proportion to his lusty girth and bulging musculature. He frequently tips the scales at a ton or more—twice the weight of a Thoroughbred race horse—an awesome massiveness that fortunately houses a kind disposition which traditionally endears him to all who work with him. While even the best of other breeds may fall into spells of moodiness or irritability, the willing, workmanlike heavy horse is known the world over for his consistent amiability.

While we regard him nostalgically today as the tiller of the fields or as the dray horse of the merchants and brewers, clip-clopping through the cobbled streets of a half century ago, the fact is that the heavy-horse breeds were not developed for peaceable pursuits. They were a by-product of war.

Prior to the Middle Ages, horses of less weight and strength adequately met the demands made on cavalry mounts. Following the fall of Roman rule, however, war became traditionally the affair of mounted men of good birth, who required larger horses to carry the weight of their increasingly elaborate armor. Protected by heavy, jointed metal skirts and head gear, and ridden by a cavalier in the full armor of the Middle Ages, the Great Horse of Europe—like the tank of modern war—mowed down anything in his path.

The evolution of armor, as well as of animals big and strong enough to bear its weight, was gradual. Medieval troops, like those of William the Conqueror in 1066, wore only iron helmets and body armor of meshed metal links. These outfits were apparently not very cumbersome, since it was the custom for young men to adjust to their added weight by turning somersaults fully garbed. Relatively comfortable as the mail may have been, however, it did not provide adequate defense against such heavy weapons as the mace. For extra protection armorers began attaching metal plates to the mail underlining, until, by the time of the Battle of Crecy in 1346, plate armor predominated. Over the following three centuries, as the knights encountered increasingly effective weapons, the armorers fashioned armor plates which were still heavier and covered larger areas of the body, until these sculptures of steel, carefully fitted and jointed, completely encased the wearer. Ultimately the combined burden of the rider's weight, his attire, and the protective fittings for his horse could amount to four hundred pounds. Obviously, the beast required to carry this load had to be vastly different from the light war horses of earlier armies. Battle tactics, too, had shifted from the intricate cavalry maneuvers suitable for light mounts to outright charges, foe against foe. To bear these new burdens of weight and strategy, medieval horsemen produced through selective breeding the equine giants whose descendants remain with us today.

The animals they originally had to work with were the large, cold-blooded descendants of Equus robustus, a coarse, lumbering species that abounded in European prehistory and which, except when man deliberately interceded, was al-

Preceding pages: Jerry Rybolt of Swayzee, Indiana, drives Beau Tress and Nancy, his fine Percherons, to day's work in fields.

most completely free of the influence of Eastern blood. The earliest distinct type bred from this background was the Flemish horse, the ancestor of all draft-horse breeds, whose closest modern relative is the Belgian.

Many of these early Flemish horses were bought or captured by the French, and their off-spring were called Norman horses. In France the Norman animals evolved into the handsome breed we now know as the Percheron. In England, where Norman mounts were introduced by William the Conqueror, they mated with native stock, chiefly the English Black Horse, and contributed to the development of the three draft-horse breeds of the British Isles: the Shire, the Suffolk, and the Clydesdale. These three, and the Belgian and Percheron, are the dominant breeds of modern draft horse.

The early descendants of the Flemish, Norman, and Black horses, the medieval destriers or war horses, were of the greatest importance to the chivalric system of war which lasted until the fourteenth century. The usefulness to the medieval knight of a good destrier is reflected in the sizable purchase price these horses commanded. As one authority notes: "The destriers, or trained battle-chargers, able to carry the immense weight of the heaviest armed nobles, cost around £ 100, or as much in modern purchasing power as a high-powered limousine." Their keep was an expensive proposition also. In 1310, when the Great Horses abounded in England, one archbishop railed against the extravagance, pointing out that the weekly cost of each animal was sufficient to support four or five poor people, not even considering the amounts expended on wages for grooms to care for the creatures. But the usefulness of the Great Horses, in war and eventually in other areas as well, outweighed the disadvantage of expense. Their popularity only grew with time, as evidenced by the fact that, two hundred years later, Henry VIII attempted to increase their numbers at a faster rate than ever, by passing laws to do away with smaller horses

and to compel a majority of landowners to maintain the larger ones for breeding purposes.

Once having emerged as a distinct type and as an animal of towering strength, the heavy horse gradually found his way into civilian as well as military use. In agriculture, the going was, at first, rather slow. The ox had been the traditional farm animal for centuries; he was used for drawing the plow and was also a source of food and hides. It took some doing for a horse to compete with these advantages. Nevertheless, there is evidence that on medieval farms heavy horses were bred not only as battle chargers but as haulers of cart and plow as well. At first they were harnessed in combination with oxen but, as the feudal method of farming private, isolated plots evolved into the enclosure method, whereby neighboring fields were linked together to form larger areas, the horses proved more effective and eventually supplanted their slower, duller competitors.

Travel in medieval times was mostly done on horseback, and under saddle the heavy horse was said to have an extremely comfortable "ambling pace." One lady of the day complained bitterly when put aboard "a cruel trotting horse" in lieu of the customary ambler that could safely carry her infant child in comfort on a pillow. Carriages were thought of as luxuries that could be afforded only by the richest of the rich. Such coaches as did exist were an awkward blend of elegance and discomfort. Drawn by sturdy horses, they bounced, jounced, and jolted along, for springs were not invented until 1690. In France the carriages were called *diligences* and were pulled by Percherons, while in the German principalities the coaches were drawn by horses that, like the Belgian, were directly related to the Flemish horse but of much lighter weight. These were called German Coach Horses and animals of this same breed were ridden by Kaiser Wilhelm's Uhlans when they marched into Belgium in 1914.

Heavy horses also were used to transport the mails, and often were ridden astride by a sixteenth-century postman who announced his

Opposite: Broad
back of big
Belgian drafter
is decked out
in parade finery.
Constrico
(above), fine
Belgian stallion
of L. C. Smith,
San Mateo,
California.
Left: Belgian
mares and foals,
Meadowbrook Farm,
Michigan.

175

presence to towns and passers-by by blowing a horn as he made his rounds. Later, the mails were carried by coach pulled by a dray horse.

The hard-working heavy horse also had more unhappy parts to play. In early times he was used to turn mill wheels and, to prevent dizziness, was frequently blinded by having his eyes bored out. In the field of amusements, too, he could have a grueling career. Early hauling competitions tested his weight-pulling ability to an often cruel degree. Wagons loaded with sand, their wheels sunk into mud with blocks of wood placed before them, sent the animals down to their knees before the burden could be budged. Even more punishing were contests in which rival heavy horses were hitched to growing trees and forced to pull until the loser collapsed.

The heavy horse, in all his many roles, was never essentially a pleasure animal. He was bred for usefulness and, unfortunately, that usefulness was fated to end. His decline began with the first military use of gunpowder. In order to protect soldiers from gunfire, armorers simply made the metal plates in armor increasingly heavy. The results for the wearer were disastrous—he ultimately lost all mobility and became more vulnerable than ever. Furthermore, these suits were a torment to wear for any length of time. Some soldiers demanded extra pay for wearing them; others refused point-blank to put them on, and still others conveniently "lost" entire suits of armor! The result was a reversion to less cumbersome arms and, subsequently, lighter and more maneuverable cavalry mounts.

A second blow to the usefulness of the heavy horse was the invention of the gasoline engine. After the great horse's decline as a military asset, he had found a comfortable niche in both farm and urban regions as a stalwart puller and hauler. During the seventeenth and eighteenth centuries the demand for, and consequent interest in, working heavy horses was so great that the general type had separated more clearly into distinct breeds. But the slow, deliberate mechani-

zation of agriculture and transportation denied the heavy horse his function in these areas as well. In 1937 in England there were upwards of one million working draft horses whereas twenty-one years later the figure dwindled to about seventy thousand and has diminished to an even smaller figure since. In America, where once more than one out of every two registered horses was a draft breed, the annual increase in registrations of all the purebred heavy horses combined is less than a thousand.

Before his decline, however, the heavy horse in America had accomplished a stupendous task. He had opened up great farming belts and given the initial burst of speed to the rapid agricultural expansion of the young country. Small wonder then that even now he remains a fixture in America's vast farming regions. He is still valued for other kinds of hauling as well. For instance, along the Pacific Coast the heavy horse is used in offshore fishing to pull the seines from the water. And nothing has replaced him in the hearts of breeders who cultivate fine strains of draft horses to exhibit each year at lavish agricultural and livestock expositions.

Today, at such celebrated gatherings as the Michigan, Ohio, and Iowa State Fairs and the Chicago International, as well as smaller, folksier affairs in New England, champion draft-horse stallions and mares gather to be shown in hand and judged on conformation. For plowing competitions, the horses are hitched in teams of two or more, according to the requirements of the contest. Today, too, they are used in exciting hauling competitions that are a more humane survival of the brutal events held in earlier times. The "horse drawing contests," as the tests are usually called, are a main attraction for every fairgoer and the giant arenas are packed with crowds of ten and twelve thousand, assembled to cheer the giant teams on to victory and to lay heavy wagers on their favorites. At smaller affairs the teams simply draw a weighted stoneboat over a specified distance. At the more

elaborate expositions, however, an apparatus called a dynamometer is used to gauge their strength. This method involves an arrangement of suspended weights which is attached to a truck. Each team is harnessed to the truck and, as the horses thrust their massive bulk forward, the weights are gradually elevated. When a certain degree of tension is reached, the truck's brakes are automatically released and the horses are able to move the vehicle for the specified distance as long as they maintain the proper tension on the dynamometer. As each team takes its turn and reaches its goal, a roar goes up from the crowd that has pulled and strained with it every inch of the way.

Just as spectacular as these exciting competitions are the great hitches once used in urban communities and now preserved in the magnificent Clydesdales owned by America's Anheuser-Busch brewery. One of these handsome teams is sometimes shown in special exhibition at the National Horse Show in Madison Square Garden. The Schlitz brewery sponsors the Milwaukee Circus Parade which features a procession of splendid heavy horses. In England the fabulous Shires of the Whitbread brewery are used to

Four-horse hitch easily pulls
wide disk harrow through overgrown field
near Zearing, Iowa. These are
Clydesdales. Known for their flashy action,
they are willing workers as well.

horse the Lord Mayor's coach at colorful London pageants. Once seen, these animals can never be forgotten. Thanks is due to public-spirited companies and private breeders who keep alive the noble tradition of the heavy horse.

THE BELGIAN

Although the Belgian gained favor slowly in America, he has recently enjoyed spectacular success. He was first imported at a rather late date (1886) by Dr. A. G. Van Hoorebeke of Illinois, and originally attracted little attention. For many years he was second to the Percheron in popularity. In the early twentieth century, however, the breed began to catch the fancy of heavy-horse users. Gradually the registration numbers increased until now the annual listings, which average about four hundred, are about double those of any other heavy-horse breed.

A descendant of the ancient Flemish horse, the Belgian is thought to be a strictly European animal with no Eastern blood. In his native Belgium he is viewed with understandable pride. Breeding is encouraged by the Government, which awards annual prizes and subsidies to the champion animals of the different provinces. Quality is also carefully regulated—stallions that stand at public stud service must receive certified approval from a Government commission.

The Belgian, averaging a height of 15:2 to 17 hands, is not the tallest of the draft-horse breeds, but he is nevertheless the heaviest. In weight he generally tips the scales at 1,900 to 2,200 pounds or more. He is what breeders term the most "drafty" looking of his kind—meaning that he is wider through the chest, deeper through the barrel, and more massive through the haunches than other types. Belgians are distinctly blocky and compact, with short, close-coupled backs, and bodies that settle low and deep into chunky, powerful legs. At one time the breed was criticized for having stubby, round hoofs, round

bones, short necks, and an aspect of over-all coarseness which was generally disfavored in heavy-horse circles. American breeders have altered these characteristics and in the past thirty years the Belgian has improved in looks more than any other heavy horse. He now is a thoroughly handsome, as well as a supremely powerful, animal.

Sorrel, chestnut, and roan are the most usual colors for Belgians. Bays, blacks, and grays sometimes appear but are commonly penalized in judging. The Belgian often has a flaxen mane and tail, and a white-blazed face. Because of these horses' massive width there is a tendency for them to roll or "paddle" when they move; since they are built strictly for power their action lacks the springy elevation that marks some of the other breeds. Their great girth and strength does not make them impractical to keep, however, nor does it affect their good temper. Hard-working Belgians eat less than most Thoroughbreds and by nature are extremely amiable horses.

THE SHIRE

From the shires of east-central England, particularly Lincoln and Cambridge, comes a towering animal appropriately called the Shire horse. He is the tallest of all breeds, averaging between 16 and 17:2 hands, nearly a hand higher than his nearest heavy-horse rival. In weight he is almost equal to the Belgian, but not nearly so compact. His back is longer and he is rangier over-all. In addition to his immense size, he is characterized by a luxuriant growth of hair about the fetlocks called "feathers." Feathering is a trait shared by only one other heavy-horse breed, the Clydesdale, and for this reason they are both sometimes referred to as the "feather-legged" breeds. In color Shires run chiefly to bays, browns, and blacks, although grays, chestnuts, and roans are sometimes seen. (The Whitbread Shires used for the Lord Mayor's coach are always matched grays.) Shires usually bear some white markings on the face and have white legs from knee or hock to hoof.

The Shire is one of the earliest heavy-horse breeds to be developed specifically for agricultural uses. The strain caught the interest of Robert Bakewell (1726-1795), an Englishman who is considered to be the first major influence leading to the improvement of farm livestock. It is probably this early start that makes today's Shires so well-formed and developed that Shire stallions often have been used to beget offspring of size and bone from mares of inadequate strength.

Shire horses were first imported to Canada in 1836, and records indicate that a stallion called Columbus arrived in Massachusetts earlier than 1844. But it was not until the 1880's that Shires began to be widely appreciated. Their popularity, once established, increased rapidly, and in 1887 more than four hundred Shires were imported to the United States. Their moment of glory was sadly short-lived, however, for soon the importations dwindled, and even today their total American registration is only about three thousand. ("Total registration" means all horses of the breed ever registered in the U.S.)

THE SUFFOLK

Most cherished by down-to-earth farm folk, although probably least celebrated elsewhere, is the Suffolk. He can be easily distinguished from other draft-horse breeds because of his unusual history and physical characteristics.

The Suffolk is the smallest of the drafters. At maturity, he attains a height of 15:2 to 16:2 hands, usually standing higher at the croup than at the withers, and a weight of 1,600 to 1,800 pounds. The purebred Suffolk, unlike other heavy horses, exists in but a single color—chestnut, of various shades, with only the sparsest of white markings. His history, too, is unusual in that he is one of the few to have been developed ex-clusively for rural use and has always fulfilled his duties "down on the farm" rather than in urban surroundings. Finally, he is the only member of the heavy-horse family whose ancestry must trace back to a single prepotent stallion—the Crisp horse of Ufford (owned by a Mr. Crisp) that was foaled in 1768. The chestnut color of the Suffolk, although it may stem from this stallion, himself a chestnut, is more likely the result of extensive inbreeding with early Norse horses.

Being a rural sort, the Suffolk has never had any pretentions to beauty. With a head that is coarse, even by heavy-horse standards, and a homely demeanor, he is devoid of glamor. He developed in the region of England for which he is named and never gained great favor in America, partly because of his size and partly because native American draft horses satisfied most modest farmers. The supply of Suffolks also was limited, and there was already a considerable demand for them in British Commonwealth countries. The three-thousand-odd Suffolks that *have* been registered in the United States, however, superbly demonstrate why the breed has been so warmly appreciated wherever it has been imported. They are willing animals that thrive on modest fare and toil contentedly throughout the day with never a hint of laziness or moodiness. They are neither giants in size nor dazzling beauties to behold, but they do an honest day's work that can put larger horses to shame, and their loyal service and friendly personality have earned them the enduring respect of their owners.

THE CLYDESDALE

From the valley of the River Clyde in Lanark County, Scotland, comes a strain of heavy horse that, like the Scottish Aberdeen Angus cattle and Black-faced Highland sheep, is esteemed above all for sheer beauty. The Clydesdale horse has a flamboyant style, a flashy, spirited bearing and

Handsome and intricate fly nets on these two Percherons help ward off insect pests.

counts for his springy, elevated action. His hocks, set unusually close together, also contribute to his spirited way of going. This peculiarity of conformation sometimes causes his rear toes to point out a little, but it also enables him to go collectedly at the walk and trot. Clydesdales usually stand from 16 to 17 hands high and are characteristically brown or bay with white markings on the legs and face. Other colors, however, are occasionally seen.

Among Clydesdale breeders, one great horse family stands above all others as producers of superlative champions and sires—the Baron's Pride strain. Although Baron's Pride himself was a famous stud, as was his distinguished son Baron O'Buchlyvie, it is his grandson Dunure Footprint that may rank as Scotland's finest stallion of all time. In 1915 Dunure Footprint supplanted his father as the champion producer of winning offspring—a position he held, unchallenged, until 1928. In one year, 1922, he was represented at Scotland's nine principal shows by eighty-two of his get, which won a total of one hundred thirty-one prizes. At the height of his best stud season, he is said to have served two mares an hour. Two cows were needed to provide his milk ration!

The first Clydes in America were imported from Canada. They found a hearty reception in the United States and by the 1870's were being imported directly from Scotland. They have consistently been favored among the draft breeds, especially for city hauling. Prosperous merchants always pointed with pride to their glamorous teams of matched Clydesdales, like the Anheuser-Busch hitch of today. The popularity of the handsome Clydesdale breed is now second only to that of the Belgian.

THE PERCHERON

If the Clydesdale is noted for the showiness that, among light-horse breeds, is associated with

high-stepping action that make him a singularly elegant animal among draft horses. In the show ring his snappy gaits and lively air are incomparable. He is, in fact, the only heavy-horse type that, when shown in hand, is not trailed by the assistant who customarily urges more sluggish animals on at the walk and trot.

Except for the Suffolk, the Clydesdale is the lightest of the drafters, averaging between 1,700 and 1,900 pounds. Like the Shire, he is a comparatively rangy animal, without the extreme width and blockiness of the Belgian. He also shares with the Shire the feathering of his legs and fetlocks. On Clydesdales, however, the texture of these hairy tufts is of a finer, silkier quality. His pasterns are notably longer and more flexible than those of other drafters, which ac-

the American Saddler, the great gray Percheron is famed for a handsomeness comparable to that of the Thoroughbred. Though his gaits are not as flashy as the Clydesdale's, he has spirited action and his beauty of line is rare among heavy horses. Neither as large as the Belgian and Shire, nor as light as the Clydesdale and Suffolk, his weight ranges from 1,900 to 2,100 pounds and his height from 16 hands up. His great size is more smoothly proportioned and cleanly put together than that of his fellows. He is neither blocky nor rangy, and, though he has a firm and powerful musculature, he never appears clumsy. He has the massive strength characteristic of great horses, but his lines are almost as sleek and graceful as those of a blooded light horse.

One characteristic peculiar to the Percheron is his color; fully ninety per cent of this good-looking breed is black or gray. The Percheron's head is another of his distinguishing features. Unlike the crude, Roman-nosed face of other drafters, it is finely chiseled, at once bold and delicate, and clearly suggests the Arab heritage that runs strong in his blood. The Percheron is the only heavy horse that has undergone a measurable infusion of Eastern blood and the result is apparent in his beauty and stamina.

The Percheron originated in the northwestern section of France called La Perche. Here his forebears, themselves descendants of the Flemish horse, were crossed with Arabs which had been captured from the Moors or brought from Palestine by the Crusaders as spoils of war.

Percherons were first imported to the United States in the early 1850's. The horses were so admired in America that for many years they were the most widely distributed of all the draft-horse breeds. Thousands of Percherons found homes on farms and in cities. They were faithful and energetic drays in rural communities, and handsome coach teams in urban areas, where they showed the same elegant style as when they were the favorite carriage horses of France in the days of the Bourbon kings. They were so popular and so in demand that many businessmen purchased them as investments. Indeed, there was a time when there were more registered Percherons in America than registered horses of any other breed. Even now, though ranking third in popularity behind the Belgian and Clydesdale, the vast Percheron numbers of past years are reflected in the total registration figure that approaches the quarter of a million mark, while the total figure for registered Belgians is not yet seventy thousand.

Percheron breeding has produced a number of sires so exceptional that they are almost legendary—among them are Brilliant, imported in 1881; Dragon, owned by Selma Farms in Virginia; and Carnot, bought by Gregory Farm in Illinois in 1909 for $10,000, an unheard-of price at that time for a draft horse. Greatest of them all was Sir Laet, whose get of eleven stallions and one mare all became grand champions at the Ohio State Fair over a fifteen-year span. At the Chicago International, between 1923 and 1934, he was the sire of nine grand-champion stallions and four mares. He sired twenty-three first-prize futurity winners at the Ohio State Fair and Chicago International, and, in 1928, 1931, and 1933, sired both the grand-champion stallion and grand-champion mare at the International—a record that has never been equaled. The prizes of his get continue ad infinitum and have established him as one of the immortal stock horses of any breed at any time in history.

Although recently the Percheron has declined in favor as a working draft horse, his stylish looks and splendid gaits have made him a favorite performer under the circus big top, and hunting people have traditionally crossed him with Thoroughbreds or other smaller, lighter-boned mounts to beget hunters of substance, good looks, and endurance. It is not surprising that the Percheron, who so outstandingly combines power with grace, and hardiness with beauty, was considered by many to be the king in the golden age of the working draft horse.

AMERICANS

While it is true that horses had ceased to be native to the American heath for some ten thousand years before they returned in the ships of European adventurers, there are nonetheless four breeds of horses that can be called "American" in that they were created here and are genetically purebreds because when mated together they will faithfully reproduce their own types. These horses are the Morgan, the American Saddle Horse, the Tennessee Walking Horse, and the Standardbred. The earliest of these is the Morgan, whose blood figures to some extent in the background of the other three.

Excepting for Poseidon, the Greek deity said to have engendered the first horse, there probably has been no sire in equine history who inspired more legend, or stirred up more controversy, than the pint-sized but potent New England stallion known today as Justin Morgan.

So fraught with contradictions is the background of this truly remarkable horse that it is not inappropriate to start by stating that, in the first place, his name was not Justin Morgan. That was the name of the tubercular innkeeper-singing master in whose care the horse first appears. Morgan, a slender and solemn personage, and a musical composer of no mean talent, called this stallion Figure, and there is no reason to believe that he was ever called anything else during a lifetime of twenty-eight or twenty-nine years, most of which he spent in the school of hard knocks. It is not known when Figure became Justin Morgan. The change seems to have been caused by neighbors calling him "Justin Morgan's horse," and eventually contracting that to plain Justin Morgan.

Much of the lore surrounding Figure, or Justin Morgan, as we might as well call him from now on, came into being long after the gallant little stallion died, the unattended victim of a fatal kick from another horse, or perhaps the victim of wolves. His last owner, a farmer named Levi Bean, apparently considering him a worn-out hack, had reduced him to the lowly chore of pulling a manure spreader, and at the time of his death he had been pastured outdoors for the winter with other animals considered unworthy of barn space.

It was not until people started taking note of the spectacular successes of his progeny that the facts, such as they are, about Justin Morgan's own origin and career began to come to light. It is no small tribute to this mighty little horse that today—a century and a half later—they are still being investigated.

On two points, at least, there is no controversy: first, in his lifetime he was a performer of truly Bunyanesque feats; and, second, he was a sire of such prepotency as to stamp his own unique type indelibly on his successors to this very day. That he was considered a valuable sire in his own time, however, seems dubious in view of the evidence that the succession of wagoners, loggers, peddlers, and farmers who owned him after the demise of the man Justin Morgan often stood him for fees of from $2 to $5 to satisfy their tavern bills.

It is not certain just when or from whom the original Justin Morgan acquired his stallion. Some authorities say that the singing master made an excursion to West Springfield, Massachusetts, his native home, in 1795 and returned with the horse to Randolph Center, Vermont, that same year. The stallion was said to be a two-year-old at this time, and it was thought that he had been acquired in payment of a debt.

From all descriptions Justin Morgan blended Arabian characteristics with those of the Dutch-bred light draft horses of the period. He stood a scant 14 hands and weighed between 800 and 900 pounds. His fine head, crested neck, short back, large intelligent eye, and well-set tail suggested a strong Arabian influence. Yet his short, heavily muscled legs, thick barrel, and hairy fetlocks were more typical of the Dutch type. All of these

qualities Justin Morgan faithfully passed on to his modern-day descendants.

Despite the tireless efforts of Morgan enthusiasts, the facts concerning the founding sire's pedigree are still not certain. He was foaled in West Springfield, Massachusetts, in 1789, 1790, or 1793, and his sire is thought by some to have been True Briton, a stallion of Arabian or similar blood, who, as often happened in those less rigid times, bore a variety of names—Beautiful Bay, Traveler, Hero. It is known that at the approximate date of Justin Morgan's birth there existed a famed racing stallion named True Briton—the same horse that defeated Old England in that celebrated pre-war match race. He was owned by a New York Tory named James DeLancey, whose expert horsemanship, combined with True Briton's dashing speed, soon made the charger's exploits during the Revolutionary War renowned in both the British and Continental armies. An audacious American patriot contrived to steal the horse, so the story goes, and ran him up into Connecticut, where it is possible that he might have sired Justin Morgan; John Morgan, a relative of Justin's, certified that this True Briton was indeed the correct sire. On the other hand, quite a number of dissenting experts assert that the sire was a Dutch-bred horse called Young Bulrock; Justin Morgan's son always claimed his father referred to the animal as a "Dutch horse."

The horse's dam is an even greater mystery. Possibly she was a mare of the Wildair* strain (part Arabian, part Thoroughbred), or simply an unknown mare from the Connecticut Valley. Perhaps out of sheer frustration, the Morgan Horse Register accepts as fact that Justin Morgan was foaled in 1789 by True Briton out of a Wildair mare.

Around Randolph Center, the young dark-bay stallion soon made a name for himself. At work he was prodigious at clearing land of rock and stumps, in plowing and hauling logs to the mill. After hours he was matched against anything and everything in weight-pulling contests. An eyewitness report states that on one occasion the undersized Morgan leaned into the harness and dragged off a log that horses of 1,200 pounds and more had been unable to move. He also took on all comers in races under saddle and in harness, the usual distance being eighty rods—a quarter of a mile. Racing from scratch, a mark drawn in the dirt road, starting literally at the drop of a hat, he was never once headed. Furthermore, he always performed whatever task he approached with a willing good nature that has marked all subsequent Morgans as among the kindest and most generous of all breeds. (The only bad thing ever said of him is that he disliked dogs and chased them out of his pasture.)

So great was Justin Morgan's prepotency

* Wildair, also owned by James DeLancey, was an imported stallion "of the blood." On the maternal side, his modern-day descendants include the famous Thoroughbred sires Nearco and Nasrullah.

at stud that today Morgans are the only full-fledged breed (that is, not simply a substrain or offshoot) ever to be founded by, and named after, a single horse.

Justin Morgan's blood was perpetuated chiefly through three sons—Sherman, Bulrush, and Woodbury—each of whom founded a family. They were at stud in various Vermont, Massachusetts, and New Hampshire communities year after year, and the combination of longevity and prepotency in their strains resulted in an abundant yield of young Morgans. Bulrush, for example, was thirty-six when he died in 1858. One of Woodbury's sons, Gifford Morgan, sired an estimated thirteen hundred foals, and another, Green Mountain Morgan—winner of first prizes at the Kentucky, Ohio, and Michigan state fairs—also became a distinguished sire.

Sherman, however, was the most famous and successful of Justin Morgan's offspring. Noted for his racing speed, he begot Black Hawk, who was the trotting-horse champion of his day. Tradition has it that Black Hawk was never beaten, and when he retired his stud fee was $100, the highest figure known up to that time. Known in the Standardbred stud book as Vermont Black Hawk 5, he earned a total of more than $34,000 in stud fees and his blood still figures in the modern world of harness racing.

In the 1800's there was a great demand for harness horses and, for fifty years, Morgans were tops both over the road and on the track. Black Hawk's son, Ethan Allen, succeeded his father as a nationally celebrated trotter. In 1853,

as a four-year-old, he was named Champion of the World when he trotted the mile in 2:25 1/2, but the peak of his long career came when he was at the advanced age of eighteen. In June, 1867, at the Fashion Course on Long Island, Ethan Allen trotted against the hitherto unbeatable Dexter and won in three consecutive mile-long heats in 2:15, 2:16, and 2:19.

In the years that Black Hawk and Ethan Allen were dominating the trotting tracks, thousands of other Morgans were doing all manner of work in all parts of the United States and Canada. From 1850 to 1860, Vermont raised more purebred horses than any other state. The Morgans provided Union soldiers of the Civil War with the only cavalry mounts that equaled the Thoroughbred and part-bred horses of the South. The First Vermont Cavalry, raised in a matter of six weeks, was comprised of more than one thousand Morgans and fought in some seventy-five battles and skirmishes, including Gettysburg, Cedar Creek, Cold Harbor, and the Wilderness Campaign. Of the original Morgan cavalry recruits, some two hundred survived the war and a few of these actually got back to Vermont.

In the decades after the Civil War, the Morgan's popularity as a roadster and all-around farm horse, as well as a stock horse on Western ranches, continued unabated. The larger Standardbreds, however, with their dynasty of Hambletonians, and the rich racing blood of Messenger, rapidly took over the trotting tracks and caused a curious crisis for the Morgans. To give the Standardbreds more bottom—endurance—

they were crossed with Morgans, and to increase the Morgan's speed they were mated with Standardbreds. The intermingling was of inestimable value to the Standardbred but proved to be the near-ruination of the Morgan. Since there was no Morgan register, nor any organization to set standards for the breed or record data, whole families of Morgans were absorbed into the Standardbred register, where their fundamental identity as Morgans was forgotten.

The survival of the Morgan owes much to the work of a few dedicated individuals, the pioneer among them being D. C. Linsley of Burlington, Vermont, who spent years ferreting out the history of Justin Morgan and his descendants, and published a book titled *Morgan Horses* in 1857. Linsley's labor of love was followed up by another Vermonter, Colonel Joseph Battell of Middlebury, who gathered still more information about the breed, and, at about the turn of the century, brought out the *Morgan Horse and Register*. Aside from devoting the major part of his life to the study of the horse, Battell gave a large farm at Weybridge, near Middlebury, to the Federal Government for the perpetuation and improvement of Morgans.

In the 1880's, Morgans found still another friend, a Texas rancher named Richard Sellman who began raising Morgan stock (he owned some four hundred) and did much to cultivate the breed in his part of the country.

The Morgan Horse Club was formed in 1909, but the breed's popularity—as, indeed, the popularity of all horses—declined with the rise of the automobile. The club's 1925 meeting was attended by a paltry five members and annual registrations plummeted to seventy-five. For a time the fate of the breed looked dismal, indeed. Not until the 1940's did Morgans enjoy a renaissance that was largely owing to the dedication of Charles A. Stone and his son Whitney Stone, who kept the Morgan register going and whose interest encouraged Morgan breeders.

Further credit for the resurgence goes to the United States Morgan Horse Farm (a result of Battell's contribution) which had for decades been trying to rescue and improve the breed. The farm provided stallions for the cavalry-horse program of the remount service, as well as for private breeders, and Government Morgans achieved impressive records in the three-hundred-mile endurance rides designed to test the military horses of the times. Fortunately, when the Government ended its program in 1951, the farm was taken over by the University of Vermont.

The contemporary Morgan, probably bred to a point of greater refinement than the original Justin, sometimes possesses a style and elevated action that can barely be distinguished from the Saddle Horse. But his basic conformation and nature remain unchanged. He is still a relatively small horse, usually of about 15 hands, and characteristically runs to dark colors—browns, bays, blacks, and, less frequently, chestnuts. White markings are rarely prominent.

The polish of show-ring Morgans in no way denies a more fundamental virtue of the breed —namely, its all-purpose fitness for an amazing variety of duties. The Morgan is the embodiment of the handy, durable, using animal that will do almost anything asked and will accept with affection the full range of handling, from the inattention of a blase owner to the annoyances of small children. He can be ridden or driven, hunted or used for Western stock work, or just kept for family fun.

With all the Morgan's versatility, it is easy to understand why annual current registrations have climbed to the fifteen hundred mark, and why nearly fifteen thousand Morgans are registered from all fifty states (California is now the leader in production of the breed), not to mention Canada, Puerto Rico, Japan, France, Spain, and Israel. In the United States, the high point of the Morgan owner's year is the National All-Morgan Show held in Northampton, Massachusetts. When the show was first held in 1939, to celebrate the one hundred and fiftieth anniversary of Justin Morgan's presumed birthday, the breed was represented by one hundred horses. In recent years the entries number more than five hundred in eighty-odd classes, and draw Morgan fanciers of all ages to what has the atmosphere of an enormous family reunion.

If there are Cinderella aspects to the story of the Morgan, this noble little horse has left them far behind and has assumed a rightful place as one of our most cherished breeds.

THE AMERICAN SADDLE HORSE
AND THE TENNESSEE WALKING HORSE

The American Saddle Horse, also called the Kentucky Saddle Horse, the Saddlebred, the Saddler, and the gaited horse, is primarily a riding horse—a designation that, while accurate, is about as inadequate as describing William Shakespeare as a writer. Saddlers are the consummately fashionable riding mounts of all time, the true peacocks of the horse world, and their show-ring performance has been stylized to a sophisticated elegance. Their heads have a regal, lofty bearing that suggests a fiery inner excitement—and, perhaps, a slightly scornful view of humbler, less dazzling rivals. They have an artful, supremely high-stepping action—hoofs barely touching the ground before the knees and fetlocks flex sharply into another stride with a vertical lift that seems to reach for a piece of sky. They circle the ring at collected gaits—not so intent on ground-covering speed as on the splendor and elevation of every regal step.

For use under saddle, there are two types of gaited horse—the three-gaited variety and the five-gaited. Three-gaited horses perform at the walk, trot, and canter—the walk being brisk and lively, the trot moderate and showy, and the canter a highly controlled rocking-chair motion at a slow and collected pace with minimal forward distance covered at each stride. The five-gaited horse, in addition to these three natural gaits, performs at the slow-gait and rack. Both of these are distinct four-beat gaits in which each foot strikes the ground singly, creating a smooth flow of action which the rider can sit in comfort without posting or bouncing. The rack and slow-gait involve an identical pattern of footwork from the animal, but in the latter the pace is slow and tautly constrained, each step high and precise, the legs seeming to hover magically in the air. The high degree of control involved in the slow-gait usually precludes an exactly even one-two-three-four rhythm to each full stride, and the careful listener will be able to detect a slight but regular hesitation in the footfall.

At the order to "rack on," the five-gaited horse commands a full-throated cheer from horse-show spectators, for at that instant he shoots forward with an explosive burst of speed, abandoning the restraint of the slow-gait. The rack is fast, free, and gliding—sometimes at the fantastic rate of about 2:19 a mile, if the track is larger than the limited circle of most show rings whose turns inhibit speed. Here the one-two-three-four rhythm of each hoofbeat is exactly even and, despite the blistering speed, the action continues to be spectacularly elevated with each leg flexing sharply and reaching to phenomenal vertical heights. To see five-gaited horses performing at their best is an experience not soon forgotten.

The Saddler's conformation is as handsome as his gaits are peerless. His head is well-formed, neck long and extravagantly arched and proud, as is the tail, back short and strong, and the body well-muscled and round. Saddlers are tall horses, averaging about 16 hands, and solid colors predominate—usually black, bay, brown, or chestnut, although there are grays as well. White markings, on the nose and legs only, are abundant. Structurally, there is little difference between the three-gaited horse and the five-gaited, though the latter is usually larger, with greater width about the chest to supply the strength for the two extra and highly demanding gaits.

Earl Teater is the
dean of American Saddle Horse
trainers and riders.

The beauty of three- and five-gaited horses is not seen only under saddle. Another member of the breed, the fine-harness horse, which possesses the same qualities of conformation and performance, is shown at the walk and animated park trot pulling a lightweight four-wheeled show vehicle. In judging his performance, a certain emphasis is placed on his mannerliness, for it would be unthinkable, especially in classes where ladies are to drive, for a refined, pleasure harness horse to show the high-strung fire that is not uncommon among gaited horses.

The rarefied magnificence of the American Saddle Horse is a result of selective breeding and training. In addition, a number of "beauty aids" are employed for the show-ring appearance. For example, except in states where the practice has been outlawed, it is the custom to perform an operation on Saddler's tails, breaking the vertebrae in such a way that the tail, when it has healed, is held in a poised arch. The procedure is augmented by strapping the horse into a tail-set—a brace which holds the tail in its arch when the horse is in his stall. Then, shortly before the Saddler is ready to enter the ring, he is gingered. A handler chews the ginger until it has reached the proper consistency, and inserts it into the horse's anus, causing an irritation that prompts him to keep his tail lifted high, indeed.

Three-gaited Saddlers are shown with a shaved mane and natural tail shaved close at the top along the bone, and pulled quite thin at the bottom. Five-gaited horses are shown with a full, flowing mane decorated with two ribbon streamers, and, if their natural tails are insufficiently long and sweeping, with false tails.

The foot of the Saddler is, of course, crucial to his elevated action. His pasterns are much longer and more flexible than other horses'. In addition, his toes are allowed to grow to extreme length and he wears specially weighted shoes.

The artificiality of the Saddler's preparation may seem a strange folly to those who prefer to think of horses as natural beauties, but the end effect is so breathtaking that even the harshest critic hesitates to find fault with anything that has contributed to it.

The Saddle Horse was developed gradually, largely by Kentucky horsemen, in a half century or more of selective breeding. The origins of the Saddler go back to horses of colonial days, the Canadian and Narragansett pacers, and the amblers imported from England. Kentucky settlers crossed these colonial horses with other strains—Morgan, Thoroughbred, and Arabian, relying heavily on the blood of imported Messenger and Mambrino. The great Kentucky landowners wanted a horse who could carry them tirelessly

on daylong inspection tours of their vast tracts, whose gaits would be easy, and whose appearance would be admired at Sunday-go-to-meetin' time. The American Saddle Horse they developed was the perfect blend of strength, comfort, and classic beauty.

Tom Hal, a Canadian pacer, was one of the important early horses in the Saddler background. Foaled about 1806, he was bought by a Dr. Boswell of Lexington, Kentucky. On one occasion Dr. Boswell wagered that he could ride Tom Hal to Louisville, more than eighty miles away, between sunup and sunset. He completed the feat handily; then, the next day, rode back to Lexington.

According to the best accounts available, Tom Hal lived to the age of forty-one. He founded a family of Saddlers that included Bourbon Chief, whose son, Bourbon King, for decades was held to be the greatest Saddle sire of this century. The Standardbred and Tennessee Walker also bear the mark of Tom Hal's fine career as a sire.

Another horse of destiny was a Thoroughbred foaled in 1839 named Denmark, who eventually was established as the foundation sire of the American Saddle Horse breed. (The National Saddle Horse Breeders Association was formed in 1891 and brought out a registry listing fourteen founding sires. Later the number was increased to seventeen. In 1908 the Association, by then called the American Saddle Horse Breeders As-

sociation, reduced the number to one and selected Denmark as the sole sire.) Bred to the "Stevenson mare," a colonial pacer, Denmark sired Gaines Denmark in 1851. Although technically it is Denmark who is the foundation horse of the Saddler, his magnificent son should be given the credit for the honor. Gaines Denmark was such an outstanding horse that John Hunt Morgan selected him as his favorite charger during the Civil War. During the years before the war, Gaines Denmark produced his finest offspring. In the first four volumes of the Saddle Horse Register 7,311 of the listings trace their ancestry to Denmark and, of these, 7,291 do so through Gaines Denmark, making him one of the most distinguished progenitors the breed has ever known.

Gaines Denmark's closest rival as a top Saddler stallion was a descendant, through his dam, of Tom Hal, and, through Black Hawk, of Justin Morgan—a horse called Cabell's Lexington, foaled in 1863. Cabell's Lexington sired a host of top show horses, but his own performance record was no less enviable. He was defeated only once in the ring—by Middleton's Drennon, who was never registered—and won over such famed contemporaries as Montrose and Washington Denmark, the latter prized as the finest show horse of the mighty Denmark family and never bested except by Cabell's Lexington.

Montrose, foaled in 1869 and also of Denmark

These Saddle Horses show varied gaits, all highly controlled, legs reaching maximum elevation, fetlocks flexing sharply.

blood, was renowned as one of the most beautiful stallions of the day and became the first Saddler to sell for $5,000. Montrose was not without competition, however, for the fine Black Squirrel, foaled in 1876, offered exciting rivalry both in the ring and at stud. A daughter of Black Squirrel produced the immortal Rex MacDonald, a gleaming blue-black stallion who inherited his grandsire's handsome looks and style and became such a show-ring favorite that he is credited with reviving lively interest in gaited horses at a period when they were suffering something of a decline. Rex MacDonald's father, Rex Denmark, was also a considerable performer and apparently had a temperament to match his success. According to one account, a rude spectator had the gall to spit in Rex Denmark's face during a show. The horse was enraged and "with his mouth open, with lightning speed dashed at him and only a strong halter and the man's flee to safety, no doubt, saved this fellow from severe injury . . . The fool went away pale as a corpse, weaker but wiser."

Another brilliant performer was Harrison Chief, foaled in 1872. Sired by a Standardbred trotter, Harrison Chief accomplished his extraordinary success as a fine-harness horse and it is unlikely that he ever had a saddle on his back. He was defeated only four times, but even more important than his record in the ring was his career at stud. With amazing uniformity he passed

on his qualities to his get and the result was a family of "Chiefs" whose blood is almost as valuable to Saddler history as the Denmarks. One of his greatest sons was Bourbon Chief, sire of the incomparable Bourbon King and his two full brothers, Montgomery Chief and Marvel King.

There are many names that have earned a place on the honor roll of Saddlers who have contributed excitement to the arena and substance to the breed, but, in this century, there is no name that signals greatness and splendor more than that of Wing Commander. Wing Commander is owned by Mrs. Frederick Dodge Van Lennep of Dodge Stables, one of the world's most famous sportswomen and an investor of millions in superb horseflesh. During his show career Wing Commander was ridden by that master of Saddlers, Earl Teater. The bold, spirited, young chestnut first burst upon the scene in the 1946 show at Lexington and set audiences on the edge of their seats as he entered the ring with explosive speed and brilliance. When he took off in a rack, mane and tail flying, feet a blur as he flashed by, the crowd was electrified by a speed and action that has never been equaled in the history of the show ring. After Wing Commander's victory in this three-year-old stakes, Carey Ward, an authority on Saddle Horses, said of him: "I never thought I'd live to see as great a horse as Bourbon King, but I've lived to see a horse that will be greater."

This prophecy became a fact. During the years 1948 to 1954, at all the major shows, Wing Commander was the undefeated champion five-gaited horse. He was the World's Grand Champion Five-Gaited Saddle Horse from 1948 to 1953 at the Kentucky State Fair and, from 1947 to 1954, at the Chicago International, where he also won the $1,000 Five-Gaited Stallion Stake from 1946 to 1954. In all, he has totaled over two hundred championships in nine years of competition and, like Man O'War and Greyhound, his name has become a legend among horsemen. Now at stud, he has already proved an exceptional sire by producing dozens of prize-winning offspring.

The Saddler has come a far distance from the days when he was used as an all-around horse on Southern estates. Nowadays his true milieu is the show ring. But the fact that he is born to be seen, and is seen at his best on center stage, should not imply that the gaited horse is inherently a frail, fussy, glossy-coated fop—nothing could be further from the truth. He is not often used outside the show ring because he is an expensive creature, often costing $25,000, with a price of $50,000 no longer unusual. Nevertheless, when given a chance, Saddlers can accomplish a host of feats of which their public would never dream them capable.

The breed's wide range of ability is partly due to its extraordinary degree of endurance. Tom Hal demonstrated this on his round-trip trek to Louisville, as did subsequent Saddlers in their work on plantations and, more recently, in the arena. The racing Thoroughbred is asked to go full tilt for two minutes at a gait that is natural to all horses. The Saddle Horse must compete at highly educated, and therefore extremely wearing, paces for forty minutes, an hour, sometimes more. Astral King, in 1915, contending as a nine-year-old for the world crown in the Championship Stake at Louisville, had to fight for two hours and five minutes before he was chosen the victor. Wing Commander won the Five-Gaited World's Grand Championship Stake at the 1948 Kentucky State Fair in forty-five minutes. A year later it took him an hour and fifteen minutes to repeat the success.

The breed's educability is another reason for its great potential. A horse like the Saddler who is receptive to learning in one area is likely to be at least reasonably so in others—jumping, for example, is an ability Saddlers often pick up with a flourish. On numerous occasions they have proved astonishingly good in the hunting field.

In order to give an exciting show performance the Saddler is usually conditioned to a state of tension and alertness, and few efforts are made to turn high-ranking winners into docile pets. Yet, despite the fact that they are deliberately kept "revved up," they have inherently agreeable natures and will respond to calm treatment and affection.

Among admirers of the Tennessee Walking Horse there is an old adage that goes: "Ride one today, and you'll own one tomorrow." A vast number of people have done precisely that, for the Walking Horse is a supremely companionable and comfortable mount. His popularity has increased with amazing rapidity—the Tennessee Walking Horse Breeders Association with its official register was not organized until as recently as 1935 and already its numbers have grown to a phenomenal sixty thousand.

Historically, the Walker and the Saddler began at the same time—long before 1835, when adventuresome settlers were first bringing civilization to Tennessee, Kentucky, and Missouri. At the outset of the nineteenth century, Tennessee breeders brought quality to their stock through crossings with Thoroughbreds, Arabians, Morgans, Saddlers, and Standardbreds, mingling the lines of the Hals, the Denmarks, and the Copperbottoms (another strain that was influential in early American horse breeding). The Tennesseans wanted to produce a horse, who, like the Saddler, would be able to undertake all-day rounds over the endless acreage without taxing the rider— and could also make an attractive showing on social occasions. In fact, the traditional uses and breeding background of the Saddler and the Walker were so closely associated that for many years there was little distinction between them in show events. At Tennessee's first State Fair, held in Nashville in 1877, there were simply classes for "saddle horses." By 1910 the Fair offered classes for "plantation saddle horses"—the designation "plantation" being synonymous with Tennessee Walking Horse and a name which has remained with the breed. Early plantation horses were also referred to as "turn row" horses because they were used to inspect crops by rows.

194

Given the close identity between the Saddler (especially the five-gaited horse) and the plantation horse, what, then, constitutes the difference between the two breeds? Although a novice would have difficulty in distinguishing a first-class Walking Horse from a good five-gaited horse, when more average horses are compared, differences in conformation will be apparent. The Tennessee Walker is generally a less refined animal than the gaited horse. His head is plainer, and carried lower on a shorter and less boldly arched neck. His back is longer, his tail carried lower, and his body and legs tend to be somewhat coarser. Another minor but quite consistent characteristic of the Walker is the look about the eye. The lids are commonly wrinkled and sloping, giving him a sage and melancholy expression.

Unlike Saddlebreds, Walking Horses are of a wide variety of colors—chestnut, black, roan, white, brown, bay, gray, even a Palomino gold, often with generous white markings, including splashes of white on the body, particularly among the roans.

If the Walker is thought to be a shade coarser in appearance than his gaited cousin, he more than compensates for it with a temperament that is to be coveted by every other breed with the possible exception of the Morgan. Wherever Walkers go their superb dispositions earn them friends. Frequently called "the gentlemen of equines," even their most high-strung representatives behave graciously at the hands of ladies and children.

Together with his fine nature, the Walker is differentiated by the swift and graceful running walk for which he has been named—and which offers the most sublimely relaxing ride ever produced by a horse under saddle. Technically, the gait is a vastly accelerated walk in which each foot strikes the ground separately, like the rack and slow-gait among Saddlers, in a four-beat rhythm. Although the footwork pattern of the plantation horse's walk and the Saddler's gaits is much the same, the effect produced by the horse's action is quite different. The Walker's stride, although it has noticeable elevation, is not nearly as high as the Saddler's and, in the length of its forward reach, far exceeds the Saddlebred's. His running walk is more extended and flowing with a distinctly freer, looser movement from shoulder to hoof. The legs of the Walker, unlike those of the Saddler, move separately and unrelatedly, so that the Walker's back remains perfectly horizontal. A pleasant, gentle, rocking-chair motion results which anyone from an aging grandmother to a tiny child can enjoy for hours without the slightest strain.

The running walk demands great strength in the forequarters and neck, and the effort of keeping the back horizontal and steady produces a distinct nod of the horse's head. This is to be expected of all Tennessee Walkers and, in fact, if the horse's jaws are relaxed, it is even possible to hear the "pop" of the teeth as his bobbing head causes them to knock together.

The speed of this exceptional gait is officially between six and eight miles an hour, but in the show ring it is at least twice as fast. Excessive speed is to be avoided, however, as it will unbalance the horse's movement and edge him toward a pace or a disjointed trot. Care should also be taken to guard against the horse's cutting himself with his own feet. The stride of each leg is so long at the running walk that it is possible for a hind hoof, which is about to land, to reach as much as two feet farther forward than the front hoof which is about to rise. Under these circumstances, it is common for the hind foot to clip the front (called forging) and cause injury.

In addition to the running walk, the breed is commonly shown at a normal, flat-footed walk and a nice, easy canter, and is capable of trotting, although rarely asked to do so.

When the Tennessee Walking Horse Breeders Association met in 1935 to establish a register, it was discovered that a majority of the Walkers in the first volume of the register traced their lineage to a Standardbred trotter named Black

Allan. Under the designation Allan F-1, he was established as the foundation sire of the breed.

Foaled in Lexington, Kentucky, in 1886, Black Allan led a star-crossed life in his early years, much like Justin Morgan (to whom he is related through his dam who was descended from Black Hawk). As a trotter he was a failure, chiefly because he infinitely preferred pacing. As a pacer he was equally bad for precisely the reason that he became so valuable to the Walking Horse breed—his gait was so loose that he could not keep to a strictly lateral pace, and finished every race by cutting his front legs to ribbons because of the extended, syncopated action of his rear legs. Thus Black Allan fell upon hard times and, in 1900, was swapped for some livestock and $20.

His fortunes changed for the better, however, when James R. Brantly of Manchester, Tennessee, favorably impressed by Black Allan's pedigree in the Trotting Registry, decided to buy the stallion to breed to his fine Walking mare, Gertrude. Out of this union was born Roan Allen F-38—one of the greatest Walkers of all time—and many succeeding Allens. (Somewhere along the line the spelling was changed from the original version to "Allen," but no one knows why.)

Roan Allen also became a famous sire. He lived until 1930 and persons who saw him perform say that in addition to the flat walk, running walk, and canter, he could do the square trot, fox trot (a somewhat disjointed version of the normal square trot), pace, and rack. He was that fantastic rarity, a seven-gaited horse.

Hunter's Allen F-10 was another of Allan's sons who made Walking Horse history. He won top honors at the Tennessee State Fair in 1912 and repeated the same sweeping victory at the Bedford County Fair in Shelbyville, Tennessee, in 1924, when he was twenty years old. Those who saw the performance exclaim that the fine old stallion "walked up a storm," beating top competition that included two of his own sons. And the quality of his offspring cannot be doubted—his get won the stakes class at the Ten-

nessee State Fair ten times out of the fourteen years between 1920 and 1933.

The most highly prized honor for a Walker is to win the Grand Championship at Shelbyville, Tennessee, which calls itself the Walking Horse capital of the world. Every year since 1939 it has held its annual "Celebration"—a horse show which is said to boast more entries than any other show in the country. In 1964 some sixteen hundred Walkers were exhibited for eight straight days of competition, with a crowd of twenty thousand spectators on closing night.

Obviously, the Tennessee Walker is prime show-ring material, but he is outstanding chiefly because of his wonderful suitability as a pleasure horse. His gaits make him a joy to ride and his nature makes him a joy to own—an enchanting blend which increasing thousands of horsemen are discovering to their satisfaction and delight.

*The Tennessee Walker's
unique gliding gait covers ground
smoothly and tirelessly.*

AMERICAN-STYLE

Shortly after dusk one evening in early September, 1940, an anonymous electrician switched on a newly installed bank of floodlights at what had been, until then, a bankrupt auto-racing plant on Long Island, New York, and thereby started a revolution in the American sporting world. It is doubtful whether any among the handful of hopeful promoters or the slim crowd of forty-five hundred spectators who witnessed this event at Roosevelt Raceway ever could have guessed the extent to which big-city populations would take night harness racing to their hearts.

For years Standardbred harness racing had been regarded as a "country" sport, suitable only for county fairs and similar rustic celebrations. Wasn't it a fact that before automobiles, the animals that raced in harness meetings were the same mundane creatures that took the village doctor on his rounds and pulled the better-heeled farmer and his family to church on Sundays? They were a far cry indeed from the costly, aristocratic Thoroughbreds who dwelt in pampered luxury in the stables of America's so-called "first families" and lived only to race their owners' silks.

Yet in the twenty-five years that have elapsed since the innovation of night harness racing at Roosevelt Raceway, this concept has been completely altered. The sport, which sputtered through the war years, took off immediately after peace came, and at a rate of climb that exceeded even that of Thoroughbred racing. It is still going up. Figures for 1964 showed that more than twenty-one million harness fans wagered in excess of $1,000,000,000 and, incidentally, returned some $100,000,000 to the treasuries of fifteen states. This represented an increase of nearly sixteen per cent over the previous year.

In the years between 1960 and 1965, no fewer than eleven big new centers of night harness racing opened their gates in such diverse locales as Pompano Beach, Florida; Phoenix, Arizona;

and Philadelphia, Pennsylvania. A $4,500,000 plant in Windsor, Ontario, and another $6,000,000 track in western Pennsylvania opened late in 1965. Unable to build fast enough to cope with the growing demand, harness-race promoters have also leased such major Thoroughbred tracks as Hollywood Park and Santa Anita, in California, and Chicago's Washington and Sportsman's Parks during their off-season months. In other places, harness-racing seasons have been extended. New York now has barely a score of "dark dates" between the close of one session in December and the commencement of a new one in January.

A good measure of the appeal that harness racing has always had for its adherents is that it is a peculiarly American sport. It may be true, as some horse authorities, like John Hervey, have long contended, that the sport of racing wheeled vehicles reaches even farther back into antiquity than does mounted racing. It is a well-established fact, for example, that in the ancient Greek Olympics the sport of chariot racing, which was incorporated into the games in about 1000 B.C., antedated horseback racing by some two centuries. Still older records attest to the existence of chariot racing in Mesopotamia around 3000 B.C. Much later, an informal game of road racing behind speedy road horses enjoyed a brief vogue in eighteenth-century England. But the evolution of harness racing as it is practiced today, and the development of the fast, sturdy Standardbred harness horse both took place in the United States and nowhere else. In contrast to Thoroughbred racing, which was imported directly from England, harness racing and Standardbred horses have been exported from this country to become widely popular in France, Germany, Italy, Holland, Belgium, Austria, Hungary, the U.S.S.R., Scandinavia, Japan, Australia, and New Zealand.

The word "Standardbred" actually has come to have two meanings. Originally, it meant a harness horse of any breed that could travel a mile within a certain margin, or "standard," of

speed. This is still true, the standard having moved up through the years to a present outside limit of 2:20. No harness horse that has not qualified under that standard may be raced in an officially recognized meeting.

In its second and more widely employed meaning, the word refers to the pedigreed family of horses bred specifically for the purpose of equaling and bettering the time standard. It is not necessary, as many suppose, for a horse to be a Standardbred in order to be eligible to race, as all flat-track racers are required to be Thoroughbreds, but the success of the Standardbred strain in harness racing has been so complete that the appearance of a so-called "nonstandard" horse on a harness program today is rare indeed.

In contrasting Thoroughbred racing with the Standardbred sport, it must be kept in mind that the Thoroughbred runs at a gallop, which is the natural gait of all horses when urged to extend themselves fully, while harness racers go in one of two highly controlled gaits. These are the pace and the trot. The horse that performs at either of these gaits well enough to race successfully is the end product of many generations of selec-

tive breeding and hours of patient handling.

What is a trot? What is a pace? In a trot, the horse's "diagonal legs"—the front and rear on opposite sides—move in the same direction at the same time. In a pace, the legs on one side swing forward in unison while those on the other side move rearwards. Less than a second separates Adios Butler's record 1:54 3/5 for pacing the mile from Greyhound's trotting mark of 1:55 1/4. However, the general run of pacers is slightly faster than that of trotters. The pacer's side-wheeling stride gives him a split-second advantage over a trotter in moving away from a start. Otherwise, around a track they are about equal in speed.

Virtually all Standardbred horses are born with a natural tendency for pacing or trotting. A few can even do both.* Certain families within the breed tend to produce one or the other gait almost exclusively. The get of the mighty Adios, who at the time of his death in 1965 had sired winners of $14,563,130, included sixty-five pacers who broke or equaled the two-minute mile and only one trotter to do so. Other stallions, like Rodney, who have produced many fine

---

* Such exceptional horses are called "double-gaited." Most noteworthy to date was Steamin Demon of the late 1950's, who paced the mile in 1:58 4/5 and trotted it in 1:59 1/2, both marks within a few seconds of the record.

trotters, will come up with almost no pacers in their progeny.

It is useful to a trainer, therefore, to know the yearling's family proclivity for one gait. But this is a far from infallible guide. There have been many cases where a horse doing poorly with one gait has been successfully switched in mid-career to the other. A famous example was Dr. Stanton, an unsuccessful six-year-old trotter sold for a paltry $500 and converted to the pace. The astute buyer had noted something in the animal's gait that suggested he would benefit from a change—an observation that paid off to the tune of $171,922. It is an interesting point that when a Standardbred's gait is changed, it is almost invariably from the trot to the pace, not vice versa.

The development of these gaits dates from long before the birth of harness racing as a sport in the nineteenth century. They are the outgrowth of human vanity which demanded smooth, speedy action coupled with snappy appearance and durable performance. So, essentially, the first trotters and pacers were nothing more than classy road horses.

Such horses actually were called "roadsters," a name later inherited by the sporty little open automobiles of the hip-flask era. The Norfolk trotter developed in England, and the Canadian and Narragansett pacers, which evolved on this side of the ocean, were classic roadsters that have long since vanished as breeds, although traces of their blood remains in the background of the Standardbred. There also is no question that the valiant little Morgan appears far back in the Standardbred ancestry.

Unlike the Thoroughbred breeders, the early developers of the Standardbred were concerned more with performance than pedigree. Nevertheless, it is to a Thoroughbred stallion that the modern Standardbred owes most in terms of bloodlines. This was Messenger. In the twenty years from 1788 to 1808 that Messenger stood in the American stud, it was noted that many of

his descendants—not all of them pure Thoroughbreds, by any means—were naturally inclined to the trotting gait and had a kindly disposition that suited them for training to harness. To students of equine genealogy this comes as no great surprise, since Messenger's Thoroughbred line in England was one widely used in developing fine road horses. It appears today in the background of the dashing Hackney horse.

In 1849, a great-grandson of Messenger, three times inbred to him, finally turned up with an almost unfailing ability to transmit the trotting instinct. This was Rysdyck's Hambletonian, who became the foundation sire of an estimated ninety per cent of today's Standardbred family.

Rysdyck's Hambletonian, better known as Hambletonian 10 (there was a preponderance of horses named "Hambletonian" at the time, some of them Thoroughbred, others partly bred, and most of them related to Messenger), was dropped at his dam's side on the farm of Jonas Seeley, a well-to-do horse breeder in Chester, New York. His sire, Abdallah, was a proven getter of good trotting horses; his dam was a well-bred, though crippled, animal known as the Kent Mare, who, like Abdallah, traced back to Messenger. Hambletonian 10 grew to become a strong, but by most accounts, exceptionally ugly horse. In any event, Mr. Seeley thought so little of him that he sold him to one of his hired hands, William Rysdyck, in return for a promissory note for $125. It turned out to be the best investment Bill Rysdyck ever made and the worst transaction of Mr. Seeley's career as a breeder. After a brief and only modestly successful career at fair meetings around Orange County, New York, Hambletonian 10 was retired to stud. He produced harness racers of such quality that in a few years his stud fee rose to the almost unprecedented sum of $500. His father, Abdallah, had been the first stallion to sire a trotter capable of doing a mile in 2:30, a very creditable time considering the slow tracks and heavy, high-wheeled sulkies of the mid-1800's. But Hambletonian 10, in his twenty-

Above:
Mares and foals
thrive on
the luxurious
Bluegrass at
Castelton Farm,
Kentucky.
Left: Foal
rests beside his
dam at Hanover
Shoe, in
Pennsylvania.

four-year career in the stud, was to sire no fewer than forty 2:30 trotters among the staggering total of more than thirteen hundred foals he begot.

Harness racing had its start long before Hambletonian 10's day. At the beginning of the nineteenth century it was well-rooted in New England, which had banned running races as immoral, but tolerated harness racing because the horses did useful road work and were not merely frivolous and sinful toys of the idle rich. It flourished in New York State as well, where, in what was then the peaceful country hamlet of Harlem, a gelding of unknown parentage named Yankee trotted the first under-three-minute mile in 1806. By 1839, the mark had been lowered to 2:32 by a horse named Dutchman at a meeting in Hoboken, New Jersey. The present standard for qualifying —2:20—was first achieved by Flora Temple in 1859. And finally, in 1884, a trotter named Jan-Eye-See dazzled the harness world with a new record of 2:10.

The following year, however, saw the first of two mechanical improvements that revolutionized the entire sport in less than a decade. This was the leg harness perfected by a railroad engineer named John Browning and known as hopples (sometimes "hobbles"). Its function was to keep pacers from going off stride and breaking into a canter. A broken stride requires that the offending horse be taken back and to the outside until the correct gait is restored, an adjustment usually sufficient to lose the race. Trotters had been more popular with the harness crowd because they were less inclined to break than pacers, but with the introduction of hopples the pacer immediately began to gain in favor. (Today nineteen out of twenty pacers wear hopples. Those that do not are called "free-legged.")

The other major change came about in 1895. The high-wheeled sulky which had been standard for about fifty years (and frequently depicted in Currier & Ives lithographs) was replaced by a prototype of the modern racing machine with its low seat, small wheels, and pneumatic bicycle tires. Until the introduction of this newfangled racing "bike," a two-minute mile was considered to be virtually impossible. But within a year more than four seconds were cut from the existing record of 2:08 1/4, and in 1897 the pacer Star Pointer cracked the two-minute barrier with a sizzling 1:59 1/4.

In the year 1900 emerged the pre-eminent horse of his era, perhaps the great pacer of all time: Dan Patch. No Thoroughbred from Eclipse to Kelso ever dominated flat-track racing as this fabulous animal dominated pacing. In the nine years the mighty brown horse was at the track, he broke the two-minute barrier thirty times— more times by far than any harness horse has achieved since. As a seven-year-old in 1904, he set a mark of 1:56 1/4. At the age of eight he lowered it to 1:56. At nine, he did 1:55 1/4, a high-water mark that stood for thirty-three years, until it was finally lowered to an even 1:55 in 1938 by Billy Direct. Besides Billy Direct, only three other pacers—Adios Harry in 1955, Adios Butler in 1960, and Bret Hanover in 1965—ever went faster than old Dan Patch and all four of them did it in the modern era, pulling vastly improved vehicles over vastly improved tracks. Old-timers believe that under today's racing conditions Dan Patch might have topped his records by as much as two full seconds. Even so, his best time remains less than a full second over the current world record.

Harness racing's progress was not uninterrupted. In the 1860's it underwent difficulties similar to those which were later to afflict the Thoroughbred establishment: fixed races, doped horses, and other unsavory doings. Much of the trouble could be blamed on a scandalous lack of organization in the industry. But it moved with commendable speed to police itself, and by 1870, before too much damage had been done to its reputation, it had formed a national association to regulate tracks and races. This is why harness racing was virtually untouched by the tidal wave of repressive legislation that swept the Thorough-

Above: Crack driver Harold Miller is a picture of concentration as he pilots horse down stretch. Below: President Grant handles reins of speedy Standardbred.

bred scene around the turn of the century, and which saw major-league running races temporarily confined to Maryland and Kentucky. It proved to be helpful that harness horses were classed as "useful" beasts, rather than as race horses, and while there was some wagering around the harness tracks it was not on such a scale as to kindle the wrath of the reformers.

It was the automobile, not the law, that eventually put the skids under harness racing. As cars took over the highways, the day-to-day need for harness horses dwindled proportionately. By the late thirties the sport was back to its humble beginnings as a minor fairgrounds attraction. It was waning even further that night in 1940 when the lights flicked on at Roosevelt Raceway.

The lights changed everything. By operating at night the harness-racing people avoided direct competition with the major Thoroughbred tracks. Although in some cases they were after the same betting dollar, they succeeded in bringing out hosts of new horse fans—persons whose daytime occupations prevented them from attending the Thoroughbred ovals. Nighttime patrons also seemed to be in a more relaxed mood than daytime flat-racing fans. By the end of World War II, the sport's promoters began building luxurious eating and drinking facilities into the multimillion-dollar plants that were springing up in the big cities, wherever there was legalized pari-mutuel betting. Today, in spacious, beautifully appointed dining rooms overlooking the race track, harness fans are able to enjoy an evening that is considerably more festive than a mere tussle with the tote board. As a result, the harness track also has become an eminently suitable place to which to escort a lady.

Two other changes since 1940 have done much to enhance harness racing's popularity with big-city fans. The first of these was the automobile-mounted starting gate, introduced at Roosevelt Raceway in 1946 and now in use at all pari-mutuel tracks. This innovation virtually eliminated the numerous and boring false starts which resulted from the difficulty of bringing all the horses into an even line across the track.

The other was the change-over from the old practice of deciding each event on the basis of several heats—a procedure long since abandoned by the Thoroughbred-racing crowd—to the modern method of running each race as a single contest. (Heat racing is still seen around the Grand Circuit, but even these have been reduced to the best of three heats.*)

Both of these departures from the past helped to speed up the sport, and while there was grumbling among the diehards the game became vastly more appealing to metropolitan racegoers, many of whom were already hopelessly entranced by the fast action at the Thoroughbred tracks.

What probably contributed more than any other single factor to the swift ascent of harness-racing popularity, however, was the seemingly inexhaustible supply of "pleasure dollars"—betting money—provided by the postwar economy. Money and recreation time have established harness racing as complementary to, rather than competitive with, Thoroughbred racing. It is a known fact that racing fans who have had a good day at the "flats" will often try to extend their winning streak at the harness tracks in the evening, while losers who are not completely "tapped out" will head the same way in the hopes of recouping their losses. This is very noticeable in New York, where fleets of public limousines appear in the late afternoon at the exits to Aqueduct race track to ferry the faithful on to Roosevelt or Yonkers Raceways.

Harness horses have yet to attain the refinement of the Thoroughbred. For although the

* The Grand Circuit, organized in 1873, is sometimes called the "major league" of harness racing. It can best be described as a movable meeting in which the top horses and drivers visit at some twenty of the Circuit's fifty member tracks and fair meetings for varying periods of time. Many important stakes races, not all of them wagering affairs, are Circuit events. The Hambletonian, held annually at the Du Quoin State Fairgrounds, in Illinois, is one.

sport dates back to the beginning of the 1800's, the Standardbred breed is little more than a hundred years old. Its progress, accordingly, has been dramatic; in the fifty years between Hambletonian's earliest impact on the Standardbred family and the appearance of Dan Patch, record time for the mile was reduced by nearly thirty seconds. During the same period, improvements in the Thoroughbred, with two centuries more selective breeding in his background, were reflected in mere seconds and fractions thereof. Better vehicles can account for only a part of the Standardbred's dramatic improvement. Startling evidence of how the breed itself had gained in speed came in 1940 when Mrs. Frances Dodge Johnson (now Mrs. Frederick Van Lennep) trotted the champion Greyhound, *under saddle*, to a world record of 2:01 3/4 for the mile. Saddle racing of trotters had long since passed out of the picture here (though it is still practiced in France and elsewhere), but in the old days any trotting horse that covered the mile with a rider up in less than three minutes was considered phenomenal.

The horse that evolved from the predominantly Thoroughbred Hambletonian 10, and the pot-

pourri of Morgan and roadster types that went before, is a truly remarkable animal. Although he is generally a coarser type than the Thoroughbred, with a larger head and thicker legs, the Standardbred is particularly adapted to his own style of racing. Standing as a rule between 15 and 16 hands, and ruggedly built, the average harness racer is a far more durable animal than the more delicately put-together Thoroughbred. As a result, his career at the track is not only longer than that of the average runner, but will involve many more races per season. Part of the reason for the Standardbred's great stamina is the way he is conditioned. In contrast to the Thoroughbred race horse, who may be worked only a few furlongs twice a week, the harness horse customarily works many miles. Even on the night of a race he works out three times before going to the post.

The Standardbred is by nature an extremely kind and tractable creature, probably because he spends relatively more time with people than the shy, high-strung Thoroughbred racer. He also is a disciplined animal, carefully trained to perform in a mannered way. This does not mean that the good Standardbred is less mettlesome or more

mechanical than the runner. The best harness horses are as dead game at their own sport as any other competitive horse.

One thing that is immediately noticeable about harness racing is that the people in it—not just the trainers and their helpers, but the owners and their families—are generally much closer to their horses than are the masters of most Thoroughbred stables. The gentler disposition of the harness horse enables the owner to participate actively in his training, at least to the extent of jogging him at the beginning of a workout.

A fair number of owners have known the thrill of racing their own horses. Since neither the weight nor the age of the driver is an important consideration, and the danger, while present, is far less than in Thoroughbred racing, driving is possible for almost any owner who has the time and patience to learn the technique.

This is not so easy as it sounds, however. To drive at a pari-mutuel track, the would-be driver must first meet the rigid requirements of the United States Trotting Association (USTA), a governing body similar to The Jockey Club in the Thoroughbred sport. He must also meet the

requirements set by the various state harness commissions in the places where he wishes to race. He will usually begin learning under the guidance of an experienced driver and pick up his first racing experience at the nonwagering fair meetings, of which there are still some four hundred or so thriving in different parts of the country. When he has acquired competence, he will be issued a preliminary license, which he holds for at least a year. During this time he must participate in a minimum of twenty-five wagering contests. Such drivers are called "apprentices" and they are so denoted in the race program by the letter "P" following their names. (This is similar to the asterisk which indicates a "bug boy," or apprentice rider, on a Thoroughbred race card.)

It is true that harness racing, even at its best, has a more plebeian flavor than the Thoroughbred game. A scattering of socially prominent names does grace the Standardbred scene: persons like E. Roland Harriman, Norman Woolworth, Elbridge Gerry, Dunbar Bostwick, and Frances Dodge Van Lennep. But these individuals are patrons for love of the sport, rather

Preceding pages: Pacers go into turn at Santa Anita track in California. Above: Standardbred works at Lexington, Kentucky.

210

than for any social distinction which may attach to it. Mr. Woolworth, for example, takes a very active part in the training of his horses, as does Mr. Harriman, who also underwrites the annual Grand Circuit visit to the picturesque little Historic Track at Goshen, New York, a town that once was the very hub of harness racing. The Messrs. Gerry and Bostwick are both crack amateur drivers. Mrs. Van Lennep's unique achievement with Greyhound has been cited.

Another name that will long be remembered in harness-racing circles is that of the "Cinderella Man," Harrison Hoyt, a Connecticut hat manufacturer, prominent in the sport during the 1940's. Hoyt, a long-time horse fancier but a newcomer to harness racing, had his initial success as an amateur driver (technically, one who has accepted no recompense for at least ten years) with a trotter named Louis Cobb, an animal he originally acquired as a pleasure roadster. In 1946, Hoyt visited the annual sales at Harrisburg, Pennsylvania, and bought a likely-looking yearling named Demon Hanover, which he trained and drove himself. After a few successes in amateur competition, he decided to take on the pros. His wins with Demon Hanover continued, and now, as word of the animal's potential greatness began to get around, he was under increasing pressure to hand the reins over to a professional driver. Hoyt, however, elected to remain in the sulky himself. He was still sitting there in 1948 when Demon Hanover won the Hambletonian—the Kentucky Derby of the sport—in straight heats, a feat never performed before by an amateur.

Viewed from the professional angle, harness racing possesses another distinction unique in the sporting world: a large number of drivers train the animals they race. Not only that, many of the leading professionals are breeders and owners—even track operators. It is rather like having Thoroughbred jockeys own, breed, and train their mounts, and acquire a piece of the race track as well.

Perhaps more than any other, Delvin "Del" Miller, now semiretired after a highly successful driving career, typifies the modern harness-horse man. Not only was Miller a prime mover in forming the half-million-dollar syndicate that purchased the great stallion Adios in 1955, he was also the founder of The Meadows raceway, a prosperous harness-racing operation in Pennsylvania, of which he is president.

Miller is but one of a sizable group of crack reinsmen whose expertise in horsemanship is not surpassed in any other division of the equine world. Robert Farrington, who in 1964 set a high-water mark of 312 wins in a year, and Stanley Dancer, the first driver whose winnings for a single year (also 1964) topped a million dollars, are two of the more notable. George Sholty, Billy Haughton, Ralph Baldwin, and Del Insko are also among the outstanding figures seen nightly at big-city harness tracks. Age is no bar to successful participation in the harness game. While a few well-known jockeys like Eddie Arcaro have ridden well into their forties, and that most exceptional exception, Johnny Longden, rode until nearly sixty, most riders are finished by the time they reach their early thirties. They have lost the war of the waistline. In harness racing, where the almost frictionless sulky eliminates weight as a factor, middle-aged drivers are more common than youthful ones. A distinguished example is Frank Ervin, who at age sixty drove the sensational Bret Hanover to the record two-year-old winnings of $173,298 during the 1964 season. He went to the post twenty-four successive times without tasting defeat.

Not the least of harness racing's appeal is that one doesn't have to be a millionaire to get into the sport. While the cost of owning and racing harness horses is rising (last year's yearling sales were made at prices as high as $65,000, a little more than a third of the price paid for the top Thoroughbred yearling), it remains a considerably less expensive proposition than the running game. It can, in fact, be embarked on for $10,000 or so. And this investment is considerably less risky than buying a Thoroughbred, since harness racers are far less subject to breakdown. Purses, too, have been growing apace with attendance and betting handle. In 1964, nearly $50,000,000 was paid out in prize money. Big stakes events like the Hambletonian, the Messenger, and the Cane Futurity, are firmly established in the $100,000-plus bracket, and the lifetime earnings of the top horses are now edging toward the million-dollar mark. The trotter Su Mac Lad, for example, closed out his 1964 season with a lifetime bankroll of $814,199 and is still active in racing. Barely a dozen Thoroughbreds have ever earned more.

Harness horses are acquired in any number of ways. Like Thoroughbreds, they may be bred privately or acquired as yearlings. Important yearling sales are held every year in California, Delaware, Illinois, Kentucky, Michigan, New Hampshire, New York, Ohio, Pennsylvania, and in Canada, the most important being those conducted in Harrisburg, Pennsylvania, and Lexington, Kentucky. Average 1964 prices ranged from as little as $696 in Felton, Delaware, to $5,851 at the mid-autumn sales in Lexington.

Unlike the Thoroughbred industry, which numbers more than a hundred major breeding establishments, the Standardbred breeding business has only two giants: Lawrence B. Sheppard's Hanover Shoe Farm in Hanover, Pennsylvania, the largest horse-breeding plant of any kind in the country, and Mrs. Van Lennep's Castleton Farm, in the Kentucky Bluegrass. There are a few other fairly large farms, but most of the remainder range from medium sized, with a stallion or two and perhaps twenty-five brood mares, to very small, with only a few mares.

Should the prospective harness-horse owner elect not to go over the longer and riskier route of buying and training a yearling, he may decide to purchase a mature horse. This can be done by private contract, or at many of the auctions where yearlings are sold. Some noteworthy bar-

gains have been picked up this way. The trotting mare Proximity, bought as a three-year-old for $500, went on to lifetime earnings of $252,390. A bargain on an even grander scale was the all-time money champ Su Mac Lad, who was bought at the age of five for a reasonable $35,000.

If he does not choose to buy at all, the would-be harness man may lease a racer. If he has already started a horse at a meeting, he is also eligible to claim one, as with Thoroughbreds.

The training of a harness horse begins a few days after he is foaled, when he is first accustomed to the halter and to the idea of being handled by men. But it is not until the latter months of his yearling year—Standardbreds, like Thoroughbreds, have a common birthday on January 1—that real breaking begins. The young horse is first introduced to the bridle

212

and gets used to the feel of the bit in his mouth. Later, a piece at a time, other parts of the rather complicated harness are added. Often the yearling will simply wear them standing in his stall to become accustomed to the sensation. Or he may be led around inside the barn to give him the idea of moving in harness.

The next step is to attach extra-long reins. Walking behind the young animal, the trainer guides him left and right, and teaches him to start and stop, much as a plowman controls his horse. This phase of training is called "line driving" and it usually goes on for a week or so. When the trainer judges that the horse is ready, the youngster is hitched to a jogging cart, a vehicle similar to a racing sulky, but heavier and more comfortable for the driver.

If he has not already been shod, he now gets his first set of shoes. This is one of the important features of a horse's preparatory period, for how he is shod will determine the balance of his stride. While he is being readied for the track, therefore, he is shod and reshod with a wide assortment of shoes and toe weights until just the right balance is struck. In general, trotters wear heavier shoes than pacers—about eight ounces as against five. Toe weights, which help a trotter to extend his stride, are clipped to the surface of the front hoofs and weigh from one to ten ounces.

In his initial workouts the youngster will be jogged slowly, but as the trainer develops the gait and the horse improves, the tempo is increased. Soon the trainer knows whether his charge is progressing at a satisfactory rate. If not, it may be wise to postpone further schooling. Some horses mature more slowly than others and may do better with more time to "come around." In such cases the shoes are removed and the horse is returned to pasture. He will get another chance next year to show what he can do.

If the youngster is responding well his training will be intensified and geared to track conditions. Every other day he will be jogged up to four miles, with a short "brush," or burst of top speed, at the end of the workout. This will continue until he is capable of making a mile in three minutes or so.

At this level he is worked toward faster and faster times, but the workouts are reduced to two a week. By the time he reaches the track, the fledgling harness racer will have worked a total of several hundred miles and been brought to within a few seconds of his racing potential.

A newcomer to the harness track, on seeing a trotter or pacer in full racing regalia for the first time, will wonder how the horse can move at all. Actually, this racing gear has evolved after more than a century and a half of experimentation, and

every item contributes to the speed and protection of the horse.

For both trainer and horse, life around a harness track is an active affair. Work starts early in the morning and may not end until after the last race at 11:30 p.m. Regardless of weather, the harness trainer gets to the track around 7 a.m. to go over the training routine with the second, or assistant, trainer and the stable hands. He personally checks each horse to see that it is sound. Then he, and often the second trainer and a groom or two, start working the horses out. This may be continued until the lunch hour. The afternoon is taken up with chores like supervising the shoeing of the horses that will go out that night, perhaps a session with the veterinarian, and, necessarily, a careful study of the form of all the opposing horses on the night's race card. Knowledge of one's opponents in the harness game is as vital as knowing one's own horse.

Post time at most night harness tracks is 8:30 p.m., but long before that horses will be seen on the track limbering up for the races. Each race on the program is color-coded, and the color indicating each race is prominently displayed, usually along the inside rail facing the stands. If, for example, yellow is the color for the third race, each horse wears a yellow saddlecloth with his program number on it. His head number—a metal disc mounted at the back of the head—likewise will be yellow. In this way, fans watching the horses working out are able to identify their possible choices well in advance of every race.

Almost invariably, each horse that is to race starts preparing about two hours before his event. He is worked in three separate phases. First, he is jogged slowly the "wrong way" (clockwise) for a distance of two and one-half to three miles with a jog cart and minimal harness, then turned the "right way" (counterclockwise) and opened up for perhaps two and one-half miles. He is returned to the paddock, where all the horses on the evening program assemble, and is sponged

down and cooled out in the same manner as a Thoroughbred race horse.

About a half hour later, he reappears on the track, again hitched to a jog cart, and usually with a trainer in the seat and most of his racing gear in place. He will be given a couple of "scores"—practice starts in which he is hustled away from the approximate starting line as he would be in an actual race—then worked another mile, this time at a somewhat faster clip than in the initial warm-up. The same sponging-down and cooling-out routine is followed again.

In the horse's third and final pre-race appearance, he is hitched to a racing sulky and wears full racing harness. His regular driver will be at the reins as he goes another mile at a rate of speed that is only eight or ten seconds off the anticipated pace of the actual race in which he is to compete. This last workout will be only thirty or forty minutes before the event itself. Once more, the horse is cooled out.

By the time he shows up in the parade to the post, the harness horse has worked from four and one-half to five miles, but again he is limbered up briefly before he moves to the starting gate. At this point one might think the horse had nothing at all left for the race. This is not the case. The experience of many years has shown that the Standardbred race horse requires every bit of this elaborate warming-up procedure to be loose enough to trot or pace at his best.

Most harness tracks are a half mile in circumference, although there now appears to be a trend favoring slightly greater lengths, say, five-eighths of a mile. There are also a few which are a mile around. The famous "Red Mile" at Lexington, Kentucky, where both Adios Butler and Greyhound set their respective pacing and trotting records, is one. The Du Quoin, Illinois, State Fairgrounds, scene of the classic Hambletonian, is another. Some other mile tracks are at the leased facilities of Thoroughbred plants, where the "deep" running surfaces must be rolled to make the smooth, hard roadbeds on which

Harness racing is often a family affair. Boy silhouetted inside barn is bringing water to his father's Standardbred.

harness horses compete.

Although on occasion they are contested at both greater and lesser distances, most harness races are one mile. Because a mile track has only half the turns of a half-miler, and because these turns are wider and more gradual, there are different racing strategies for bigger and smaller loops. For example, it is a rare thing to see a horse attempt to pass others on the sharp turns of a half-mile track, although at the mile ovals it is not at all uncommon. The longer straightaways of mile tracks also can be used to greater advantage by a big-striding animal than those of a half-mile plant. In fact, in the early days of harness racing, "speedways," long straight thoroughfares, were the preferred tracks. For a while, New York's Third Avenue served as one.

Generally speaking, however, the principles that govern successful harness-racing driving are universal. These include such factors as the driver's knowledge of racing tactics, his nerve and skill in maneuvering at close quarters, and, perhaps most important of all, his knowledge of what he can expect from his horse. In harness-racing language, it is said that the average good trotter or pacer can be "used" only twice in a race. In plain English this means that only twice during an event can a horse be extended to his greatest effort. Only the superstars of the harness-racing breed can be called upon more often than that. How and when the driver "uses" his horse frequently determines how he finishes.

In all forms of horse racing conducted on a circular track, it is axiomatic that the horse traveling nearest the inside rail has the shortest path to the finish. This is particularly true in harness racing because of the four-foot width of the sulky. It is plain to see that when the horses come abreast of the starting gate the radius of the circle in which the outside horse will be going is forty or more feet greater than the track of the inside horse, depending upon the number of starters.

The starting, or post, position of the horses is

216

determined earlier by the luck of the draw. Normally, the inside, number-one spot is considered to be best.*

In the start, the horses are led by a mounted marshal to the extended arms of the mobile gate mounted on the starter's car in the backstretch. The starter sits in the car, facing the gate. As the car moves forward, each horse lines up behind the number indicating his assigned post position. Gradually the speed picks up from about eleven miles per hour for the first eighth of a mile to not less than eighteen miles per hour for the second. In the final sixteenth of a mile the gate and horses are traveling at about thirty-five miles per hour. As the start is reached, the car speeds away at about fifty, and, folding its wings, moves to the outside to clear the track for the race.

Once the horses are away, the horse on the rail may be taken back to allow one or more horses to go ahead and act as "windbreakers." This stratagem is called "covering up." Horses in the outside spots move rapidly to the rail, and the first time past the stands on a half-mile track, they are not infrequently in single file, tight on the rail. Meanwhile, the shrewd driver, stop watch cupped in one hand, is calculating the reserve strength he can sense in his own horse against what he is able to tell from the way the others are going. At precisely the right moment—perhaps it will come in the last quarter of a mile or less—he must know when to pull out cleanly for the lead and ask his animal for the all-out effort that will bring him home a winner. At the same time, since harness racing is conducted at very close quarters, he must exercise care to see that his flying sulky does not crowd another, cut in too quickly, swerve in the homestretch, or otherwise commit an infraction of the rules that could cost him the race or result in a dangerous collision. He must also keep such control of his horse that he will not "break."

As with Thoroughbred racing, each step of the way is carefully supervised. The presiding officials at a harness track are called judges. Their powers are similar to those of the stewards of a Thoroughbred meeting in that they have the authority to change the results of a race in cases of unfair driving, and to suspend the drivers who commit violations of the rules.

The judges arrive at decisions not only by their own observation of the race, but by the evidence given them by patrol judges stationed around the racing enclosure, and by the record of the motion-picture film patrol, again as in Thoroughbred racing. Similar, too, is the employment of the photo-finish camera.

In this chapter an effort has been made to establish the ways in which Thoroughbred and harness racing differ, and those in which they are alike. To sum these up simply, it can be said that the differences are man-made, while the similarities stem from the traits of the horses.

The harness horse runs at a gait for which he may have an inherited tendency, but which must be developed by man down to the last ounce of weight in the horse's shoes. Every step in a race is planned for him. Every move is under the driver's tight control. While in Thoroughbred society an endless argument rages over the relative importance of jockeys, there is no such debate in harness circles about drivers. It is an accepted fact that the clever driver who knows how, and when, to get the most out of his horse will win time and time again over the driver who may have the better animal but who spends its energies foolishly, permits it to break needlessly, or gets caught in a traffic jam when he should be making his move. Few who have studied both sports would disagree that the human element is more important in harness racing than it is in the Thoroughbred sport, and that this is the principal difference between them.

They are alike in that, with all human considerations being equal, the ultimate margin of victory must be provided by the animal itself. In horse racing, regardless of what kind, it is inbred generosity and will to win that marks the better horse and shows the way to the winner's circle.

* Except on a very wet track. Racing surfaces being concave, there is a tendency for water to run inward toward the rail, making the inside going difficult.

13 MODERN

HORSE SHOWS

Wherever there have been horses, there have been men whose pride of ownership has compelled them to demonstrate that their animals were the best that could be had—the best looking, or the best riding, or the best hunting, or the best jumping. A hundred and fifty years ago the only opportunity to match horses was at country fairs, where the best blood of the stable mingled in the rural "midways" with cows, hogs, sheep, poultry, newfangled farming contraptions, and the baked goods and jams put up by the ladies of the community. Today, a far cry from the folksy atmosphere of the past, the major horse show is a glittering, sophisticated, full-dress affair with as much pomp and protocol as a debutante ball and a range of participants that includes celebrities, millionaires, grade-school children, suburban housewives, the old guard of professional horse dealers and trainers, international jumping teams, and just plain ordinary citizens who love and ride horses. In fact, there is probably no other event in the country that brings together such a wide and enthusiastic variety of entries in an atmosphere of sporting camaraderie. It has not been unusual, for example, for a teen-age shower of hunters to find herself riding in an event against Mrs. Robert F. Kennedy, or for a modest owner of Hackneys to discover such companions in the show ring as the renowned Mrs. William P. Roth, whose Why Worry Stables is one of the great plants in the country. There is a place in the horse-show world for all—regardless of age or income—and in that world is a sense of fun and healthy rivalry, of spotlight showmanship and traditional elegance that attracts people of both simple and cultivated tastes.

At the highest level, the horse show is a prestigious affair that may occupy for a full week the facilities of such showplaces as Devon, Pennsylvania, a lavish complex of stadium, stables, and fashionable stores which has been specially constructed for the purposes of horse shows, or the giant arenas of such urban centers as New York City (The National Horse Show), Washington, D.C. (The Washington International), Louisville (The Kentucky State Fair), Kansas City (The American Royal), Chicago (The Chicago International), and Dallas (The Dallas Charity). The first night of the National at Madison Square Garden is a highlight of the social season that is considered to rival the opening of the Metropolitan Opera, and the traditional opening ceremonies are a dazzling spectacle. The entire arena is draped in bunting. The national flag of each country taking part in the international competitions is prominently displayed. The United States Army Band opens the festivities, marching into the arena and then playing the national anthems of the United States and its foreign visitors, as their riding teams assemble in formation.

Ladies in long gowns and gentlemen in white tie—perhaps distinguished members of the horse-show world or other dignitaries—are on hand to present the sparkling silver trophies and thousands of dollars in prize money offered to the winners. Gala dinners, parties, and the Horse Show Ball complete the whirl of events organized to entertain the exhibitors.

Lavish events such as these are high points of the horseman's calendar, but there are hundreds of less elaborate, although equally picturesque and challenging, shows taking place the year around throughout the United States. These are generally two-day affairs, sometimes held at an old hunt club, as in Virginia, Grosse Pointe, and Connecticut's Fairfield and Litchfield Counties, or in the parts of Long Island still reminiscent of F. Scott Fitzgerald—perhaps at a riding stable, a private estate or farm, or a local fairgrounds, where the big event is still a neighborly community affair, with everyone pitching in to help. Here there are few frills. The air is clean and crisp, the fields likely to be slowly turning bronze with the autumn chill. Station wagons are packed with food and drink for the hungry horsemen.

Preceding pages & opposite: In FEI
and open jumping, fences may exceed five feet.
Faults, such as touching or knocking
down obstacles, are scored against each horse;
rider's form is not taken into account.

Children exclaim over their first blue ribbon, and seasoned professionals watch with keen eyes the performance of the horses they hope to take to the Garden *next* year. These events are the real backbone of the horse-show game, and in recent years they have flourished with such success that the whole sport of showing has enjoyed a phenomenal boom. In 1959 there were four hundred and twenty-five recognized shows conducted, with a distribution of $1,453,322 in prize money. Five years later, in 1964, there were six hundred and fifty-one recognized shows distributing $2,179,280, and 1965 put the number of recognized shows over seven hundred.

The single most important influence in the success of horse shows is the American Horse Shows Association, founded in 1917 at the instigation of Reginald C. Vanderbilt, its first president. Since that time the Association has been a guiding force in promoting the sport, in keeping the activity clean and fair, in preventing injustices to riders and cruelty to horses, and in establishing nationally uniform regulations under which contestants compete, whether in the wilds of the Dakotas or at Madison Square Garden.

To insure that the interests of all horsemen are fairly represented—whether their show stock is Western horses, Kentucky Saddlers, hunters, jumpers, or specialized breeds—the Association has established eleven geographical zones in the United States, with a chairman in each zone responsible for supervising horse-show activities and voicing the problems that may arise.

Diversified interests are also represented by individual committees, the scope of whose attentions may be indicated if we review the list:

Arabian Committee
Combined Training Events Committee
Dressage Committee
Equitation Committees (Hunting Seat, Saddle
    Seat, Stock Saddle Seat)
Hackney Committee
Harness Committee
Hunter Committee
Jumper Committee
Junior Exhibitors Committee
Morgan Committee
Palomino Committee
Parade Horse Committee
Polo Committee
Roadster Committee
Saddle Horse Committee
Shetland Pony Committee
Walking Horse Committee
Welsh Pony Committee
Western Committee

LEADING WITH THE RIGHT FORE-FOOT.

All shows which are officially sanctioned by the AHSA are said to be recognized shows. This means that they have been duly licensed by the Association and that the show dates have been cleared on the horse-show calendar. The show management must follow procedures established by the AHSA, even to details that do not directly relate to what is going on in the ring, such as filing a record of class results with the Association, and seeing that a blacksmith and veterinarian are on the show grounds. The classes themselves must be governed by AHSA rules (or, in some instances, equivalent regulations which it recognizes) and the entire contest officiated by duly licensed judges. In addition, licensed stewards must be on the premises to supervise the show, seeing that no regulations are infringed and acting as counsel to management and exhibitors. These prescriptions are safeguards for the horse, the owner, and the rider, and any exhibitor who is the victim of a breach of the regulations of a recognized show may file a protest with the AHSA, whereupon a hearing will be conducted to determine whether there has indeed been an injustice.

The rules of the Association also afford a certain protection to horse-show management by barring unscrupulous, dishonest exhibitors from the ring. One year a show which had not previously sought recognition dispatched its show secretary to the offices of the AHSA to submit its application for membership. He was asked why and gave a straightforward answer: "Two months ago you suspended Mr. X for a year and that exhibitor cannot show in recognized shows in that period. I am mighty afraid we are going to be asked to accept his entries and we don't want him. The only way we know to prevent taking him is to join the Association. Then we cannot accept his entries."

Shows which are not members of the AHSA are said to be unrecognized shows. This label does not prejudice the show, but it does mean that neither the management nor the exhibitors can enjoy the assurances offered by the association. It is significant, in fact, that while many shows do not go to the trouble of joining the Association, they do not hesitate to avail themselves of its guidelines and almost invariably conduct their classes in accordance with its rules.

Sidesaddle position, once considered de rigueur for proper equestriennes, has fallen from favor and is now seen only at shows and in the hunting field.

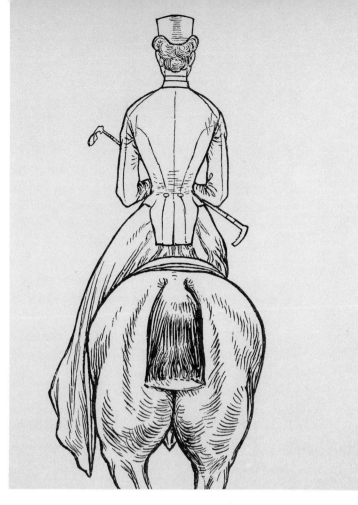

The problem is, however, that while most unrecognized shows choose to adhere to AHSA regulations, there may be some deviations from the standard procedures for which the rider might be unprepared. And, because the show is not under the supervision of the AHSA, a contestant has no official recourse, no matter how unjust he feels a decision may have been. Nor has he any assurance as to the quality and integrity of the judges who are evaluating his performance. AHSA judges must undergo a written test to demonstrate their knowledge of the various qualities desirable in the kinds of horses they will be examining. In addition, comments testifying to the character of a candidate for judge are invited from those who know him. Evaluating these often makes the judge's task in the ring look like child's play, as may be seen from reports on a man who was seeking credentials in the Saddle and Walking Horse Divisions:

Answer No. 1 "Not capable or honest enough to be a judge."
No. 2 "Impartial, proper temperament and has the knowledge to render sound decisions."

Rider's upper, or right, leg is supported by bar, concealed by rider's habit, which extends outward from saddle and curves upward to catch the thigh.

No. 3 "Fairly good prospect."
No. 4 "He is a crook."

Obviously there were conflicting views in this case which would require careful deliberation to settle. Other reports may express unanimous opinions—favorable or unfavorable—but in all instances the AHSA does its best to ascertain the qualifications of its judges.

The rules established by the Association are what may be called the common law of showing. They define the specifications of every type of class, the manner of scoring and the basis on which judging is to be conducted, the limitations on the eligibility of horses or riders to enter an event, and circumstances which constitute grounds for disqualification. Additionally, they try to cover procedure in cases where the unexpected occurs, such as a horse throwing a shoe, or a horse or rider breaking a piece of equipment, or the interruption of a class by some calamity or act of God.

Since a huge week-long event offers harsher competition than a limited, one-day show, the AHSA gives its member shows ratings of "A," and "B," and "C," based on the amount of prize

223

money and the number of classes each one offers. Winning contestants in member shows are awarded points which are totaled at the end of the year. The exhibitor with the greatest number receives the coveted High Score Award for his division, announced at the annual AHSA ceremonial dinner. Points at "A" shows have the highest value. Points at "B" shows are worth half as much. Points at "C" shows are worth half as much as "B" points.

The AHSA has approximately ten thousand members and has recorded some twenty thousand horses. Its dues are $10 for adults; $5 for children. Horsemen who are seriously interested in showing are wise to avail themselves of its services and its leadership. The horse-show world owes much to the exceptional ability and dedication of the officers of the Association.

The horseman going to his initial show, whether as an exhibitor or a spectator, is bound to be at a loss unless he first familiarizes himself with the language and law of the sport. Consider, for example, the apocryphal story of the little boy who was asked by his aunt why he had not entered a certain class. He replied, much to her confusion, "Good heavens, I can't. I'm not a maiden anymore!" He meant, of course, that he was ineligible for the event because he had already won his first blue ribbon in that class.

Recognized horse shows offer a wide variety of classes, which are usually grouped into general divisions. Some divisions are categorized according to the breed of horse involved; thus a single show might contain an Appaloosa Division, an Arabian Division, a Morgan Division, a Saddle Division, a Walking Horse Division, and so on, covering as many breeds as the show can handle within its time span and concentrating especially on those which will attract a large number of exhibitors. In these breed divisions it is always the performance of the horse, not the rider, which is the foremost consideration. Under saddle, the horses will be asked to perform at their customary gaits (usually, the walk,

trot, and canter are required) with special emphasis on the particular gait for which the breed may be famous—such as the walk of a Tennessee Walker, or the extra two gaits of a five-gaited horse. In addition to studying a horse's action, the judges will look at his conformation, assessing the degree to which he possesses the ideal physical characteristics of his breed.

Individual classes will often stipulate conditions of eligibility for the horse, or the circumstances under which he is to be ridden. Some events, such as those in the Arabian Division, may call for the entries to perform in native costume. Other classes may demand that amateurs, or ladies, or owners, are to ride. In some cases the breed types are required to be shown in Western tack. Other competitions call for English tack. All these specifications must be clearly stated by the horse-show management when it sends out its entry blanks and prize list describing the events to prospective exhibitors.

Not all divisions, however, evaluate the horse in terms of his breed. Nor in all divisions is it always the horse that is being judged. In some cases the rider's performance is under scrutiny. In others, both horse and rider are considered.

The Equitation Division is a highly popular group of classes organized chiefly to meet the interests of junior horsemen (under eighteen years old) whose insatiable passion for horses and showing has been largely responsible for the incredible horse-show boom of recent years. In some cases, in fact, there have been so many entries that special hours have had to be set aside for elimination classes to reduce the group to a manageable size.

Equitation classes are for horsemanship alone, and usually are open only to youngsters who have not reached their eighteenth birthday, although occasionally there are classes open to riders under twenty-one. The rider is tested solely on his mastery of his horse and his correctness of form. Whether or not he is on a fractious or inferior horse, his skill at enforcing control and discipline is what will count with the judges. Naturally, a wise contestant will try to mount himself on a horse that shows off his ability, but if he is a poor rider he will not deceive the officials by relying on a well-trained animal, for judges often ask contestants to change their mounts in order to establish just how much of the performance is due to the horse's talent and how much to the rider's.

Equitation classes are held for each of the three types of riding seat—hunter seat, saddle seat, and Western-stock seat. In saddle- or stock-seat classes, entries are tested on the flat—no jumping required. Saddle-seat contestants are asked to walk, trot, and canter, and those in stock-seat events to walk, jog, and lope. In addition, entries may be asked to execute figure eights, serpentines, circles, or other drills which will demonstrate their degree of accomplishment.

In hunter-seat equitation, riders are tested over jumps, usually about three feet high. Jumping faults are not scored against a contestant unless they result from improper horsemanship. After each contestant has performed his round over fences, the judges usually select finalists to return to the ring where they may be requested to work on the flat in routines similar to those in saddle-seat and stock-seat events.

Since it would not be fair to have championship riders consistently pitted against newcomers, eligibility for the classes may be restricted according to the contestant's show-ring history. A maiden class, for example, is open only to those who have not yet won a blue ribbon in the division in a recognized show. A novice class is open to entries who have not won three firsts, and a limit class is open to non-winners in six. An open class is open to all—within the age limit.

Class designations may apply to horse or rider, depending on whose performance is being judged. A junior exhibitor whose mount wins a first prize in the Saddle Horse Division, for example, is still eligible for maiden class in equitation if he has won no victories in this category.

There are several famous classes in equitation in which every child aspires to become a winner, such as the hunter-seat event known as the AHSA Horsemanship Class, or simply "the Maclay," which is sponsored by the American Society for the Prevention of Cruelty to Animals, and whose trophy is donated by the late Alfred B. Maclay, a former president of the American Horse Shows Association. The AHSA Medal Class, sponsored by the Association and open to its members under eighteen, and the NHS "Good Hands" Class, a saddle-seat event sponsored by

*This horse has moved in too close to
fence for smooth flight, but rider has done
well to give him a loose rein.*

the National Horse Show, are other notable equitation events.

The art of equitation, at its highest level of competence, can be seen in the Dressage Division. The name dressage is French and means training. Dressage differs from equitation in requiring not only more highly skilled mastery by the rider, but precision response from the horse, as well. Until recently, dressage was looked upon by American horsemen as a rather effete enthusiasm of European riding masters, but recently it has become a popular element of American shows, especially for those interested in international or Olympic competitions. To encourage youngsters to enter this specialty, the Professional Horsemen's Association, the American Horse Shows Association, and the United States Equestrian Team all offer special events in dressage for junior exhibitors.

The essence of dressage is the delicate relationship between horse and rider, which is based on precision control and response. Both performers are under scrutiny by the judges. Both must exhibit the ultimate refinements of high-level training. The horse must pick up—instantly and accurately—the signals he is given, and the rider must demonstrate perfect form, using the aids of leg and hand so subtly that they are imperceptible to the onlooker. No clucking or use of the voice is permitted. The appointments of horse and rider must meet the specifications of the class.

The primary emphasis of dressage is on the performance of intricate drills and exercises on the flat, although entries are sometimes asked to take a simple three-foot jump. Each entrant takes the track individually, performing a routine that lasts about ten or fifteen minutes, following each step of the instructions which have been posted in diagram beforehand. It is always wise for the rider to memorize the drill, so that he need not rely on the directions of the announcer; in some cases it is mandatory that the rider execute the course from memory.

The course is set up within a marked rectangular enclosure. Regulation dimensions for a large arena are 198 by 66 feet, and 132 by 66 for a small one. Situated around the enclosure are alphabetical letters to indicate the route the rider is to follow and the point at which he is to commence a new gait or figure, or change direction. For judging the basic gaits the horse and rider are called upon to perform at a walk, trot, and canter, executing each gait in its ordinary, extended, and collected forms. At the canter it is expected that both simple and flying changes of lead will be completed with ease, and sometimes instructions will call for the contestant to move at the counter-canter, in which the horse circles in a canter on the wrong lead.

In addition to the serpentine, the figure eight, and the circle, which are basic figures in the dressage drill, there are additional movements involving terms which may be less familiar to horsemen unacquainted with this division. A volte, for example, is a small circle twenty feet in diameter, unless otherwise noted. (The normal circle is sixty-six feet, the width of the arena, unless otherwise noted.) A turn on the forehand requires the horse to pivot on a single foreleg. A turn on the haunches is a pivot on a single rear leg. In the pirouette, usually performed at the canter, the horse's forequarters describe a circle around his hindquarters which remain at the center of the figure. It is important that the horse not break the rhythm of his gait while executing the movement. His forelegs must continue to canter even though they are not carrying him forward but in a circle, and his rear legs, in order to hold the extremely tight pattern, must be raised and lowered at exactly the same spot on the ground.

The passage is a very collected, very elevated, very cadenced trot, characterized by a faint hesitation of each leg before it descends to the ground—almost as if the horse were dancing to an old-world Viennese strain. The piaffer is a trot in place—the collected, elevated motions of

the trot performed with no forward movement.

The shoulder-in requires the horse to trot forward along the wall of the arena with his haunches parallel to the rail and his shoulders, neck, and head curved in toward the center of the ring. He does not face the direction in which he is going, but by trotting so that his inside legs cross in front of his outside legs, he can proceed straight ahead, parallel to the wall.

In the haunches-in, or travers, the horse moves with his head parallel to the rail and his haunches curved to the inside. This time the horse's head faces the direction of motion, and the outside legs cross over the inside legs to keep him moving directly ahead and parallel to the rail.

The haunches-out, or renvers, is the inverse of the travers. The hindquarters are curved to the wall instead of to the center. Head, neck, and shoulders remain parallel to the wall and the horse again faces the direction of motion.

The pass, also called the transversal or two-track, is a movement in which the horse trots forward and to the side at one time, thus carrying him on an oblique, forty-five degree path away from the wall. His body is not curved, but points straight forward, although his head is slightly turned in the same angle as his direction.

Dressage is in no sense "trick" or circus riding. All its movements are completely natural to an agile, supple horse and may frequently be performed "by accident" by frisky horses playing at pasture. In fact, the purpose of dressage training is to develop flexibility and balance in the animal, as well as obedience and technical accomplishment. Dressage can, in fact, be regarded as a form of enlightened calisthenics.

Novices should not be discouraged by the demands of expert performance. There are many levels of dressage, ranging from the "A" tests, designed for newcomers, to the "D" tests designed for those of superior skills. The next step is the perfection of the Olympic level, or the incredible mastery of the *haute ecole*, of which the Lipizzaners from the Spanish Riding School in

Vienna are the most renowned example.

In the Hunter Division, the performance of the horse is the judges' only consideration; faults of horsemanship are not taken into account unless they reflect a mistake by the animal. The entries are generally required to take a course of fences which simulate actual obstacles encountered in the hunting field—stone walls, brushes (hedges), chicken coops, gates, post-and-rails, logs, and so forth. These jumps average about four feet. The object of the class is not to see how high the horse can jump, however, but to judge the evenness of the horse's pace and the smooth, flowing grace with which he negotiates the barriers— what horsemen call his "brilliance over fences." A hunter, after all, must be a safe, comfortable mount with plenty of endurance. If he takes a fence in an awkward and therefore hazardous manner, this will be scored against him even though he may actually clear the hurdle with room to spare. On the other hand, if he jumps with a smooth, even action, he will not necessarily be penalized for nicking the barrier.

Eligibility for the most prominent classes in the Hunter Division may be based on a number of conditions. Classes for young hunters, for example, are open only to horses five years old and under. Green-hunter events may be entered by horses of any age who are still in the first or second year of showing over jumps in recognized-show classes. Those in their first year of competition are usually tested over jumps of about three feet six inches and second-year entries go over fences of three feet nine inches. Both these classes are excellent proving grounds, but because they are so popular among professional horsemen who want to display the promising prospects they are offering for sale, the competition is a good deal more rigorous than the class definitions might imply.

Working-hunter classes are for more experienced animals, and here the fences reach a solid and respectable four feet. The events are usually divided into the lightweight, middleweight, and heavyweight categories— the lightweights being horses able to carry up to one hundred and sixty-five pounds, middleweights up to one hundred and eighty-five pounds, and heavyweights up to two hundred and five pounds.

Events for model hunters are based purely on conformation. No performance is required and a horse is judged simply on the degree to which his appearance approximates that of the ideal hunter. The word model, therefore, appropriately describes this event, and it is used in many divisions to describe a class in which conformation is the criterion of evaluation. Similar contests among Western and draft types are often called halter classes, because the only equipment the horse wears in them is a halter.

The so-called Corinthian classes and appointments events are—competitions in which horse and rider must appear in absolutely correct hunting attire, right down to the sandwich case and beverage flask carried on the saddle. Every detail of the prescribed hunting equipment must be worn or carried in proper position—hunt whips, gloves, spurs, boot tops, hats, tack, the whole ensemble. The magnificent hunting livery in which the riders appear makes this one of the most colorful and beautiful moments of any horse show. The only difference between a Corinthian and an ordinary appointments class is that in the former the rider must be a member in good standing of an actual, recognized hunt.

Events in the Western Division are primarily calculated to test the balance, agility, and the willing, workmanlike manners of a horse trained for practical cow work. Some of these contests closely reproduce tasks actually performed on the open range, such as roping and herding. Others establish the horse's ability through the performance of rigorous reining routines which are a sort of Western version of dressage drills. These classes are in no sense rodeo events. There is no wild-bronc riding or bull riding in the Western Division of a horse show. Rather, the emphasis is on displaying the talents of a trained animal moving through his working routine.

In classes in which the horse works cattle, a bunch of steers is held in the arena by riders who are not contestants. As the exhibitor commences his performance, these riders abandon the herd and the competing horse and rider work the steers in accordance with the judge's instructions. Horses are judged on a basis of one hundred and fifty points: fifty points for cow work; fifty points for reining (responding to the rider's guidance); twenty points for conformation; twenty points for manners; and ten points for appointments. The horse will be faulted for signs of nervousness, such as switching his tail or tossing his head, or of overeagerness, such as tugging at the bit or anticipating the rider's signal, as sometimes happens when a horse is overtrained. The horse should, of course, respond willingly and work smoothly, keeping his feet well under him so that he will not spraddle at a sudden turn. And he should have a soft, responsive mouth, reacting to every command.

Roping contests in the Western Division of a horse show follow the basic pattern of roping contests in the rodeo except that the rider's roping time does not count. Hence, while the rider must be a competent roper in order to show his horse effectively, his skill is of less importance than the horse's ability to help him make the catch. A time limit of two minutes is permitted for each entry. Within this limit, the rider may throw as many loops as necessary to demonstrate satisfactorily his horse's accomplishments. Again, the horse must show mannerliness and quiet behavior—especially when he is behind the barrier and as he awaits the rider's return after the calf has been tied. But once in action, the horse will be judged on his ability to rate the calf, to stop, and to keep the rope taut so that the calf cannot scramble away.

There are many different types of reining contests but the primary purpose of them all is to measure a horse's willingness and ability to obey the rider's signals immediately. Each entry nego-

tiates an intricate pattern of circles, figure eights, loops, straightaway sprints, and sudden halts, performing simple and flying changes of lead. He may be asked to back, to pivot, and to change direction by reversing almost in place, rolling back on his hocks and wheeling his forequarters around, as well as to execute the diagramed course at whatever gaits are specified.

Barrel racing is a clocked event in which the horse with the best time wins. Here the entries race at full speed in a cloverleaf pattern, circling three barrels placed in the ring in the form of a triangle, then rushing back over the finish line.

Classes for Western riding and trail horses evaluate the horse on the basis of his behavior in situations that might be encountered during a day's ride—such as fording shallow water, jumping a fallen log, riding through brush, or coming upon a gate which the rider must be able to open and close without dismounting.

Other stock-horse classes may simply test the entries at the walk, lope, and full gallop. These are usually divided into lightweight and heavyweight sections—the lightweight category being for horses weighing 850 to 1,100 pounds, and the heavyweight for horses over 1,100 pounds.

At U.S. Equestrian Team training camp in New Jersey, team members practice for trail ride in three-day event.

229

Parade-horse classes are among the most colorful events in the Western Division. The entries show at only two gaits—the walk and the parade gait, an extremely slow, elevated, cadenced trot —hopefully performed to the stirring music that would be played in the real parades led by these eye-catching horses. The parade horse must have exceptionally good manners, since there must be no danger of his cutting up within the ranks of a brass band or around a crowd of spectators. Emphasis is not placed on a multiplicity of gaits, for more important considerations in judging the parade horse are his flashy looks and dazzling trappings. Brilliant markings and a richly colored coat mark the good parade horse, and he should carry a saddle and bridle heavy with silver decoration. The rider should be in colorful costume, often wearing fancy boots, hats, guns, spurs, serapes, and other equipment of an Old West, whose days are called to mind as these horses march by in all their showy splendor.

For sheer excitement, none of the many different horse-show competitions can surpass the classes in the Jumper Division. The sole purpose in these competitions is to determine which horse can jump the highest. Horsemanship, style, manners, gait, conformation—nothing counts except getting over the obstacle cleanly. The spectators watch in hushed silence as horse and rider enter the ring and, with nerve-wracking intensity, gauge every obstacle and measure each stride with infinite precision, trying to approach the fences just so, in order for the horse to sail over without touching or knocking down a rail. As an entry completes a flawless round, the crowd cheers with abandon to show its approval of a job well done.

The obstacles vary from simple post-and-rails, brush fences, and gates, to exotic concoctions of bull's-eye targets and brightly painted barrels that would loom as nightmares to less expert horses and riders. Some of the hurdles will be ordinary vertical jumps. Others will be spread fences, in which several rails or elements of the jump will be placed a measured distance apart and at successively increasing heights, all to be cleared in one bold leap. Still others will be broad jumps—various kinds of wide, low obstacles, such as the Liverpool (a hedge or other barrier with water beyond). The entire course will be set up in a twisting pattern, with irregular distances between the fences so horse and rider will continually have to check and readjust their pace. And although the jumps may start out at a not-too-fearful four or five feet, they soon soar to incredible heights of six and seven feet as the bars are raised to break the tie between two or more horses that have jumped the previous round without a fault.

The Jumper Division may incorporate handicap classes for maiden, novice, and limit jumpers, but usually the two main categories offered are for green jumpers and open jumpers. Classes for green jumpers are open to horses which have not been shown in the Jumper Division at a recognized show prior to January 1st of the current year, and the jumps are approximately three feet nine inches. Open classes are open to all, and the fences are of more formidable dimensions. The skilled jumpers that enter these are often referred to simply as "open horses."

Showgoers should observe that the Jumper Division uses not one but two sets of rules by which events may be scored. The show management must clearly specify in its entry blanks and show program which type of scoring is being used. One method is according to AHSA regulations, and the other is the FEI standard, governed by the *Federation Equestre Internationale*—the official international horse-show organization which rules such worldwide competitions as the Olympics and the Pan-American Games. (The AHSA is the representative body of American horsemen to the FEI.)

There are many aspects in which the AHSA and the FEI methods concur and others in which they diverge, and the horseman seriously interested in open jumping or stadium jumping (the

James Day, member of Canadian riding team, takes his big brown jumper over a beautiful fence in stadium jumping at popular Devon show, near Philadelphia.

*This family class is only a
beginning for many youngsters, who soon learn
to jump fences far taller than themselves.*

international term for these events) should, of course, familiarize himself thoroughly with the details of each system. Only the major points will be summarized here, so that the viewers may have some knowledge of what is going on.

In the majority of classes held under AHSA rules it is not customary for the entries to be clocked as they make their rounds, and time does not count unless specified. Nor in most cases are there any rules governing the minimum weight that must be carried by the horse. A fall by the horse or rider or both will cause elimination, and faults will be calculated on the following basis:

> Touch of obstacle with any portion of horse's
> body behind stifle.................... ½ fault
> Touch of obstacle with any portion of horse's
> body in front of stifle, or with any part of rider
> or equipment....................... 1 fault
> Touch of standard or wing in jumping obstacle
> with any part of horse, rider, or equip-
> ment............................. 1 fault
> Knockdown of obstacle, standard, or wing with
> any portion of horse, rider, or equipment. 4 faults
> Placing any foot in Liverpool, ditch, or water
> and/or knockdown of any obstacle placed be-
> fore, in, or beyond water or ditch...... 4 faults
> First disobedience (refusal)........... 3 faults
> Second cumulative disobedience ...... 6 faults
> Third cumulative disobedience..... Elimination

The winner of the class is the horse with the least number of faults. Sometimes, of course, there are ties and, if the tie involves an award for first place, it is mandatory that the contestants jump-off until one surpasses the other. If the tie does not involve first place, the exhibitors may elect to settle the matter by tossing a coin or by choosing to jump-off; thus the oft-heard call from an impatient announcer, "All right, gentlemen, will you jump or toss?"

Special events may be scored by other AHSA systems. In the Touch-and-Out, each horse begins his round and continues over the course until he touches a fence or commits any other fault before finishing. One touch or other fault disqualifies the entry and the horse that has gone over the greatest number of fences "clean" wins.

The Knock-Down-and-Out is a similar class, except that the eliminating factor is a knock-down, or a fault (other than a touch) listed

above. Touches are not counted at all. Thus the winning horse covers the most obstacles without knocking down a rail or bar.

The Touch-and-Out and the Knock-Down-and-Out have been classic events in the Jumper Division for many years. In the past two decades, however, the AHSA has sought to devise more ingenious and varied classes to keep pace with the types of competitions offered by the FEI. Among its most exciting new events is the High Jump—a class in which a single jump (and a practice fence) is placed in the ring. The fence is set at a starting height of approximately four feet six inches or five feet. Each horse has three tries in which to clear the obstacle, and touches do not count. If the entry clears it on the first try, he is awarded three points, on the second try two points, and on the third try one point. Failure to clear after three tries means elimination. The animal that jumps the greatest height, with the greatest number of points, is the winner.

Under FEI regulations, an important factor to bear in mind is that most of the classes are timed. In the case of ties, the horse with the best time wins. Also there is a weight minimum required of the riders. A horse ridden by a male must carry one hundred and sixty-five pounds including tack, and if he is ridden by a female the minimum is one hundred and fifty-four pounds including tack. Perhaps the most important difference from the AHSA rules is that a fall by horse or rider or both does not cause elimination, but is penalized by faults. The horse and rider may recover themselves and proceed.

Under FEI rules, touches are of no consequence. Other faults are usually scored as follows:

> First disobedience................... 3 faults
> Obstacle knocked down.............. 4 faults
> Flag (used as marker) knocked down or both
> obstacle and flag knocked down....... 4 faults
> One or more feet in water or on marking lath
> measuring broad jumps.............. 4 faults
> Second disobedience................. 6 faults
> Fall of horse, or rider, or both........ 8 faults
> Third disobedience.............. Elimination
> Exceeding time allowed—for each commenced
> second (unless breaking time limit is stipulated
> to cause elimination)................ ¼ fault

FEI classes include a wide variety of competitions which have become horse-show favorites the world over, especially at the Olympics where the cream of every nation's jumpers may compete in these grueling tests. Two of the highlights are the Puissance and the Six Bars.

In the Puissance, the course consists of from six to eight fences, some of them vertical, and some spread fences, but no out-and-out broad jumps, such as a ditch or Liverpool. None of the jumps, except the first, may be lower than four feet seven inches (1.40 meters), and the event is not timed. In case of ties, there are compulsory jump-offs over fewer fences, which have been raised and broadened. In a really exciting contest, the jumps finally are reduced to two (the rules state that there may not be fewer than this), one of which is a straight vertical jump and one a spread fence. The thrill of the crowd increases with every notch that the jumps are raised and broadened until one horse emerges as the winner.

In the Six Bars, six vertical fences are placed in a row. They may all be four feet high, or they may become progressively higher, starting at three feet nine inches and ending at five, or start-ing at three feet nine inches and ending at four feet six, with several fences of duplicate heights. Again, the event is not timed and the jumps may be raised to phenomenal heights as horses that are tied return to the course to prove their skill and spirit.

The horse show is, in a sense, all things to all horsemen. In a single arena a man may see practically every type of horse and every type of rider —and what feats of beauty and daring may be accomplished when they work in concert. There are the precision and skill of the expert equitation rider, and the alert obedience and agility of his horse as they work through their demanding routines. There, among the jumpers, is Pegasus still earthbound, floating wingless over obstacles man constructs to take his measure. There is the gliding grace of the hunter; the educated and special way of moving of the gaited horse; and the beautifully developed structure which is to be found in the best of all the breeds. The horse show is a perfected display of perfected combinations—of horse and rider, of fun and formality, of art and science, and, most of all, of courage and character.

AND TOMORROW

We often think of the preautomotive era in America, particularly the second half of the past century when the westward push was in progress, as being the heyday of the horse in this country. But actually it was in the year 1914 that the combined horse and mule population of the United States reached a high-water mark of about thirty million animals, nearly one for every three persons in the land. Strangely, this was almost thirty years after Karl Benz and Gottlieb Daimler had successfully pioneered their sputtering little one-cylinder cars, and a good two decades after automobiles had become a fairly common sight around American metropolitan centers.

The reason was that mechanization had yet to hit the farms, although the appetite of an exploding population placed such a demand on the farming community that huge new segments of virgin land were being brought under cultivation every year. As the auto industry had yet to come up with a useful, reasonably priced tractor (its steam-driven predecessors had proved highly impractical), the demand for horses of the heavy working variety reached its peak at this point.

World War I gave tremendous impetus to the internal-combustion engine—particularly the powerful, rugged-duty type employed in heavy armored vehicles. And it also hastened the techniques of mass production. In 1917 Henry Ford was able to bring out the first line of serviceable, low-priced tractors. The following year, more than one-hundred and thirty thousand tractors of various manufacturers went to the farms. That same year there were more than twenty-one million horses in use by American farmers. In the years between World War I and World War II that number was cut in half, and since the end of World War II it has fallen below a million.

Horses and mules do remain, and will probably continue to remain for some years to come, in certain agricultural specialties like tobacco farming in the South, where mules are still widely employed because they can thread their way nimbly between the planted rows without damaging the delicate leaves. Cotton raising also has lagged considerably behind other areas of agriculture as far as mechanization is concerned, and the take-over of machinery from the mule is far from complete, particularly on the smaller plantations of the Southeast.

Sometimes terrain dictates the use of horses. In a number of the steeply sloping vineyards, such as are found in New York State's Finger Lake wine country, draft horses are still used at harvest time to pull the heavy wooden sledges loaded with trays of grapes. And in a number of lumbering operations, horses or mules are employed to "snake" out the logs.

Then, too, there is the special case of the Amish people, whose religion interdicts the use of motors in any form. A visit to their magnificently tended farmlands in Pennsylvania, Delaware, Indiana, and elsewhere is like stepping a half century back into the past. Here may be seen not only teams of superior plow horses working the fields, but also the industrious Amish farmers and their families going about their daily rounds in buggies drawn by fancy-stepping Standardbred trotters and pacers.

In recent years there has been a minor revival in the breeding of draft horses, more or less on a hobby basis, among a group of nostalgically inclined farmers in various parts of the country. They have recently brought out their own publication, *The Draft Horse Journal*, and registrations in some purebred strains like the Belgian have risen in the past few years. Since no real need, including that of recreation, is really behind this *petite renaissance*, the development must be regarded as interesting but not numerically significant because, with the exception of the special cases cited earlier, the working farm horse in America is dead. It is an unhappy comment on a long career of service to mankind that his epitaph, during the past half century, has ap-

Preceding pages: Tennessee riding club on outing. Horse still is used in Pennsylvania to pull four-wheel Amish carts (right) and for ranch work in West.

Left: In the heart of New York, many enjoy
bridle paths of Central Park; one of "New York's finest"
dismounts to call precinct headquarters. Below:
Fine team of Hackneys takes St. Louis brewer August A. Busch Jr.,
leading horse enthusiast and former polo player, and
family on jaunt around estate. New York's horse-drawn cabs,
like the one at bottom, still serve a purpose
for sightseers and romantic couples.

peared principally on the labels of pet-food cans.

In fact, throughout the United States there are few jobs left, besides the herding of beef cattle, in which the horse can be said to play a useful role on a large scale. Several cities, like New York and Boston, still have mounted police. Formerly, the well-schooled police mount and his rider were used to control outbreaks of mob violence and just one such combination of horse and man was considered as effective psychologically as half a dozen men on foot. Actually, in recent history, few rioters have been physically injured by police horses—these mounts being selected for their

kindness of disposition and carefully trained not to step on pedestrians, whether hostile or friendly. Nevertheless, the appearance of mounted policemen at the scene of public demonstrations has inspired angry shouts of "Gestapo" (a rather inaccurate epithet considering that no one has ever reported seeing a Nazi plainclothesman riding a horse), and in the past decade or so they have been used sparingly for such duty. In New York, which still has some two hundred and seventy mounted policemen, they are used mainly to handle traffic in areas of heavy congestion, like the Fulton Fish Market, where they can be seen

*Diving horse (left) looks far down
from his perch at Atlantic City's Steel Pier.
But he never fails to make the plunge.*

240

more easily by motorists than foot policemen, and to patrol lonely regions of the park system.

Aside from these, and the handful of Old World fruit and vegetable hucksters who stubbornly cling to their decrepit wagons and superannuated horses, the horse has vanished from the city as a useful animal—unless, perhaps, the small but valiant fleet of horse cabs can be considered to be performing a valuable service for romantic young couples.

In view of the virtual demise of the horse as man's working partner, it may seem ironic that the year 1966—a year in which men were striving to wire the moon for television—should also be the Chinese "Year of the Horse." The truth is, however, that the horse is a long way from extinction. As a matter of fact, he is staging an amazing comeback. Most of this has taken place in the past dozen years, which have witnessed a sensational increase both in horse population and in equestrian activities.

Generally speaking, this boom—it has been estimated as exceeding in total financial value even the great postwar bonanza in private boating—stems from two principal areas of investment. The first has been the dizzying ascent of

Opposite: Husky team of Belgians draws heavy circus
wagon in Milwaukee's big annual parade. Wagons are brought
from famous circus museum at Baraboo, Wisconsin, while
horse teams come from all parts of the country. Left:
Jousting is popular in Maryland. Below: George Hanneford Jr.
executes somersault from one horse to another at
Ringling Brothers' circus. Horses are still a major big-top attraction.
Bottom: Chicago polo players race upfield. Thoroughbreds,
once excluded by size, now are widely used.

Thoroughbred, Standardbred, and Quarter Horse racing. The monetary worth of the farms, racing plants, and animals involved in these sports exceeds $5,000,000,000. The other great category of growth has been in pleasure horses. Quantitatively, at least, this is where the largest expansion in equine activity has taken place. For example, in the year 1953, according to the *American Racing Manual*, 9,062 Thoroughbred foals were registered with The Jockey Club. By 1964, the figure had almost doubled to 17,022. Though these figures do represent a whopping percentage increase, they are almost negligible numerically when compared to the rise in the number of pleasure horses in the same span of years. This was an increase of from two million to three and a half million animals. (These are official Government figures based on actual registrations kept by breed associations and similar organizations. Most authorities are agreed that the true total of pleasure horses in the 1960's may approach five million.) The trend shows no sign of abating. On the contrary, it can be expected to accelerate because of the increasing number of children—the horsemen and women of the future—entering the equestrian ranks.

In recent years, the financial problems which were associated with keeping a horse have been greatly eased for families of modest incomes. A principal reason for this change has been the community stable. Families can now maintain a horse for as little as $1,000 a year, which is much less than it would cost to operate a private stable. And in warmer climes, like that of Southern California, horses are merely parked in the backyard at even less cost.

(The diminishing cost of owning a pleasure horse is in sharp contrast to the spiraling expenses of the racing world. In the past decade, which saw the first $1,000,000 stallion syndication, no fewer than twenty-three Thoroughbred stud horses have been syndicated at sums ranging from $1,000,000 to $2,500,000. There were nine such deals in 1965 alone.)

In the past ten or fifteen years, the pleasure horse has been promoted as never before in its history. The United States Pony Clubs, for instance, which were started for youngsters twelve years ago, now have some seven thousand members in twenty-five states. For $4 a year these clubs teach riding and grooming, using as instructors veteran horsemen who contribute their services gratis. Much larger than these are the extensive 4-H horse programs, which flourish where agriculture is a principal occupation.

Attendance and participation in horse shows of all kinds has risen proportionately to the over-all boom. Attendance at United States Horse Shows Association meetings in 1965 reached an all-time high. The horse also fared well in other sporting areas. The ancient game of polo, once a major sports attraction in the East, was some years ago driven westward by the urbanization of its Long Island stronghold. Today, around Chicago and Milwaukee and in the Southwest and California, it is staging a strong comeback. Another throwback to olden times is the sport of jousting, in which a rider going full tilt endeavors to spear with his lance tiny rings which are suspended over the course from archlike supports. It is currently popular in Maryland and Virginia, and in certain parts of Canada. Coaching—driving teams of spirited road horses hitched to antique coaches—is a diversion of a number of prominent businessmen like printer John Cuneo, of Chicago, and brewer August Busch Jr., of St. Louis. Hunting to hounds is hitting new peaks of popularity with some thirty-five hunts being organized in the past ten years alone. Trail-riding expeditions, complete with pack animals, are also widely enjoyed as a vacation activity in America.

It is obvious that the great increases in "pleasure dollars" and leisure time which have marked the postwar economy have made possible a parallel expansion in recreational activities. But why have so many Americans turned for this purpose to the horse? In *The Horse in America*, Robert

Strong-backed, strong-minded mule still has no peer as pack animal. These are being packed for Rocky Mountain trek.

West Howard observes: "The Horse has become a means for Man to achieve mental therapy and maintain physical health in his technological environment." This point is surely well taken. But it should be added that in achieving these practical ends American men and women who ride also experience the vague, but delicious, sensation that comes from reliving traditions of another age.

In recent years, a concern with the American past has been manifest in literature, on the stage, and in motion pictures. A night does not pass without television screens coming alive with the exploits of pioneers like Daniel Boone, daring soldiers like John Mosby, Western lawmen like Wyatt Earp. And what city, town, or village which can boast of three native generations is worthy of its salt unless its anniversary dates are duly observed in elaborately costumed pageants for the ladies and much sprouting of beards by the male element (whether or not the community happened to have been founded in a clean-shaven era)?

Our forefathers dreamed of the future in which we now live. Now that these times are upon us—albeit in rather Quixotic form—our escape is to dream in the past. There is not a single object, inanimate or alive, that symbolizes that past more than does the horse. He is a flesh-and-blood antique, a living and breathing tradition, and an incarnate monument to the American heritage.

*Exceptional sure-footedness
makes mules ideal for carrying visitors down
precipitous slopes into Grand Canyon.*

INDEX

Italic numbers refer to illustrations.

PICTURE CREDITS

All pictures are by Walter D. Osborne except the following:

CHAPTER ONE
13—New York Public Library. **15**—New-York Historical Society, May, 1834. **24-25-26-27**—American Museum of Natural History. **28** (left)—Pictorial Parade; (right)—American Museum of Natural History. **29**—American Museum of Natural History.

CHAPTER TWO
30-31—Metropolitan Museum of Art, gift of Cornelius Vanderbilt, 1887. **33**—New York Public Library (from *The Hittites* by O. R. Gurney). **34**—Fleming, Art Reference Bureau. **35**—Culver Pictures. **36-37**—New York Public Library. **39**—New York Public Library. **40-41**—Culver Pictures. **43**—Vatican, Alinari, Art Reference Bureau. **44** (top)—Metropolitan Museum of Art, gift of Mrs. J. Insley Blair, 1947; (bottom)— Cleveland Museum of Art, Holden Collection. **45**—Metropolitan Museum of Art, Cloisters Collection, 1954. **46**—New York Public Library. **47**—Marburg, Art Reference Bureau. **48**—Museo del Prado. **49**—Baltimore Museum of Art, William Woodward Collection.

CHAPTER THREE
54-55—British Museum. **57**—Baltimore Museum of Art, William Woodward Collection. **63** (top)—Culver Pictures; (bottom)—Endpapers from *Sir Archie,* University of North Carolina Press, 1958. **70**—New York Racing Association. **73**—National Museum of Racing, Saratoga Springs, New York.

CHAPTER FOUR
85—Culver Pictures. **86**—New York Graphic Society. **87**—Culver Pictures. **89**—Culver Pictures. **90-91**—Culver Pictures. **92-93**—New York Graphic Society. **94**—Culver Pictures. **96**—Frederic Lewis Photographs. **97**—Culver Pictures.

CHAPTER FIVE
101—Library of Congress. **102**—New York Public Library. **104**—Kennedy Galleries. **106** (top)—New York Public Library; (bottom)—New-York Historical Society. **109**—New York Public Library. **110**—Kennedy Galleries.

CHAPTER SEVEN
139—Kennedy Galleries. **144** (top)—Poster from the Bella K. Landauer Collection, New-York Historical Society; (bottom)—Woolaroc Museum, Bartlesville, Oklahoma.

CHAPTER TWELVE
205 (bottom)—New-York Historical Society.

CHAPTER THIRTEEN
222 (right)—Library of Congress. **223** (right)—Library of Congress.